Wild Yankees

WILD YANKEES

The Struggle for Independence along Pennsylvania's Revolutionary Frontier

PAUL B. MOYER

CORNELL UNIVERSITY PRESS
ITHACA AND LONDON

Copyright © 2007 by Cornell University

All rights reserved. Except for brief quotations in a review, this book, or parts thereof, must not be reproduced in any form without permission in writing from the publisher. For information, address Cornell University Press, Sage House, 512 East State Street, Ithaca, New York 14850.

First published 2007 by Cornell University Press
First printing, Cornell Paperbacks, 2015

Printed in the United States of America

Library of Congress Cataloging-in-Publication Data

Moyer, Paul Benjamin, 1970–
 Wild Yankees : the struggle for independence along Pennsylvania's revolutionary frontier / Paul B. Moyer.
   p. cm.
 Includes bibliographical references and index.
 ISBN 978-0-8014-4494-4 (cloth : alk. paper)
 ISBN 978-1-5017-0070-5 (pbk. : alk. paper)
   1. Susquehanna Claim, 1753–1808. 2. Frontier and pioneer life—Pennsylvania—Wyoming Valley. 3. Indians of North America—Pennsylvania—Wyoming Valley—History. 4. Wyoming Valley (Pa.)—History. I. Title.

F157.W9M75 2007
974.8'01—dc

2007021948

Cornell University Press strives to use environmentally responsible suppliers and materials to the fullest extent possible in the publishing of its books. Such materials include vegetable-based, low-VOC inks and acid-free papers that are recycled, totally chlorine-free, or partly composed of nonwood fibers. For further information, visit our website at www.cornellpress.cornell.edu.

Cloth printing   10 9 8 7 6 5 4 3 2 1
Paperback printing   10 9 8 7 6 5 4 3 2 1

For my parents
Robert William Wagner Moyer
Linda May (Potteiger) Moyer

Contents

List of Illustrations	ix
Acknowledgments	xi
A Note on Terminology	xiii
Abbreviations	xv
Introduction: A Farmer's Revolution	1
1. "Among Quarrelsome Yankees, Insidious Indians, and Lonely Wilds": Natives, Colonists, and the Wyoming Controversy	13
2. "A Great Many Wrangling Disputes": Authority, Allegiance, Property, and the Frontier War for Independence	37
3. "A Dangerous Combination of Villains": The Social Context of Agrarian Resistance	65
4. "All the Difficulties of Forming a New Settlement": Frontier Migration, Land Speculation, and Settler Insurgency	94
5. "A Perfect Union with the People": Cultures of Resistance along the Revolutionary Frontier	120
6. "Poor and Ignorant but Industrious Settlers": Frontier Development and the Path to Accommodation	148
7. "Artful Deceivers": Yankee Notables and the Resolution of the Wyoming Controversy	175
Epilogue: Closing the Revolutionary Frontier	196
Selected Bibliography	201
Index	211

Illustrations

Maps
Map 1. The Connecticut Claim, 1754–68   15
Map 2. The Wyoming Valley, 1760–85   38
Map 3. The Expansion of Connecticut Towns, 1785–1800   103
Map 4. Pennsylvania's Upper Susquehanna Valley, 1790–1810   123

Portraits
Figure 1. Timothy Pickering   71
Figure 2. John Franklin   73
Figure 3. Thomas Cooper   125

Acknowledgments

This project first germinated in my mind during a graduate research seminar I took with Carol Sheriff at the College of William and Mary. It was with her guidance and encouragement that I developed the idea of examining the intersection between daily life and agrarian unrest—a concept that has guided this project ever since. When I selected the Wyoming controversy for the topic of my doctoral dissertation, I was ably supported in my endeavors by James Whittenburg, Leisa Meyer, James Axtell, the late John Selby, and Alan Taylor. Jim Whittenburg is everything anyone could want in a dissertation committee chair, and Leisa Meyer pointed me in the direction of examining the relationship between agrarian unrest and the frontier process. Alan Taylor, besides offering insightful comments on my dissertation, put it all into perspective by reminding me that it was only one of many drafts I would turn out on the way to publishing a book.

I have also had the good fortune to land among a very supportive group of scholars here at SUNY Brockport. In particular, two of my colleagues stand out for the help they gave me in transforming my dissertation into a book. Steve Ireland read and commented on each of my chapter drafts and greatly assisted me in clarifying my arguments. Lynn Parsons provided invaluable assistance in helping me to hone my prose. Thanks also to Alison Kalett and the rest of the staff at Cornell University Press for all of their help in making this book a reality. I should also mention that I greatly appreciate the effort the press's anonymous readers so obviously put into evaluating my manuscript.

A number of institutions also contributed to the completion of this project.

I would like to thank the staffs of the Historical Society of Pennsylvania, the Connecticut Historical Society, the Pennsylvania Historical and Museum Commission, the Wyoming Historical and Geological Society, the Tioga Point Museum, the New York Historical Society, the Swem Library at the College of William and Mary, and SUNY Brockport's Drake Library for their assistance. A special word of appreciation needs to go to Bob Gillam of Drake Library's interlibrary loan division for the speed with which he obtained research materials. I would also like to express my gratitude toward The College of William and Mary and SUNY Brockport for the research grants they awarded to me.

Last but not least, there are a number of individuals who I need to thank for their support. My parents, Robert and Linda, have encouraged my love of history and my choice of it as a profession in so many ways. I would also like to thank my wife, Christine, and my children, Bridget and Ethan, for putting up with me for all the years I took time away from them to devote to this project. Chrissy, the good news is that this book is almost done. The bad news is that I already have a second one in mind. Finally, I would like to extend my gratitude to the employees and patrons of Brockport's Java Junction. Much of the thinking and editing that went into this book was accomplished there with cup of coffee in hand.

A Note on Terminology

I use the terms *settlers*, *farmers*, and *backcountry inhabitants* interchangeably throughout this work to designate non-Native frontier inhabitants, knowing full well that Indians also settled, farmed, and inhabited the land. I refer to those who held land under Pennsylvania as Pennamites, Pennsylvania claimants, or at times, just Pennsylvanians. Likewise, I use the terms *Connecticut claimant*, *Yankee*, and *New Englander* interchangeably to designate settlers who held land under deeds issued by Connecticut land companies. However, I reserve the terms *Wild Yankee*, *Yankee insurgents*, and others for those Connecticut claimants who actively resisted Pennsylvania. In the name of verbal variation I also use the terms *frontier*, *backcountry*, and *hinterland* interchangeably. Moreover, when referring to the region on which this study focuses, I employ the terms the *Wyoming region*, *Northeast Pennsylvania*, *Pennsylvania's Northeast frontier*, or simply the *Northeast frontier*. In cases where I am specifically talking about the Wyoming Valley, I stick with that designation. Finally, although I employ the phases *agrarian unrest*, *agrarian resistance*, and *agrarian insurgents* throughout this work, I do not use the word *agrarian* to indicate that backcountry settlers were fighting for some radical, leveling vision in which landed property would be equally distributed to all; rather, I simply use it as a synonym for rural, backcountry, or frontier.

Abbreviations

CCP	Connecticut Claims Papers (2 vols.), Historical Society of Pennsylvania
CRP	Samuel Hazard, ed., *Colonial Records of Pennsylvania*, 9 vols. (Harrisburg, 1852).
HDP	Henry Drinker Papers, Historical Society of Pennsylvania
HSP	Historical Society of Pennsylvania
JTP	Jason Torrey Papers, Wyoming Historical and Geological Society
MPLA	Minutes of the Pennsylvania Landholders' Association, Historical Society of Pennsylvania
PA1	Samuel Hazard, ed., *Pennsylvania Archives*, First Series, 12 vols. (Philadelphia, 1854).
PA2	William H. Egle, ed., *Pennsylvania Archives*, Second Series, 18 vols. (Harrisburg, 1890).
PA4	George Edward Reed, ed., *Pennsylvania Archives*, Fourth Series, 4 vols. (Harrisburg, 1900).
PA9	Gertrude McKinney, ed., *Pennsylvania Archives*, Ninth Series, 10 vols. (Harrisburg, 1931).
PMHB	*Pennsylvania Magazine of History and Biography*
PHMC	Pennsylvania Historical and Museum Commission
RPLA	Records of the Pennsylvania Landholders' Association, Historical Society of Pennsylvania
TPM	Tioga Point Museum

TPP	Timothy Pickering Papers, Massachusetts Historical Society Microfilm Publications
SCA	Susquehannah Company Account Books, Connecticut Historical Society
SCP	Julian P. Boyd and Robert J. Taylor, eds., *The Susquehannah Company Papers*, 11 vols. (Ithaca, NY, 1962–71).
USDT	United States Direct Tax of 1798, National Archives and Records Service Microfilm
WHGS	Wyoming Historical and Geological Society
WMQ	*William and Mary Quarterly*

Introduction

A Farmer's Revolution

The Wyoming Valley occupies a roughly twenty-mile stretch of the Susquehanna River between the mouths of Nanticoke Creek and the Lackawanna River. "Wyoming" is a corruption of the Delaware word *Maughwauwam*, which translates into "the large plains." The name certainly described the wide, fertile flats that bordered each side of the Susquehanna before the land rose into the mountains that boxed in the valley. But this depicts Wyoming in only its strictest geographical sense. In the eighteenth century, people came to use the term to refer to a much larger area of hill and valley country covering Northeast Pennsylvania. By the nineteenth century, the meaning of the word *Wyoming* had changed in a far more telling way. By then, many Americans believed that it meant, not "the large plains," but "a field of blood." Considering the region's turbulent history, it is no wonder that its name acquired such a sanguinary association.[1]

No event did more to link Wyoming with bloodshed than the battle that took place there on July 3, 1778. On that day about three hundred American militia led by Colonel Zebulon Butler confronted an invading force of more than seven hundred Indians and Loyalists in a desperate bid to save their homes from destruction. The battle was joined near the west bank of the Susquehanna late in the afternoon. The two sides exchanged fire for about half an hour before the invaders' superior numbers tipped the contest in their favor. Indian warriors enveloped the Americans' battle line and began to cut off their line of

---

1. Charles Miner, *History of Wyoming* (Philadelphia, 1845), xi, xv.

retreat. Realizing their peril, the militia broke and fled. Some ran through the fields and woods; others attempted to make their escape by swimming the river. Many of the fugitives were chased down, killed, and scalped by their victorious foes. By the time the sun had set, the raiders had killed or captured more than half of the militiamen who faced them that day. In the days that followed, they drove Wyoming's remaining inhabitants out of the valley, burned their homes, slaughtered their livestock, and destroyed their crops.[2]

The American press dubbed the battle the "Wyoming Massacre" and circulated stories of Indian savagery and Tory treachery. These tales spoke of Indians burning prisoners alive or of forming them in circles and splitting their heads open with tomahawks one by one. Some of the most lurid reports concerning this so-called massacre focused on brutalities perpetrated by Loyalists. The *Pennsylvania Gazette* related how Partial Terry, a Wyoming Valley resident who had joined the British and returned the valley as a Tory raider, "murdered his father, mother, brothers and sisters, stripped off their scalps, and cut off his father's head." Another account concerned the fate of Henry Pensell, one of the American militiamen who fought at Wyoming. After fleeing the battlefield, Henry came face to face with his Tory brother, John, whom he begged for his life. Showing no mercy, John called his sibling a "damned rebel," shot him dead, and scalped him.[3]

Though the Battle of Wyoming and the exaggerated stories of murder and mutilation it generated certainly helped to darken the valley's name, it was by no means the only time that the Wyoming Valley became the scene of violence. Those killed in the battle mingled their blood with Indians and colonists who had already died vying for possession of the region. In April 1763, the Delaware chief Teedyuscung perished in a fire that consumed Wyoming's main Indian settlement and that was likely set by colonists who coveted the valley. Several months later, a Delaware war party took their revenge and "most cruelly butchered" a group of pioneers from Connecticut who had occupied the site of the destroyed Indian village.[4] Dozens of people were killed and wounded and hundreds more violently dispossessed in the years preceding the outbreak of the Revolutionary War. This time, however, the combatants were not Indians and colonists but competing groups of settlers from Pennsylvania and Connecticut.

---

2. My description of the Battle of Wyoming is based on an account of the engagement included in Miner, *History of Wyoming*, 217–28.

3. Both of these stories of alleged Tory and Indian atrocities are taken from Miner, *History of Wyoming*, 225–26; and Gregory T. Knouff, *The Soldiers' Revolution: Pennsylvanians in Arms and the Forging of Early American Identity* (University Park, PA, 2004), 195–96.

4. Anthony F. C. Wallace, *King of the Delawares: Teedyuscung, 1700–1763* (Freeport, NY, 1970), 258–61; Extract from the *Pennsylvania Gazette*, Oct. 27, 1763, SCP 2:277.

In March 1770, Pennsylvania settlers killed one Connecticut claimant and wounded two more in a gun battle. Early in the following year Connecticut claimants replied by gunning down Pennsylvania deputy sheriff Nathan Ogden.[5] In December 1775, almost three years before his defeat at the Battle of Wyoming, Zebulon Butler led four hundred Connecticut settlers against a force of more than five hundred Pennsylvanians and won a victory that left several of the enemy dead and wounded.[6] Of course, America's war for independence added to the region's growing list of victims. Besides those killed at the Battle of Wyoming, others died in a grinding conflict of ambushes, raids, and counter-raids that cost many more lives. Casualties continued to mount in the decades following the Revolutionary War. In August 1784, a party of Connecticut claimants ambushed a detachment of Pennsylvania militiamen, wounding three and killing one. Soon after this incident, Pennsylvanians laid their own ambush and shot a Connecticut settler.[7] Nearly a decade later, Connecticut claimants gunned down Pennsylvania landholder Arthur Erwin in cold blood.[8]

This long history of violence was the product of a bitter contest over property and power known as the Wyoming controversy. Although the dispute took its name from the blood-soaked Wyoming Valley, the struggle encompassed all of Northeast Pennsylvania. Connecticut's land-hungry inhabitants ignited the conflict in the early 1750s when they took steps to establish settlements west of the Delaware River. They justified the move by resurrecting long-dormant territorial claims contained in their colony's seventeenth-century charter. The New Englanders organized the Susquehannah and the First and Second Delaware companies to orchestrate the distribution and settlement of land in the colony's western claim. These companies, in turn, purchased large tracts of land along the Delaware and Susquehanna rivers from the Iroquois at the Albany Congress of 1754. Pennsylvania resisted these efforts in court and, later, when Connecticut settlers began arriving in the contested region, with force.

Through the late 1760s and early 1770s, Yankees (settlers who held property under the Connecticut claim) struggled against Pennamites (settlers loyal to Pennsylvania) for possession of the land. At times, the contest turned violent and dozens of people were killed, wounded, or brutally stripped of their property.

5. Charles Stewart to John Penn, Jan. 21, 1771; Deposition of William Sims, Jan. 21, 1771; Deposition of William Nimens, Jan. 25, 1771; and Deposition of Peter Kachlein, Jan. 31, 1771, *SCP* 4:153–54, 155–57, 163–64.
6. *SCP* 5:l–lii; Extract from the Connecticut Courant, Jan. 22, 1776 and Sheriff William Scull and Others to Governor Penn, Dec. 30, 1775, *SCP* 6:422–25, 425–26.
7. John Boyd and John Armstrong, Jr., to John Dickinson, Aug. 7, 1784 and Deposition of Eliphalet Emmons, Aug. 9, 1784, *SCP* 8:22–24; Deposition of James Moore, Sept. 14, 1784, *PA1* 10:657; John Franklin's Diary, July 3–Dec. 7, 1784, *SCP* 8:155–56.
8. Proclamation of Governor Mifflin, June 20, 1791, *PA9* 1:135–36.

The dispute became even more ominous and threatening to Pennsylvania when a number of notorious backcountry rebels and Indian killers from western Lancaster County, known as the Paxton Boys, joined forces with the Yankee invaders. In 1773, Pennsylvania official William Maclay, frustrated in his attempts to impose the colony's authority over the region, pointedly observed that "if Hell is justly considered as the rendivous of Rascals, we cannot entertain a Doubt of Wioming being the Place."[9] The colony of Connecticut joined the fray in 1774 when it officially annexed the Susquehannah and Delaware companies' purchases and, in 1776, recognized them as Westmoreland County. The Continental Congress upheld Connecticut's jurisdiction and what had been Northeast Pennsylvania seemed well on the way to becoming part of Connecticut. But the New Englanders had no time to celebrate as the Revolutionary War descended on them. The Battle of Wyoming was only the worst of a string of Indian-Tory raids that devastated the region. That many of these invaders were one-time occupants of the valley who had been dispossessed by the New Englanders only served to intensify the brutality of the conflict.

Though the British and their Indian and Loyalist allies severely weakened Connecticut's hold on the Wyoming region, it was the newly established government of the United States that finally tore it from its grasp. In December 1782, a national court established under Article IX of the Articles of Confederation placed the contested area back under Pennsylvania's jurisdiction. In perhaps the only positive reference to Wyoming, United States secretary of foreign affairs Robert Livingston wrote a letter to Lafayette in which he upheld the court's decision "as a singular event" that would help to usher in a day "when all disputes in the great republic of Europe will be tried in the same way, and America be quoted to exemplify the wisdom of the measure."[10] Livingston's optimism was sorely misplaced. The "Trenton Decree" only served to set off another round of conflict as Connecticut settlers, fearing dispossession, banded together to defend their farms. Between 1783 and 1785, Yankees battled Pennamites who entered the region seeking to establish new claims or reentered it trying to secure old ones. This round of conflict ended with the Connecticut claimants driving their foes from the valley.

In the late 1780s, Yankee settlers turned their attention from fighting Pennamites to resisting the state of Pennsylvania and powerful nonresident land speculators who claimed land under it. These backcountry insurgents, or "Wild Yankees" as they became known, mounted a two-decade-long resistance move-

---

9. William Maclay to James Tilghman, Apr. 2, 1773, *SCP* 5:80.
10. The quotes from Livingston's letter to Lafayette are taken from Robert J. Taylor, "Trial at Trenton," *WMQ* 26 (Oct. 1969): 521.

ment in which they threatened, assaulted, and even killed those who sought to impose Pennsylvania's authority and soil rights. As late as 1801, Tench Coxe, a leading American economist and one-time assistant secretary of the treasury, warned that Northeast Pennsylvania was a home to "men worse than savages or beasts of prey" and that, until the region's disputes were resolved, "property [there] will continue but a vexatious name."[11] Only after the turn of the century did Pennsylvania and its leading landholders finally manage to bring together the right blend of force and compromise to end the insurgency.

Thus, to many, Wyoming stood as a powerful symbol of tragedy and failure. It was a place where the promise of peaceful relations between Indians and Europeans had been betrayed with violence. It was a place where bitter property disputes obscured a vision of the frontier as a site where people could make a new start. Finally, Wyoming was a place where the prospect of building a revolutionary republic that would serve as a beacon of freedom to the world was darkened by fears that American independence had set loose forces that would lead the fledgling nation toward chaos and ruin.

In this book I explore the nexus of frontier and revolutionary conflict that earned Wyoming such a dark place in the minds of early Americans. I contend that the key to unlocking the full meaning of the Wyoming controversy lies in understanding the settlers who made Northeast Pennsylvania their home. These pioneers were among the tens of thousands of people who made their way into the backcountry between the mid eighteenth and the early nineteenth centuries and who stood at the center of events that transformed American society. They were integral to a dramatic surge in territorial expansion that saw European colonists, African slaves, and their descendants occupy and improve more land in North America than in the previous 150 years of settlement. In addition, they participated in a revolution that saw America break its political bonds with Britain and establish a new republican society. These migrants also took part in the bitter conflicts generated by these developments—conflicts in which settlers, Indians, land speculators, and government officials fought over property, the nature of American society, and the meaning of the Revolution.

Because of its duration and depth, the Wyoming controversy provides a good lens through which to examine settlement and conflict along the early American frontier. The dispute emerged in the mid eighteenth century and lasted into the first decades of the nineteenth, allowing an analysis that spans the colonial, revolutionary, and early national periods. It also involved a large cast of characters, including the colonies (and later states) of Connecticut and Pennsylvania,

---

11. Tench Coxe to Henry Drinker, Edward Tilghman, and Samuel Hodgdon, July 22, 1801, *SCP* 11:146.

several Connecticut-based land companies, powerful speculators, thousands of settlers, Indian peoples who claimed or occupied land in the contested region, British imperial officials, and the government of the United States. Finally, Northeast Pennsylvania was not unique in that it experienced conflict during the revolutionary era. It is unique, however, in that it experienced just about every variety of violence the revolutionary frontier had to offer: violence between whites and Indians, between white settlers, and between ordinary backcountry inhabitants and powerful gentlemen.

The Wyoming dispute joined a broad stream of agrarian unrest that plagued America's revolutionary frontier: a crescent-shaped swath of territory from Maine to Georgia that settlers and land developers claimed and occupied during the era of the American Revolution. Contention over property among settlers and landlords sparked much of this unrest. In the 1740s and 1750s farmers in northern New Jersey fought over land with the colony's powerful proprietors. About a decade later, backcountry inhabitants in South Carolina's Rocky Mount District and North Carolina's Granville District violently resisted the claims of nonresident speculators. Farther north, in the 1760s, settlers known as "Liberty Men" or, later, "White Indians," embarked on a six-decade struggle against powerful proprietors for possession of lands in Massachusetts's District of Maine. Likewise, in Northwest Pennsylvania, frontier inhabitants battled land developers for property between 1795 and 1810. Around the same time, speculators and small farmers fought for possession of the land in western Kentucky's Green River Country. In the 1830s, settlers calling themselves "Nullifiers" came to blows with land developers in western New York's Holland Purchase. Finally, starting in the mid eighteenth century, New York's Hudson Valley experienced nearly a century of conflict between landlords and tenant farmers that culminated in the antirent movement of the 1830s and 40s.[12]

As was the case with the Wyoming controversy, backcountry land disputes often intertwined with jurisdictional conflicts among colonies and states. Starting in the 1730s, a border dispute between Pennsylvania and Maryland fueled

12. Brendan McConville, *These Daring Disturbers of the Public Peace: The Struggle for Property and Power in Early New Jersey* (Ithaca, NY, 1999); Rachel N. Klein, *Unification of a Slave State: The Rise of the Planter Class in the South Carolina Backcountry, 1760–1808* (Chapel Hill, NC, 1990), 36–37; Alan Taylor, *Liberty Men and Great Proprietors: The Revolutionary Settlement on the Maine Frontier, 1760–1820* (Chapel Hill, NC, 1990); Elizabeth K. Henderson, "The Northwestern Lands of Pennsylvania, 1790–1812," *PMHB* 60 (1936): 131–60; Stephen Aron, *How the West Was Lost: The Transformation of Kentucky from Daniel Boone to Henry Clay* (Baltimore, 1996), 150–69; Charles E. Brooks, *Frontier Settlement and Market Revolution: The Holland Land Purchase* (Ithaca, NY, 1996), 176–232; Reeve Huston, *Land and Freedom: Rural Society, Popular Protest, and Party Politics in Antebellum New York* (New York, 2000); Thomas J. Humphrey, *Land and Liberty: Hudson Valley Riots in the Age of Revolution* (DeKalb, IL, 2004).

contention over land along the lower Susquehanna River Valley. Likewise, in the 1760s, New Englanders holding deeds issued by New Hampshire challenged the jurisdictional authority of New York and the soil rights of its settlers and land speculators. Over the next three decades these "Green Mountain Boys" waged a successful struggle for property and power that ultimately led to the creation of the state of Vermont. Finally, a territorial dispute between Pennsylvania and Virginia over lands to the south of Pittsburgh in the 1770s brought settlers from the two colonies into competition over property.[13]

Contention over debt, taxes, Indian policy, and political power also fueled unrest in the backcountry because these issues impinged on the ability of settlers to obtain and secure freeholds. In the 1760s planters in the South Carolina backcountry styled themselves "regulators" and employed vigilante violence to battle frontier bandits who government officials seemed unable, or unwilling, to combat. In the same decade, Pennsylvania frontiersmen who earned the epithets "Paxton Boys" and "Black Boys" indiscriminately murdered Indians and violently rebelled against what they perceived as the colony's misguided Indian policy and inequitable distribution of land and political power. An even more serious agrarian insurrection shook North Carolina in the 1760s and 1770s when western "Regulators" fought against a provincial government they perceived as corrupt and inimical to the interests of backcountry farmers. In the end, their rebellion was put down with armed force at the Battle of Alamance in 1771. A similar uprising took place in central and western Massachusetts in 1786–87 where farmers, enraged over high taxes and the state's unwillingness to provide debt relief, rose up during Shays's Rebellion. In the following decade, backcountry farmers in eastern and western Pennsylvania took up arms to resist federal taxes. As was the case in North Carolina, government troops crushed both the Massachusetts and Pennsylvania revolts.[14]

---

13. Charles D. Dutrizac, "Empire, Provinces, Frontier: Perspectives on the Pennsylvania-Maryland Boundary Dispute, 1681–1738" (Ph.D. diss., University of Western Ontario, 1986); Michael A. Bellesiles, *Revolutionary Outlaws: Ethan Allen and the Struggle for Independence on the Early American Frontier* (Charlottesville, VA, 1993); Ann M. Ousterhout, *A State Divided: Opposition in Pennsylvania to the American Revolution* (New York, 1987), 247–72.

14. Rachel N. Klein, "Ordering the Backcountry: The South Carolina Regulation" *WMQ* 38 (Oct. 1981): 661–80; Brooke Hindle, "The March of the Paxton Boys," *WMQ* 3 (Oct. 1946): 461–86; Marjoline Kars, *Breaking Loose Together: The Regulator Rebellion in Pre-Revolutionary North Carolina* (Chapel Hill, NC, 2002); David P. Szatmary, *Shays' Rebellion: The Makings of an Agrarian Insurrection* (Amherst, MA, 1980); Leonard L. Richards, *Shays's Rebellion: The American Revolution's Final Battle* (Philadelphia, 2002); Thomas P. Slaughter, *The Whiskey Rebellion: Frontier Epilogue to the American Revolution* (New York, 1986); Dorothy E. Fennell, "From Rebelliousness to Insurrection: A Social History of the Whiskey Rebellion, 1765–1802" (Ph.D. diss., University of Pittsburgh, 1981); Paul Douglas Newman, *Fries's Rebellion: The Enduring Struggle for the American Revolution* (Philadelphia, 2004).

I argue that at the root of conflict in Northeast Pennsylvania and across the revolutionary frontier was a struggle for agrarian independence waged by thousands of ordinary settlers. To an American farmer, independence meant land ownership and material competency—it meant the ability to care for, and command, a household free from dependence on others. Moreover, in a time when voting rights and masculine identity were linked to property ownership, rural folk equated independence with political empowerment and manhood. In his *Letters from an American Farmer*, the self-appointed spokesman of American yeomen, Hector St. John de Crèvecoeur, presents perhaps the most articulate vision of what it meant to own land: "The instant I enter my own land, the bright idea of property, of exclusive right, of independence exalt my mind. . . . What should we American farmers be without the distinct possession of that soil? It feeds, it clothes us . . . it has established all our rights; on it is founded our rank, our freedom, our power as citizens."[15]

Crèvecoeur's evocative celebration of land ownership illustrates how the idea of independence was bound up with a set of powerful economic, social, and political aspirations that thread their way through the fabric of early American history. It was during the seventeenth century that the word *independence* first came to signify material security, masculine autonomy, and political empowerment. Not coincidentally, it was during this same century that large numbers of Europeans started to migrate to North America in search of land and opportunity. Ordinary colonists' efforts to acquire land and the economic, social, and political benefits that its possession conveyed suffuse the story of the birth and development of Britain's North American colonies. In the early Chesapeake, humble yeoman and freed servants struggled to acquire land and carve out a place for themselves as small tobacco farmers in a region increasingly dominated by a powerful class of wealthy, slave-owning planters. The Puritans who migrated to New England came in hopes, not only of building a Christian utopia in the New World, but also of obtaining land on which they could support their families. The central institution of local life in New England, the town, in addition to fostering and enforcing Christian fellowship, promoted the rise of a class of freehold farmers through the widespread (by European standards) distribution of land. Likewise, in Pennsylvania, the impression that the province offered some of the best opportunities for poor people to obtain land, live comfortably, and prosper gave birth to the colony's reputation as "the best poor man's country."[16] The ethos of independence

15. Hector St. John de Crèvecoeur, *Letters from an American Farmer* (New York, 1945), 24–25.
16. *The Oxford English Dictionary*, 2d ed., 20 vols. (Oxford, 1989), 7:847; Allan Kulikoff, *From British Peasants to Colonial American Farmers* (Chapel Hill, NC, 2000); Russell R. Menard and Lorena S. Walsh, *Robert Cole's World: Agriculture and Society in Early Maryland* (Chapel Hill, NC, 1991); Darrett B. Rutman and Anita H. Rutman, *A Place in Time: Middlesex County,*

was deeply embedded in the social dynamics of early America and, as such, represents an idea with significant explanatory power.

An interpretive framework that places ordinary people's struggles for independence at its center has profound implications for our understanding of the Revolution. In recent decades, historians have illuminated how the Revolution touched the lives of women, Indians, African-Americans, sailors, and ordinary farmers.[17] This book continues down this path and examines how the thousands of ordinary folk who made the decision to go to the frontier shaped America's revolutionary epoch and were, in turn, shaped by it. Though it was a common and widely accepted aspiration by the mid eighteenth century, the pursuit of independence took on new force and meaning among frontier farmers during the revolutionary era. First, the Revolution helped to heighten the political meanings attached to independence. In particular, backcountry settlers often conflated their struggle for landed independence with the colonies' larger struggle for national independence and perceived those who stood in their way not only as personal foes but also as enemies of the Revolution itself. Thus for many settlers the struggle for independence became, not just an individual battle for land, but a collective fight for liberty. Second, rapid frontier expansion during the revolutionary era gave thousands of settlers access to the basis of independence: land. Moreover, the rate of frontier settlement was only matched by its contentiousness. The vision of personal independence that drew settlers to the frontier also drew them into conflict with Indians, governments, wealthy land speculators, and fellow settlers who sought possession of the land. The struggles for property and power that resulted could (and often did) take on radical dimensions as frontier farmers challenged government authority, conventional property rights, and the landed foundations of elite power.

The story of the farmer's revolution does not just broaden our view of the American Revolution, it "decenters" the Revolution and demands that we envision it as a plural rather than a singular. The Revolution was not like a solar

---

Virginia, 1650–1750 (New York, 1984), 61–203; Virginia Dejohn Anderson, "Migrants and Motives: Religion and the Settlement of New England, 1630–1640," *New England Quarterly* 58 (1985): 339–83; Daniel Vickers, *Farmers and Fishermen: Two Centuries of Work in Essex County, Massachusetts, 1630–1830* (Chapel Hill, NC, 1994); James T. Lemon, *The Best Poor Man's Country: A Geographical Study of Early Southeastern Pennsylvania* (Baltimore, 1972).

17. Joan R. Gundersen, *To Be Useful to the World: Women in Revolutionary America, 1740–1790* (New York, 1996); Barbara Clark Smith, "Food Rioters and the American Revolution," *WMQ* 51 (Jan. 1994): 3–38; Colin G. Calloway, *The American Revolution in Indian Country: Crisis and Diversity in Native American Communities* (New York, 1995); Sylvia R. Frey, *Water from the Rock: Black Resistance in a Revolutionary Age* (Princeton, 1991); Jesse Lemisch, "Jack Tar in the Streets: Merchant Seamen in The Politics of Revolutionary America," *WMQ* 25 (July 1968): 371–407; Robert A. Gross, *The Minutemen and Their World* (New York, 1976).

system in which a single group of people and ideas formed a sun around which everything else revolved. People continue to think of the Revolution as something that was made by John Adams, Thomas Jefferson, and George Washington—as the rebellion against British rule that eventually transformed America's political and social order.[18] Even those scholars who demonstrate that the Revolution transformed America in ways the Founding Fathers never intended still see it as something that was essentially born of their efforts. Likewise, historians who map out the revolutionary experience of common folk, women, and slaves still tend to describe their subjects in terms of their relationship to a supposedly more central founders' revolution.[19] Instead, the Revolution should be envisioned as a series of struggles with independent and overlapping orbits that reshaped the lives of various groups of Americans. In keeping with this outlook, I contend that the violent struggle over property that beset America's hinterlands, rather than representing the byproduct of the "real" Revolution made by the Founding Fathers, *was* the Revolution for large numbers of ordinary folk. The farmer's revolution was not the result of ideas that trickled down from above, but of aspirations and experiences that bubbled up from below. Moreover, the radical potential of the farmer's revolution lay, not in concepts of liberty and natural rights borrowed from the Whig elite, but in the dynamics of an agrarian social order that existed long before America's rebellion against Great Britain and endured long after America won its independence.

This exploration of the farmers' revolution also revisits and recasts the role that the frontier played in the evolution of American society.[20] On one level, the story of America's revolutionary-era frontier is part of a much larger tale of intercultural contact between Indians and Europeans and of the former's ultimate dispossession by the latter. In this sense, the struggle for independence in early America started, and long endured, as a battle for land between Indians and

---

18. A spate of recent biographies on the Founding Fathers illustrates the continued vitality of this top-down view of the Revolution. Examples of this genre include Joseph Ellis, *Founding Brothers: The Revolutionary Generation* (New York, 2002); Ellis, *His Excellency: George Washington* (New York, 2004); David McCullough, *John Adams* (New York, 2002); H. W. Brands, *The First American: The Life and Times of Benjamin Franklin* (New York, 2000).

19. Gordon Wood's monumental *The Radicalism of the American Revolution* (New York, 1991) is a good example of how even broader conceptions of the Revolution continue to hinge, at least implicitly, on the study of America's social and political elite. Specifically, Wood's sources and perspective firmly tie his narrative of the Revolution to the vision of the Founding Fathers.

20. For studies that inform my understanding of the early American frontier, see: Andrew R. L. Cayton and Fredrika J. Teute, "Introduction: On the Connection of Frontiers," in Cayton and Teute, eds., *Contact Points: American Frontiers from the Mohawk Valley to the Mississippi, 1750–1830* (Chapel Hill, NC, 1998), 1–15; Aron, *How the West Was Lost*; Gregory H. Nobles, *American Frontiers: Cultural Encounters and Continental Conquest* (New York, 1997); Eric Hinderaker and Peter C. Mancall, *At the Edge of Empire: The Backcountry in British North America* (Baltimore, 2003).

whites. On another, it concerns the consequences of Indian dispossession: of how colonies, states, and empires tried to exert their authority over the backcountry and how they came into conflict with one another and with settlers and speculators who were bent on possessing the land. Finally, the frontier process merged with a dynamic that was foundational to rural society in early America: the production and reproduction of a socioeconomic order based on freehold farming. To white settlers the backcountry represented a place where they could reconstitute a world of independent freehold farms bound together by ties of kinship, community, and mutuality. Far more than government officials or land developers, ordinary farmers searching for land on which to establish their (and their heirs') independence became the driving force behind frontier expansion. Indeed, governments and speculators' schemes for frontier development ultimately rested on their ability to channel and promote settlers' aspirations.

An interpretive model that places independence at its center also provides a deeper understanding of the bitter social conflicts that marked the early American countryside. As has already been stated, the violence and tumult that marked the backcountry was not a byproduct of the founders' revolution, but of tensions intrinsic to agrarian society, which rose to the surface and burst forth during the revolutionary era. Simply put, the American Revolution intensified, but did not invent, the farmer's revolution. The real key to rural conflict lay in the concept of independence itself. On the most obvious level, the pursuit of landed independence brought white settlers into contention with Indians, government officials, and wealthy land speculators—contention that, in certain times and places, raised the specter of sectional, racial, and class conflict. However, just as intrinsic to the unrest that suffused the revolutionary frontier were tensions *among* ordinary white settlers and *within* rural households and communities. Once again, these tensions were anchored in the struggle for agrarian independence. The pursuit of independence could divide households and ignite gender and generational conflict, for the autonomy independence promised was a masculine one that required the subordination of women, children, and other household dependants. Likewise, though the ethos of independence envisioned a society of autonomous and interdependent households, the competitive, conflict-laden reality of achieving independence could place households at odds which each other and shake the foundations of community life.[21]

In sum, the concept and pursuit of independence was foundational to the Revolution, the process of frontier expansion, and agrarian conflict in early

---

21. My understanding of independence as a gendered, generational, and community-level conflict is informed by Daniel Vickers, "Competency and Competition: Economic Culture in Early America," *WMQ* 47 (January 1990): 3–29; James A. Henretta, "Families and Farms: *Mentalité* in Pre-Industrial America," *WMQ* 35 (January 1978): 1–32; and Kulikoff, *From British Peasants to Colonial American Farmers*, 3–4, 27–38.

America. The colonization of British North America was rooted in the concept of independence, for, without it, and its ability to mobilize hundreds of thousands of subjects, British claims to imperial dominion would have remained largely hollow. The Revolution's origins likewise lead back to the idea and pursuit of independence. What gave the revolutionary movement its force was that the logic of American independence resonated with ordinary people who had been pursuing their own struggles for autonomy. The Revolution's power emerged at the confluence of the founders' and farmers' struggles for independence and out of a process whereby common folk and Whig elites appropriated, refashioned, and at times, forwarded the agendas and rhetoric of the other. Finally, the unrest that swept the early American countryside was essentially a consequence of the pursuit of independence. Though agrarian disturbances intersected with class contention, ethnic and racial animus, and even struggles to define the meaning and legacy of the Revolution, such conflicts were only expressions of a far more intrinsic and pervasive battle for land.

This exploration of the farmer's revolution is ethnographic in nature; it scrutinizes daily routines and interpersonal relationships in order to discern how they reflect values, attitudes, and beliefs. In concrete terms, this means that it focuses on ordinary frontier inhabitants and the processes that shaped their lives: migration, farm building, the construction of kin and community networks, and (when necessary) armed resistance. At one level or another, each of these activities was linked to the pursuit of independence and, therefore, is critical to understanding the farmer's revolution. This study does not contend that material conditions determine ideas but, rather, seeks to shed light on the complex relationships that exist between behavior and values, experience and aspirations. *Wild Yankees* reflects this approach and seeks to tell the story of the frontier revolution in Northeast Pennsylvania while placing it in a larger interpretive framework. Each of its six chapters examines how an aspect of frontier experience (e.g., Indian-European contact, war, migration, and farm building) crossed paths with the struggle for independence. In addition, each chapter follows the flow of events in Northeast Pennsylvania. The first chapter sets the stage for this study by discussing the Wyoming controversy's social, political, and intercultural origins. The next four chapters focus on the dynamics of agrarian unrest in the region and take the story up to the turn of the century. The last two chapters chart the resolution of the Wyoming dispute in the first decades of the nineteenth century.

What follows, then, is the story of how Wyoming, a place the Indians called "the large plains," became "a field of blood." It is also the story of the people who fought and died for Wyoming and of how their struggles shaped America.

Chapter 1

"Among Quarrelsome Yankees, Insidious Indians, and Lonely Wilds"

Natives, Colonists, and the Wyoming Controversy

On July 20, 1775, the Reverend Philip Vickers Fithian prepared to set out from Sunbury, Pennsylvania, up the north branch of the Susquehanna River. Fithian, a New Jersey native, graduate of Princeton, and one-time tutor in the employ of the powerful Virginia planter Robert Carter, had received a license from the Presbytery of Philadelphia the previous December to make missionary tours through western Pennsylvania, Maryland, and Virginia. It was on one of these tours that the reverend made his way up the Susquehanna Valley. Fithian, contemplating the road before him, wrote in his diary: "I must now away up this long river, sixty miles higher, among quarrelsome Yankees, insidious Indians, and, at best, lonely wilds."[1]

Fithian journeyed into a revolutionary frontier in the making. His diary entry, besides expressing his foreboding of the trip that lay ahead, alludes to some of the peoples and processes that were instrumental to its formation. The reverend's reference to "insidious Indians" serves as a reminder that Native peoples occupied the eastern woodlands long before the arrival of European colonists and that the farmer's American Revolution was, in part, a product of Indian-European conflict. Next, Fithian's allusion to "quarrelsome Yankees," though specifically aimed at the Connecticut claimants who contested Pennsylvania's authority in the upper Susquehanna and Delaware valleys, brings to mind the

---

1. John A. Garraty and Mark C. Carnes, eds., *American National Biography*, 24 vols. (New York, 1999), 8:44–45; Extracts from the Diary of the Rev. Philip Vickers Fithian, July 20, 1775, SCP 6:329.

thousands of determined and factious Euroamericans who both settled and *unsettled* the frontier. Finally, Fithian's mention of "lonely wilds," though it ignores the fact that the backcountry was hardly a virgin land before the arrival of Europeans, suggests the importance of the land itself to the story of the revolutionary frontier, for possession of the land was the axis of contention between colonists and Indians and, later, among the whites who invaded, claimed, and occupied America.

Like Fithian's diary entry, events in the opening decades of the Wyoming dispute illustrate that the struggle for independence along the revolutionary frontier was born of, and shaped by, an earlier battle for land and power fought between Indians and colonists. The controversy highlights that land disputes between colonies and colonists were both products *and* catalysts of Indian dispossession. Indeed, one of the earliest casualties of the legal maneuvering and violence that marked the Wyoming dispute was Indian soil rights. Exploring the origins of agrarian unrest in Northeast Pennsylvania also reveals how a distinct culture of violence took root among the region's white inhabitants, which was, in part, an undeniable legacy of bitter, racially charged conflict between Indians and colonists. One of the most enduring links between Indian-European contact and the struggle over property and power in the Wyoming region was a brutal brand of violence that settlers first deployed against Native adversaries and, later, against competing groups of whites.

The Origins of the Wyoming Controversy

The Wyoming controversy grew out of the land and jurisdictional disputes that were endemic in British America. Imperial officials, who often possessed little knowledge of the American landscape they parceled out, issued vague or inaccurate patents that frequently interfered with earlier grants or encroached on competing claims. In addition, Indians, with their decentralized political systems, their own jurisdictional controversies, and their distinctive cultural definitions of property rights, commonly resold the same piece of land to different purchasers. Colonists, desiring to claim for themselves as much New World territory as possible, actively abetted imperial officials' geographical fictions and Indians' problematic land transactions. As a result, colonies and colonists who assumed that royal grants and Indian deeds ceded clear and absolute ownership of land often became embroiled in territorial disputes.[2] It was this set of circumstances that

2. For a discussion of Indian attitudes toward property, see William Cronon, *Changes in the Land: Indians, Colonists, and the Ecology of New England* (New York, 1983), 54–68. Examples of how disputes over royal charters and Indian deeds fueled land disputes can be found in: Alan Taylor,

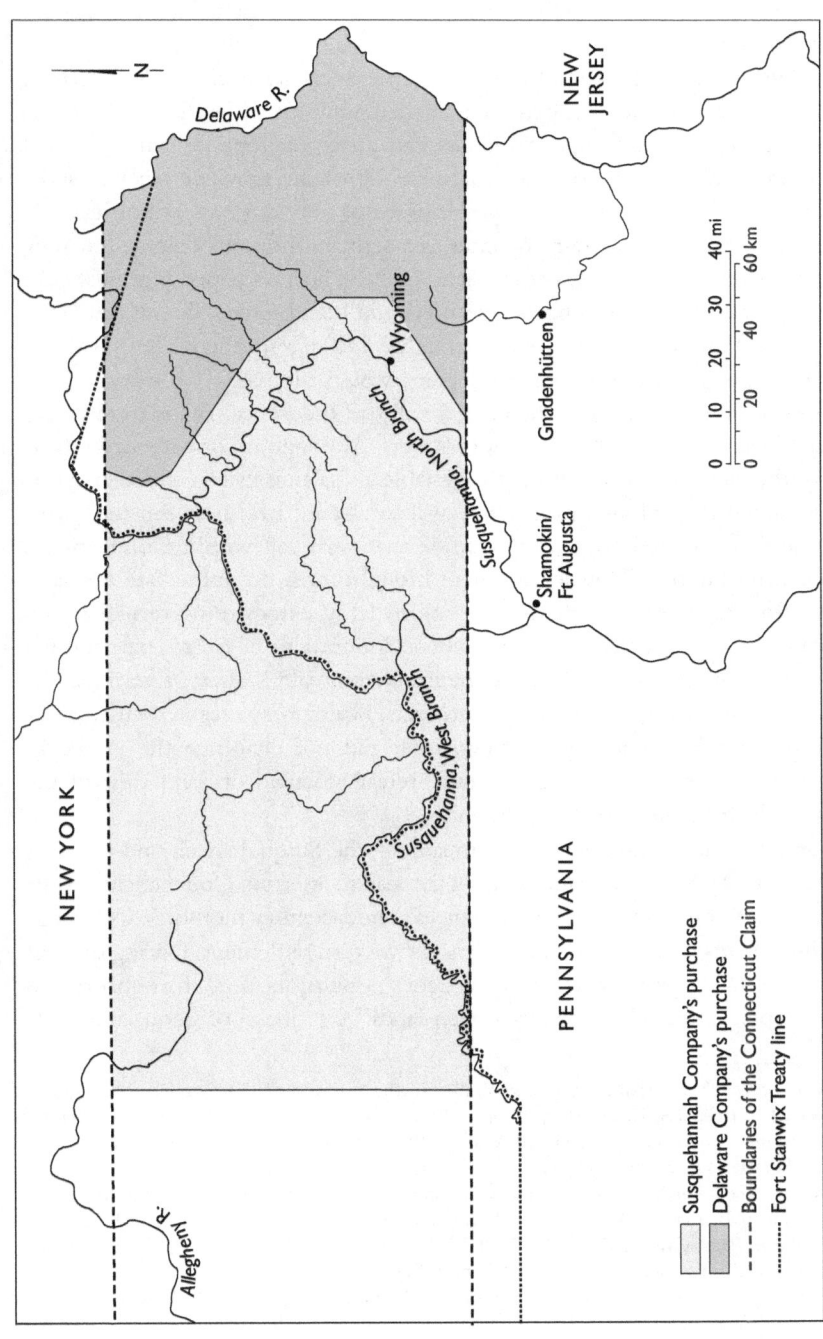

Map 1. The Connecticut Claim, 1754–68

triggered what would ultimately become a lengthy jurisdictional dispute between the colonies, and later the states, of Connecticut and Pennsylvania.

In 1662 Charles II granted a generous provincial charter to Connecticut. The colony, which owed its existence to the ambitions of its Puritan founders rather than the crown, had petitioned for the charter in hopes of gaining a royal seal of approval for their colonial enterprise. What the province received satisfied its leaders' most optimistic expectations: not only did imperial officials allow Connecticut to maintain its status as a semiautonomous colony, but they also awarded the colony a sea-to-sea land grant. Thus, on paper, Connecticut's territory extended from its border with Rhode Island to the "South Sea" (Pacific Ocean) and covered a territory roughly 120 miles wide by several thousand miles long. Connecticut's royal grant would ultimately be truncated by France's imperial claims, but the colony still had theoretical rights to territory extending as far west as the Mississippi River.[3] Although no one seemed to notice at the time, the royal grant that established Pennsylvania nineteen years later awarded the colony's proprietor, William Penn, land between the forty-first and forty-second degrees of latitude that was well within Connecticut's 1662 charter bounds. This development brought forth no immediate howls of protest from Connecticut; indeed, the colony let its extensive western claim lay dormant for almost a century. Only when Connecticut began to experience a land shortage in the 1750s did it reexamine and eventually reassert its seventeenth-century charter bounds. The New Englanders, having only recently settled a decades-long border dispute with New York, did not challenge the territorial integrity of their western neighbor but, instead, focused on land west of the Delaware River claimed by Pennsylvania.[4]

Three Connecticut-based land companies—the Susquehannah and the First and Second Delaware companies—took the lead in asserting Connecticut's western claims. A convergence of circumstances at mid-century motivated Connecticut's inhabitants to embark on bold plans for western settlement. During the first half of the eighteenth century, Connecticut's population more than quadrupled and occupied most of the colony's open lands. A shortage of good, affordable

---

" 'A Kind of Warr': The Contest for Land on the Northeast Frontier" *WMQ* 46 (Jan. 1989): 4–5, 11; Michael A. Bellesiles, *Revolutionary Outlaws: Ethan Allen and the Struggle for Independence on the Early American Frontier* (Charlottesville, VA, 1993), 27–32; Thomas L. Purvis, "Origins and Patterns of Agrarian Unrest in New Jersey, 1735–1754," *WMQ* 39 (Oct. 1982): 602–10; and Philip J. Schwartz, *The Jarring Interests: New York's Boundary Makers, 1664–1776* (Albany, NY, 1979).

3. William E. Price, "A Study of a Frontier Community in Transition: The History of Wilkes-Barre, Pennsylvania, 1750–1800" (Ph.D. diss., Kent State University, 1979), 9; Robert J. Taylor, *Colonial Connecticut: A History* (Millwood, NY, 1979), 29.

4. Price, "Study of a Frontier Community in Transition," 9; Taylor, *Colonial Connecticut*, 29, 56–59; *SCP* 1:lviii–lxii.

farmland was especially pronounced in eastern Connecticut. In addition to population pressure, an upsurge in land speculation, both within Connecticut and throughout British North America, fueled public interest in frontier expansion.[5] More immediately, the Susquehannah and Delaware companies found their origins in Connecticut residents' failed efforts to obtain permission to exploit their colony's western claim. In May 1750, the inhabitants of Simsbury sent a petition to the Connecticut General Assembly requesting a town grant west of the Hudson River in order to relieve overcrowding in their community. Although the legislature rejected the petition, other towns joined Simsbury in calling on Connecticut to assert its latent charter claims. Between 1750 and 1753, the assembly received twelve such petitions. One, submitted in March 1753 by the inhabitants of several eastern towns, contained the first mention of the Wyoming region as a potential site for settlement. The Connecticut Assembly rejected all of these entreaties for fear of upsetting their recently negotiated boundary settlement with New York and because most legislators felt that any claim based on Connecticut's 1662 charter would not stand up to close legal scrutiny. In response, the petitioners shelved their plans to obtain modest town grants from the legislature and set out on the more ambitious scheme of establishing a colony west of the Delaware River.[6]

The Susquehannah Company, which soon proved to be the most active of the three Connecticut land corporations, was born from this effort to create a new Connecticut in the west. The first meeting of the company took place in Windham on July 18, 1753. The organization that took shape there reflected the town-founding traditions of Puritan New England. The Susquehannah Company was not a legally chartered corporation, but a self-created entity whose existence depended on the consensus of its members. Moreover, in a highly democratic political structure reminiscent of New England towns, Susquehannah Company shareholders held meetings at which they voted on all major policy issues. Tempering this "shareholders' democracy" was a standing committee (much like town selectmen) who dealt with all the day-to-day business that came before the company—activities such as collecting payment for shares or surveying company townships. Finally, the company, like seventeenth-century New England towns, based itself on a concept of corporate ownership in which shareholders possessed an equal right to all the unsettled lands it held. Unlike early New England towns,

---

5. Price, "Frontier Community in Transition," 16; Richard L. Bushman, *From Puritan to Yankee: Character and the Social Order in Connecticut, 1690–1765* (Cambridge, MA, 1967), 83; *SCP* 1:xli–liii, lxv.

6. Julian P. Boyd, "Connecticut's Experiment in Expansion: The Susquehannah Company, 1753–1803," *Journal of Economic and Business History* 27 (1931): 40–41; Price, "Frontier Community in Transition," 23–25; *SCP* 1:lviii–lxiv.

the Susquehannah Company did not obtain land through the colonial assembly. Instead, it rested its claims on Connecticut's dormant charter bounds and the direct purchase of Indian lands. In addition, the company added a commercial ethic to the communal approach of seventeenth-century town corporations: its shares could be sold or traded for a profit.[7] Interest in the venture soon spread among would-be speculators and frontier settlers throughout New England, and the company, which started with only a few hundred members in the summer of 1753, expanded its ranks to eight hundred shareholders by 1754. The value of company shares kept pace with its growing membership: in 1753 shares sold for "Two Spanish Mill'd dollars," about a year later they sold for five, and by November 1754 the price had increased to nine dollars.[8]

The creation of the Susquehannah Company placed Pennsylvania and Connecticut on a collision course. At the company's July 18 meeting, shareholders agreed to send a committee of seven men to the Susquehanna Valley to find a suitable site for settlement, purchase the land from its Indian inhabitants, and survey it into towns and lots. This "Journeying Committee" departed in October, explored the Wyoming Valley, surveyed several town sites there, and made its way back to Connecticut.[9] In November Pennsylvania provincial secretary Richard Peters reported to the colony's proprietors the "disagreeable News" that people from Connecticut had been to Wyoming and "made great disturbance among the People" there with the news that they would return in the spring "with a Thousand Men and settle those lands."[10]

The Indians' Struggle for Independence

Pennsylvania's proprietors were not the only ones discomforted by the news of the New Englanders' expedition to the Susquehanna Valley. The Connecticut land companies' efforts to acquire and settle lands west of the Delaware River also upset Indians who occupied or claimed territory in Northeast Pennsylvania.

7. SCP 1:xxxii–xxxiii, lxxiv–lxxv; Boyd, "Connecticut's Experiment in Expansion": 42–43; for more on New England's seventeenth-century town corporations, see John Frederick Martin, *Profits in the Wilderness: Entrepreneurship and the Founding of New England Towns in the Seventeenth Century* (Chapel Hill, NC, 1991), quote from 4.

8. Minutes of a Meeting of the Susquehannah Company, July 18, 1753; Minutes of a Meeting of the Susquehannah Company, May 1, 1754; and Minutes of a Meeting of the Susquehannah Company, Nov. 20, 1754, SCP 1:28–29, 168, 186–87, 168; Boyd, "Connecticut's Experiment in Expansion": 42.

9. Minutes of a Meeting of the Susquehannah Company, July 18, 1753, and Minutes of a Meeting of the Susquehannah Company, Sept. 6, 1753, SCP 1:28–29, 40–41.

10. Richard Peters to the Pennsylvania Proprietors, Nov. 27, 1753, and Thomas Penn to Richard Peters, Feb. 1, 1754, SCP 1:42, 51–52.

The Six Nations, who viewed the Wyoming Valley as part of their domain and a strategic gateway to the Iroquois heartland, were, according to Pennsylvania Governor James Hamilton, "highly offended" at the prospect of it being "overrun with White People." The few Nanticoke Indians who inhabited the valley must have also felt threatened by the arrival of the Susquehannah Company's emissaries. The news also angered Delaware Indians from the Moravian settlement of Gnadenhütten who viewed the Wyoming Valley as part of their homeland. Hoping to forestall Euroamerican intrusions, and encouraged by the Six Nations, about seventy Delawares led by the sachem Teedyuscung left Gnadenhütten and occupied the Wyoming Valley early in 1754.[11]

The Wyoming region was but one of many places where Natives fought their own struggle for independence—a struggle that, though certainly not equivalent to the one waged by white settlers during the era of the American Revolution, also hinged on the possession of land. In the mid eighteenth century, Northeast Pennsylvania was not only a prize for which colonies contended, but a cultural crossroads where Indians and colonists met, intermingled, and at times, fought one another. By century's end, however, the region's Native population had largely been replaced by Europeans.[12] Many factors contributed to this process: disease, the fur trade, and warfare decimated Indian populations, set into motion ecological changes that upset Indian subsistence strategies, and undermined Indians' political autonomy. However, territorial and jurisdictional disputes between colonies and colonists contributed to this shift from a Native to a European population.

The elimination of Indian authority and soil rights in Northeast Pennsylvania was directly connected to the Wyoming controversy. After the return of the Susquehannah Company's journeying committee, both the company and Pennsylvania's proprietors made aggressive moves to secure possession of the Wyoming Valley, which placed Indians and Indian soil rights at the center of the dispute. Indeed, as Richard Peters observed, the conflict was not only "between Subject and Subject but between Indian and Englishman."[13]

The Albany Congress of 1754, which provided a backdrop for Pennsylvania and Connecticut's emerging struggle over the Wyoming Valley, drew Indians deeper into the controversy. The congress, which was supposed to improve Anglo-Indian relations and foster intercolony cooperation, only served to increase

---

11. James Hamilton to Roger Wolcott, March 4, 1754, *SCP* 1:56; Anthony F. C. Wallace, *King of the Delawares: Teedyuscung, 1700–1763* (Freeport, NY, 1970), 47–53.

12. A work that outlines the upper Susquehanna Valley's Indian population and the emergence of a Euroamerican society is Peter C. Mancall, *Valley of Opportunity: Economic Culture along the Upper Susquehanna, 1700–1800* (Ithaca, NY, 1991).

13. Richard Peters to Sir William Johnson, May 18, 1761, *SCP* 2:98.

tensions between Pennsylvania and Connecticut, between Indians and whites, and between the Iroquois (who claimed jurisdiction over the Wyoming Valley) and those Indians who made the valley their home.[14] Without asking the permission of provincial or imperial officials, agents of the Connecticut land companies purchased millions of acres of land in the upper Susquehanna and Delaware valleys from Iroquois Indians attending the Albany Congress. When the companies later sought Connecticut's sanction, the governor readily gave his approval but a more cautious legislature withheld theirs—a stance it would maintain for seventeen years. Like most private purchases of Indian land, the Susquehannah and Delaware companies' Indian deeds stood on shaky legal ground. Provincial and imperial authorities frowned on such freelance acquisitions of Indian land. In addition, rumors spread that the Indians who ratified the agreement only did so after being plied with generous amounts of alcohol. For their part, the Iroquois who signed the agreement did so without consulting the council of the Six Nations or the Indian peoples who actually occupied the land they sold. The Albany Congress ended up driving a wedge between the Six Nations and Indians in Pennsylvania who felt betrayed by the willingness of the Iroquois to sell their homeland from under their feet. Adding to the confusion, Pennsylvania's delegation to the Albany Congress also obtained a deed from the Six Nations in an effort to check the New Englanders' schemes—a deed that covered much of the land purchased by the Susquehannah and Delaware companies but that, unlike those obtained by the New Englanders, followed formal treaty protocols.[15] Thus to the conflicting colonial charters that divided Pennsylvania and Connecticut were added competing Indian purchases.

The Albany Congress marked a turning point, not only for the colonies and colonists involved in the Wyoming controversy, but also for the Indians who inhabited or claimed land between the Delaware and Susquehanna rivers. During the congress, the Six Nations formally ceded control of Northeast Pennsylvania to Europeans. More important, the conference spurred both the Connecticut land companies and Pennsylvania to redirect their energies toward recruiting white settlers to occupy their claims.

The outbreak of the Seven Years' War in 1755 interrupted both sides' plans for settlement. This imperial conflict was linked, at least locally, to the Wyoming

---

14. For a comprehensive examination of the Albany congress and its impact, see Timothy J. Shannon, *Indians and Colonists at the Crossroads of Empire* (Ithaca, NY, 2000).

15. *SCP* 1:lxxxi–lxxxix, Deed from Indians of the Six Nations to the Susquehannah Company, July 11, 1754, *SCP* 1:101–21; Shannon, *Indians and Colonists*, 108–9. For a look at the complexities of Iroquois land dealing at the Albany congress and of Iroquois-Delaware relations, see *Indians and Colonists*, 161–71; and Frances Jennings, " 'Pennsylvania Indians' and the Iroquois," in *Beyond the Covenant Chain: The Iroquois and Their Neighbors in Indian North America, 1600–1800*, ed. Daniel K. Richter and James H. Merrell (Syracuse, NY, 1987), 75–91.

dispute. The Delaware Indians, who were outraged over the moves made by Pennsylvania, Connecticut, and the Six Nations at the Albany Congress, saw the onset of hostilities between the French and the English as an opportunity to even the score. Starting with the near annihilation of General Braddock's expedition in July 1755 at the hands of French and Indian forces, Native warriors struck all along the Anglo-American frontier. Pennsylvania was particularly hard hit as Indian war parties penetrated deep into the province, killing hundreds of colonists and driving thousands of others from their homes. Encouraged and supplied by the French, Delaware Indians participated in these attacks, ravaging Penn's Creek and other white settlements along the Susquehanna Valley. The situation finally stabilized in 1758 when the war began to turn against the French and British troops arrived in Pennsylvania in force.[16]

Only after the Treaty of Easton in 1758, when the Delawares abandoned the war, did the New Englanders decide that it was safe to forge ahead with plans for settlement.[17] In the summer of 1760 word reached Philadelphia that people from Connecticut had established a settlement along the Delaware River at Cushietunk. The timing of the New Englanders' arrival was particularly bad for Pennsylvania's proprietary government: not only was the province's territorial integrity being challenged, but many feared that the intrusion would lead to another costly Indian war. The prospect of Indian-white violence became even more immediate in August 1761 when the Six Nations repudiated the purchases made by the Susquehannah and Delaware companies at the Albany Congress.[18] Tensions further increased after the Susquehannah Company resolved to send a large party of settlers to the Wyoming Valley in May 1762.[19]

As in the past, the Delaware sachem Teedyuscung led Indian resistance to the company's plans. Late in the summer of 1760, Teedyuscung met with Governor James Hamilton in Philadelphia to complain of the arrival of the Connecticut settlers and to warn that if the New Englanders did not leave, the Delawares would "turn them off." Two years later, while returning home from a treaty conference in Lancaster where he had again protested the influx of

16. For a more detailed account of Delaware attitudes, their involvement in the Seven Years' War, and how their decision to go to war was connected with the Wyoming dispute, see SCP 2:i–xvi (esp. xv); Francis Jennings, *Empire of Fortune: Crowns, Colonies and Tribes in the Seven Years War in America* (New York, 1988), 263–81; Memorandum of Conrad Weiser's Conversations with Moses Tetamy and Others, Nov. 26, 1756, and Thomas Penn to William Logan, June 21, 1757, SCP 2:2–5, 11.

17. A good description of the process by which the Delawares made peace with the English and the Six Nations can be found in Jennings, *Empire of Fortune*, 274–81, 342–48, 396–403.

18. Richard Peters to Lewis Gordon, Sept. 15, 1760, and Minutes of the Indian Conference at Easton, Aug. 1761, SCP 2:24, 111–12.

19. Minutes of a Meeting of the Susquehannah Company, May 19, 1762, and Minutes of a Meeting of the Susquehannah Company, July 27, 1762, SCP 2:130–31, 145–46.

people from Connecticut, Teedyuscung and his entourage confronted more than a hundred Susquehannah Company settlers who had recently arrived to take up land in the Wyoming Valley. He and his Indian companions traded angry words with the New Englanders and managed to scare them off with threats of violence. However, the Delaware leader had only won his people a temporary reprieve from the growing pressures of white settlement.[20]

One night in April 1763, Teedyuscung's house caught fire and he burned to death in his sleep. There is little doubt that the Susquehannah Company was behind the conflagration. More than any other event, his death symbolizes how the Wyoming dispute promoted the dispossession of Northeast Pennsylvania's Indian inhabitants. His demise was no accident but the product of a larger act of arson that resulted in the fiery destruction of the Indian settlement at Wyoming. Less than two weeks after the destruction of the Delaware village, a dozen Connecticut families took possession of the site; a month later more than 150 New Englanders were planting crops and building cabins there.[21]

Teedyuscung's assassination did not guarantee New Englanders an easy occupation of their western claims, for both Indians and imperial authorities set up new obstacles to white settlement. Fearing that the arrival of large numbers of Yankees along the Susquehanna would provoke a war with the Six Nations, the British Privy Council issued orders in June 1763 that forbade further settlement in the Wyoming region and instructed the people already there to return to Connecticut.[22] Yet news of this directive came too late for the New Englanders in the valley: shortly after the Privy Council made their decision, Teedyuscung's son, Captain Bull, led a Delaware war party that killed or captured the Connecticut claimants who occupied the site of his slain father's village. Though the attack was part of a much larger Indian uprising known as Pontiac's War, the motives for the Delaware raid on Wyoming were clearly personal.[23]

---

20. Memorandum of a Conference with Teedyuscung, Sept. 18, 1760, *SCP* 2:25; Wallace, *King of the Delawares*, 254–58; *SCP* 2:xxvi–xxvii; Conference with Teedyuscung, Nov. 19, 1762, *SCP* 2:180–83.

21. For an overview of Teedyuscung's efforts to resist the Connecticut claim, see *SCP* 2:xvii–xxxii. An account of Teedyuscung's death and the circumstances that surrounded it can be found in Wallace, *King of the Delawares*, 258–61.

22. An examination of the imperial government's involvement in the Wyoming dispute can be found in *SCP* 2:xxxiii–xlii; Instructions from the Privy Council to Thomas Fitch, June 15, 1763, *SCP* 2:256.

23. Wallace, *King of the Delawares*, 261–66; Frederick J. Stefon, "The Wyoming Valley," in *Beyond Philadelphia: The American Revolution in the Pennsylvania Hinterland*, ed. John B. Frantz and William Pencak (University Park, PA, 1998), 134–36; Alexander Graydon to James Burd, Oct. 16, 1763, and Extract from the *Pennsylvania Gazette*, Oct. 27, 1763, *SCP* 2:272, 277; George W. Franz, *Paxton: A Study of Community Structure and Mobility in the Colonial Pennsylvania Backcountry* (New York, 1989), 66–67.

The Privy Council's failure to avoid bloodshed between Indians and whites in the Susquehanna Valley illustrates that territorial and jurisdictional conflicts like the Wyoming controversy made it difficult for provincial and imperial authorities to regulate frontier expansion or, more specifically, to protect Indian soil rights. For their part, the Delawares' decision to go to war once again did not stem the tide of white settlement—the Indians raided, but did not repossess, the Wyoming Valley. The New Englanders remained determined that no one, Indians or Pennsylvanians, would keep them from occupying their claim. Likewise, Pennsylvania officials, realizing that Indians could no longer serve as an effective bulwark against Yankee intruders, turned to other methods of maintaining their hold on the valley. Indians, in sum, found themselves increasingly marginalized in the contest over the Wyoming region.

The Fort Stanwix Treaty of 1768, which established a "line of property" between Indians and whites, became an instrument through which Pennsylvania and Connecticut land companies vied for possession of Northeast Pennsylvania and extinguished Indian authority and soil rights in the region. Pennsylvania used the treaty council as an opportunity to expand and consolidate its control over the upper Susquehanna and Delaware valleys. First, the province acquired additional land between the west and north branches of the Susquehanna River from the Six Nations, which became known as the "New Purchase." Second, Governor John Penn leased one-hundred-acre tracts in the Wyoming Valley to proprietary agents Amos Ogden, John Jennings, and Charles Stewart for a term of seven years and authorized them to issue leases to settlers who promised to support Pennsylvania against the inroads of Connecticut claimants. Meanwhile, the Susquehannah and Delaware companies interpreted the Fort Stanwix Treaty (which placed the boundary of white settlement west of the Susquehanna River) as a cancellation of imperial orders forbidding the occupation of the Wyoming region and as a go-ahead for their expansionist plans.[24] Thus, the treaty opened Northeast Pennsylvania to the axes and plows of colonists and the Wyoming dispute, which had formerly been a multidimensional contest between Indians and colonists, largely became a struggle between whites.

A Brutal Legacy

Native peoples' unsuccessful struggle for land and autonomy in Northeast Pennsylvania opened the way for the contentious pursuit of power and property in

24. *SCP* 3:i–xvi; Minutes of a Meeting of the Susquehannah Company, Dec. 28, 1768, and Instructions to Charles Stewart and Others, 1769, *SCP* 3:43–47, 331–32; James Kirby Martin, "The Return of the Paxton Boys and the Historical State of the Pennsylvania Frontier, 1764–1774," *Pennsylvania History* 38 (April 1971): 126.

the region among whites. Colonists flooded into the vacuum created by the cessation of Iroquois authority over the upper Susquehanna and Delaware valleys and by the forced dispossession of Wyoming's Indian inhabitants. Soon the legal jockeying between Pennsylvania and the Connecticut land companies that had marked the earliest phase of the Wyoming dispute was joined by a bitter face-to-face conflict between Pennamites and Yankees.

Though Indians may have largely disappeared from the Wyoming region in the wake of the Seven Years' War, the legacy of Indian-white contact and conflict continued to shape events there. From the start, contention between Indians and colonists and among Euroamerican land claimants was intertwined. Specifically, the bloody, interracial confrontations that occurred during the Seven Years' War, Pontiac's Rebellion, and later, the Revolutionary War, schooled settlers in the types of violence and terror tactics they would later bring to bear against land speculators, government officials, and each other. In other words, struggle over land and independence in Northeast Pennsylvania was prefigured by decades of racialized frontier violence.

Pennamites and Yankees built on a bitter history of Indian-white conflict by engaging in a struggle that was not just violent, but *deadly*. That a legacy of interracial contention added to the intensity of the Wyoming controversy can be deduced from the fact that other regions which experienced conflicts over land and jurisdiction, but did not possess Northeast Pennsylvania's recent history of Indian-white warfare, saw much lower levels of bloodshed and death. In northern New Jersey, New York's Hudson valley, Maine, and the Hampshire Grants (Vermont) yeoman farmers and landlords became embroiled in land disputes that, at times, intertwined with questions of political jurisdiction. In none of these areas, however, was there the persistent use of deadly force that characterized Pennsylvania's Pennamite-Yankee war. The killing of a proprietary agent by backcountry insurgents in Maine was so shockingly out of the ordinary that it contributed to the collapse of settler resistance in the region. Also, unlike agrarian conflicts in New York and Vermont, where rioters did most of the dying, and government posses and militias most of the killing, Wyoming's land rioters repeatedly proved their willingness to use deadly force.[25]

Pennsylvania's notorious Indian-killer and frontier outlaw Lazarus Stewart best illustrates the connections between Indian-European conflict and Pennamite-Yankee violence. Stewart was born in 1734 in Hanover, a backwoods settlement

---

25. The murder of Paul Chadwick in Maine is detailed in Alan Taylor, *Liberty Men and the Great Proprietors: The Revolutionary Settlement on the Maine Frontier, 1760–1820* (Chapel Hill, NC, 1990), 202–5; Edward Countryman, " 'Out of the Bounds of the Law': Northern Land Rioters in the Eighteenth Century," in *The American Revolution: Explorations in the History of American Radicalism*, ed. Alfred F. Young (DeKalb, IL, 1976), 47.

in Lancaster County, Pennsylvania. His family, along with thousands of Scots-Irish, had immigrated to the frontier in the late 1720s. By the time he was thirty-seven, Stewart possessed a well-earned reputation for violence. He was wanted for multiple murder, assault, riot, arson, and treason; indeed, on one occasion he beat a constable with an axe handle and threatened another man that he would "cut him to Pieces, and make a Breakfast of his Heart."[26] But Lazarus Stewart was far more than a violent outlaw; he was also a father, a man respected by his neighbors, and a local military leader who gained his first combat experience during Braddock's ill-fated expedition of 1755.[27] Stewart first laid eyes on the Wyoming Valley during Pontiac's War—it was a gruesome introduction to a land in which he would ultimately meet his own violent death. In the fall of 1763, Pennsylvania ordered one hundred men under Captain Asher Clayton to proceed to the valley and instructed them to remove the Connecticut settlers there and destroy their crops in order to deny them to Native raiders. A company of rangers under Stewart's command formed part of this force. When Clayton's troops arrived at Wyoming, they found that Captain Bull's Delaware warriors had already destroyed the New Englanders' settlement. The war party had "most cruelly butchered" ten Connecticut claimants and plundered their homes. One victim, a woman, had been "roasted;" the rest "had Awls thrust into their Eyes, and Spears, arrows, Pitchforks, &c sticking in their Bodies." Instead of removing the New Englanders, the Pennsylvanians ended up burying them.[28]

In December 1763, just a few months after his visit to Wyoming, Stewart precipitated a crisis in the Pennsylvania backcountry when he headed a party of men from Lancaster County's Paxton district who murdered six Conestoga Indians at their village along the Susquehanna River and, a week later, cruelly butchered fourteen more who took refuge in the town of Lancaster at the county jail. One person who rushed to the jail after the killers had left was sickened by the sight of the victims—men, women, and children alike—"spread about the prison yard; shot, scalped, hacked, and cut to pieces." Though the Conestogas were Christian Indians allied to Pennsylvania, the "Paxton Boys" justified their actions by claiming that their victims had aided other Native groups who had recently attacked their settlements during Pontiac's War. On a

---

26. Oscar Jewell Harvey and Ernst G. Smith, *A History of Wilkes-Barre, Luzerne County, Pennsylvania*, 6 vols. (Wilkes-Barre, PA, 1927–30), 2:640–44; Stewart Pearce, *Annals of Luzerne County* (Philadelphia, 1866), 100–119; Deposition of John Philip De Hass, Sept. 26, 1770, *CRP* 9:682–84.

27. Harvey and Smith, *History of Wilkes-Barre*, 2:640–41; Pearce, *Annals of Luzerne County*, 101.

28. Alexander Graydon to James Burd, Oct. 16, 1763, and Extract from the *Pennsylvania Gazette*, Oct. 27, 1763, *SCP* 2:272, 277; Franz, *Paxton*, 66–67.

deeper level, the murders were the product of a sharply polarized outlook held by a growing number of white frontier inhabitants in which all Indians, regardless of their religion or allegiance, were defined as the enemy because of their race. Pennsylvania ordered the arrest of Stewart and his followers, but owing to the considerable support they received from white frontier inhabitants, none was ever brought to trial.[29] Weeks after the Paxton Boys' murderous raid, hundreds of backcountry settlers marched on Philadelphia with the intention of killing Christian Indians harbored there by the government and seeking vengeance on provincial officials whom they blamed for the poor state of frontier defense. The rioters never achieved their aims, but they did succeed in highlighting the racial enmity and rebelliousness that gripped Pennsylvania's hinterlands.[30] In 1765 the Pennsylvania frontier experienced another outburst of violence rooted in tensions between Indians and whites when Cumberland County residents, fearing that government-sponsored traders intended to sell firearms to Indians, attacked and plundered pack trains laden with trade goods destined for Native communities. Later, the rioters, who became known as "Black Boys" because of the soot with which they smeared their faces, violently resisted British troops who attempted to restore order.[31] Finally, another racially motivated mass murder occurred in January 1768 when two frontiersmen, Frederick Stump and John Ironcutter, killed and scalped an Indian family along Penn's Creek. Once again, settlers expressed their solidarity as whites and defied provincial authorities: when Cumberland County officials arrested Stump and Ironcutter, a mob descended on the county jail and set them free.[32]

29. Robert Proud, *The History of Pennsylvania in North America*, in *The Paxton Papers*, ed. John R. Dunbar (The Hauge, Netherlands, 1957), 25, 29; Sheriff John Hay to Governor John Penn, Dec. 22, 1763, and Dec. 27, 1763, *CRP* 9:102–3; James Kirby Martin, "The Return of the Paxton Boys," 117–18; Harvey and Smith, *History of Wilkes-Barre*, 2:640–41; Gregory T. Knouff, "Whiteness and Warfare on a Revolutionary Frontier," in *Friends and Enemies in Penn's Woods: Indians, Colonists, and the Racial Construction of Pennsylvania*, ed. William A. Pencak and Daniel K. Richter (University Park, P.A., 2004), 238–57; Krista Camenzind, "Violence, Race, and the Paxton Boys," in *Friends and Enemies*, 201–20.

30. For an overview of the Paxton Boys' massacres and Pennsylvania's frontier crisis, see Alden T. Vaughn, "Frontier Banditti and the Indians: The Paxton Boys' Legacy," *Pennsylvania History* 51 (Jan. 1984): 1–29; and Brooke Hindle, "The March of the Paxton Boys," *WMQ* 3 (Oct. 1946): 461–86.

31. Eleanor M. Webster, "Insurrection at Fort Loudon in 1765, Rebellion or Preservation of the Peace?" *Western Pennsylvania History Magazine* 47 (Apr. 1964): 125–40; Dorothy Fennell, "From Rebelliousness to Insurrection: A Social History of the Whiskey Rebellion, 1765–1802" (Ph.D. diss., University of Pittsburgh, 1981), 10; Lt. Col. Reid to General Gage, June 1, 1765, and June 4, 1765, and General Gage to Governor John Penn, June 16, 1769, *CRP* 9:268–69, 267–68.

32. Martin, "Return of the Paxton Boys," 121–23; Deposition of William Blyth, Jan. 19, 1768, *CRP* 9:414.

This outburst of anti-Indian violence and rebellion among Pennsylvania's backcountry inhabitants was also a symptom of their anxiety over achieving independence. Aside from any racial motivations, Stewart and his Paxton Boys murdered Indians because they perceived them as a threat to the peaceful possession of their frontier freeholds and to the enjoyment of the rights and privileges landownership conveyed. Likewise, settlers resisted provincial and imperial officials because, by their estimation, they failed to distribute frontier lands equitably or provide basic security for white settlers.[33] In March 1769, Lazarus Stewart and sixty-three frontier inhabitants added their voices to this rising tide of dissent when they sent a petition to the Pennsylvania Assembly denouncing the colony's land policies. In particular, the petitioners complained that favoritism had denied them access to lands in Pennsylvania's New Purchase. They claimed that government insiders had managed to engross thousands of acres of land even though land office regulations limited individual claimants to three-hundred-acre grants. Worse still, they accused the land office of allowing well-connected gentlemen to file their claims before ordinary settlers had an opportunity to do so, thus enabling them to secure the best lands.[34]

Complaints among Pennsylvania's western inhabitants concerning the inequities of the province's land policies set the stage for an alliance between Stewart's Paxton settlers and the Susquehannah Company, which would increase both the scope and the intensity of conflict in the Wyoming region. Stewart and his followers saw in the Connecticut claim an opportunity to obtain frontier freeholds on good terms and escape Pennsylvania's rule, and began negotiations with the Susquehannah Company late in 1769. They offered to rid the valley of Pennsylvania claimants in return for a town grant; the company eagerly accepted the deal. In February 1770 Stewart and about fifty Pennsylvanians journeyed to the Wyoming Valley and joined the New Englanders there in defiance of Pennsylvania.[35] The Paxton settlers' decision ignited a new round of warfare, wherein white settlers would train the violence they had once aimed at Indians against each other.

---

33. Richard M. Brown, "Back Country Rebellions and the Homestead Ethic in America, 1740–1799," in *Tradition, Conflict, and Modernization: Perspectives on the American Revolution*, ed. Richard M. Brown and Don E. Fehrenbacher (New York, 1977), 76–79; Camenzind, "Violence, Race, and the Paxton Boys," 201–20.

34. *SCP* 3:xv–xviii; Edmund Physick to Thomas Penn, April 19, 1769, and Edmund Physick to Thomas Penn, Sept. 28, 1769, *SCP* 3:101–2, 103 n. 2, 185; Martin, "Return of the Paxton Boys," 126–27.

35. *SCP* 4:vi–vii; Petition of Lazarus Young and Others, Sept. 11, 1769, *SCP* 3:176–77; The Executive Committee to John Montgomery and Lazarus Young, Jan. 15, 1770, *SCP* 4:5–6; Martin, "The Return of the Paxton Boys," 120, 128–30; John Penn to Thomas Penn, March 10, 1770, *SCP* 4:42–43.

Before the appearance of Stewart and his Paxton settlers, violence between Pennamites and Yankees had been limited. Pennsylvania officials had focused their efforts on arresting Yankee settlers for trespassing and disturbing the peace while Connecticut claimants busied themselves with fending off these prosecutions in court. On one occasion, Northampton County sheriff John Jennings read out a proclamation before a gathering of Connecticut claimants forbidding their settlement: needless to say, Jennings's audience did not like his message. When he finished, a Connecticut settler fired a gun over the sheriff's head but no harm came to him. On September 22, 1769, the two sides exchanged shots; however, no one was injured in the incident. But as the number of Yankee settlers grew, Pennsylvania officials became more desperate and more willing to use force. Late in 1769, Pennamites, reinforced by a cannon and a two-hundred-man posse under Sheriff Jennings, overwhelmed and expelled Wyoming's Yankee occupants. Though aggressive and heavy-handed, this act of dispossession was accomplished without serious injury or loss of life.[36]

With the arrival of the Paxton settlers early in 1770, bloodshed and murder replaced legal maneuvering as the coin of conflict in the Wyoming Valley. On March 28 a gun battle broke out between Pennamites and Yankees resulting in the death of Baltzer Stager, one of Stewart's followers, and the wounding of two other Connecticut claimants. This deadly encounter was the first act in what would become an intensifying cycle of violence. In the weeks and months following Stager's death, Pennamites and Yankees engaged one another in numerous gunfights.[37] Lazarus Stewart contributed to this mayhem on January 20, 1771, when he added a white man to his long list of Indian victims. A posse led by Northampton County sheriff Peter Kachlein and Amos Ogden's brother, Deputy Sheriff Nathan Ogden, surrounded a Pennamite fort that had recently been captured by Stewart and his followers. After days of waiting, Ogden and several other members of Kachlein's party approached the fort and tried to talk its occupants into surrendering. Stewart ended these negotiations when he placed his rifle through a loophole and shot down Nathan Ogden; others in the fort then opened fire, wounding three more Pennsylvanians. As in the past, Lazarus Stewart and his men escaped justice: the night after the killing they slipped out of the fort and fled.[38]

---

36. *SCP* 3: xxvi–xxix; Depositions of John Jennings and Joseph Morris, June 1, 1769, *SCP* 3:130–35.

37. Memorandum Book of Zebulon Butler, Feb. to May 1770 and Depositions of Amos and Nathan Ogden, May 5, 1770, *SCP* 4:81, 73–76.

38. Charles Stewart to John Penn, Jan. 21, 1771; Deposition of William Sims, Jan. 21, 1771; Deposition of William Nimens, Jan. 25, 1771; and Deposition of Peter Kachlein, Jan. 31, 1771, *SCP* 4:153–54, 155–57, 163–64.

The violence that marked the Wyoming controversy continued unabated after Ogden's murder. In the summer of 1771, the struggle for possession of the valley culminated in an extended and deadly siege of a Pennamite fort by scores of armed New Englanders reinforced by Lazarus Stewart and his Paxton settlers. On August 15 the Pennamites, having suffered one man killed and several wounded, surrendered, giving up possession of their fort as well as their holdings in the Wyoming Valley. For their part, the Connecticut claimants suffered three killed and as many wounded in gaining their victory. In a moment tinged with irony, the commander of Pennsylvania's forces in the Wyoming Valley, Captain Asher Clayton, oversaw the surrender of the Wyoming Valley to Connecticut claimants, including his old subordinate, Lazarus Stewart.[39] Though this Pennamite surrender marked the beginning of substantial levels of Yankee settlement in the Wyoming Valley, it only brought a temporary peace to the region. In December 1775, William Plunket, a Northumberland County magistrate, led more than five hundred Pennsylvanians in an effort to eject Yankee settlers and recapture the Wyoming Valley. Four hundred Connecticut claimants commanded by Zebulon Butler intercepted this force along the banks of the Susquehanna River and, in the battle that ensued, killed or wounded half-a-dozen of Plunket's men.[40]

Lazarus Stewart and his Paxton settlers, who played such a central role in precipitating the bloodshed that marked Pennsylvania's Pennamite-Yankee conflict, also took the lead in igniting a war on property. Soon after the Paxton settlers' arrival in the valley in February 1770, John Penn informed his brother Thomas that the "lawless villains" had "plundered & destroyed" the homes of proprietary tenants at Wyoming.[41] One of the New Englanders' leading men, Zebulon Butler, chronicled several of these attacks in his memorandum book. On February 23 Butler wrote that "the Boys" laid the house of Pennsylvania claimant John Solomon "Level with the Earth" and, five days later, noted that a mob of New Englanders and Paxton men destroyed the home of proprietary agent Charles Stewart. According to the testimony of Amos and Nathan Ogden, Connecticut claimants tore down the cabin of proprietary tenant Thomas Osburn, "destroyed the goods of the Family" and "shot several of the Cattle."[42] Pennamites doled out similar treatment to

---

39. Minutes of the Pennsylvania Council, July 16, 1771; John Dick to Lewis Gordan, Aug. 1, 1771; Andrew Ledlie to Lewis Gordon, Aug. 1771; Affidavit of Asher Clayton, Aug. 22, 1771; and Articles of Capitulation, Aug. 15, 1771, *SCP* 4:223–24, 230–31, 242–43, 252–54, 241.

40. *SCP* 5:l–lii; Extract from the Connecticut Courant, Jan. 22, 1776, and Sheriff William Scull and Others to Governor Penn, Dec. 30, 1775, *SCP* 6:422–25, 425–26.

41. John Penn to Thomas Penn, March 10, 1770, *SCP* 4:42–43.

42. Memorandum Book of Zebulon Butler, Feb.–May, 1770; Warrant for the Arrest of Lazarus Stewart and Others, March 20, 1770; and Depositions of Amos and Nathan Ogden, May 25, 1770, *SCP* 4:80, 50–51, 73–74.

Yankees. In November 1769, Pennsylvanians plundered the farms of Connecticut claimants and drove them from the valley. A year later, Pennamite raiders led by Amos Ogden descended on Wyoming's Yankee settlements, "destroyed much of their Corn," and "took of[f] & Carried away their horses & Cattle."[43] The struggle over property in Northeast Pennsylvania was primarily framed by white backcountry inhabitants' aggressive pursuit of landed independence. Nonetheless, for settlers who experienced decades of frontier conflict, the lessons of Indian-white warfare were close to hand and shaped patterns of violence.

As with violence against persons, attacks against property in the Wyoming Valley also drew on the precedents of racialized frontier conflict. The destruction of crops, dwellings, and other life-sustaining resources had long been a feature of Indian-European conflict. From a very early date, colonists (who could draw on concepts of total war grounded in European military culture) focused much of their war making on Indian villages, fields, and food stores rather than on Indians themselves. Indian property made an ideal military target on two counts. First, it was easier to find and eliminate than highly mobile bands of Native warriors. Second, in destroying Indians' food and shelter, Europeans struck at the heart of Indian subsistence and survival. These tactics may have been initiated by Europeans, but they were soon adopted by Indians. By as early as King Philip's War in 1675–76, the progress of Indian war parties could be measured by the burnt homes and slaughtered livestock they left in their wake.[44] The wanton destruction of property continued to shape confrontations between Indians and whites up through the eighteenth century. Growing imperial competition between England, France, and Spain served to increase conflict in the New World. Moreover, these imperial struggles invariably drew European colonists and Indians into the fray and, thus, expanded and intensified the destructive force of frontier warfare. From Pennsylvania to the Carolinas, raids and counterraids by Indians and colonial militias in the eighteenth century produced widespread devastation and dislocation.[45] The fiery destruction of the Indian settlement at Wyoming that resulted in Teedyuscung's

---

43. *SCP* 3:xxix; Harvey, *History of Wilkes-Barre*, 2:626–27, 669–71; Eliphalet Dyer to William Samuel Johnson, Dec. 15, 1770, *SCP* 4:142.

44. Adam J. Hirsch, "The Collision of Military Cultures in Seventeenth-Century New England," *Journal of American History* 74 (Mar. 1988): 1187–1212; Patrick M. Malone, *The Skulking Way of War: Technology and Tactics among the New England Indians* (Lanham, MD, 2000), 67–98; Virginia DeJohn Anderson, "King Philip's Herds: Indians, Colonists, and the Problem of Livestock in Early New England" *WMQ* 51 (Oct. 1994): 621–23.

45. A good overview of imperial competition and its impact on America's white and Indian inhabitants can be found in Ian K. Steele, *Warpaths: Invasions of North America* (New York, 1994).

death as well as the attack by Captain Bull that destroyed the valley's Susquehannah Company settlement later that year fit into this wider pattern.

Like Indian and European adversaries, Pennamites and Yankees systematically targeted each other's homes, crops, and livestock. Attacks on property in the Wyoming Valley were not isolated incidents, but widespread, and culminated in several episodes of mass dispossession. Pennamites plundered Yankees' homes and forced them from their lands late in 1769 and again in September 1770. In the latter episode, about 150 Pennsylvanians led by Amos Ogden descended on Wyoming's Connecticut settlers and "robbd them of their money, some Cloaths, destroyed much of their Corn, took of & Carried away their horses & Cattle."[46] Yankees struck back and drove Pennsylvania claimants from their farms in the spring of 1770 and again in the summer of 1771.[47]

Settlers dressed and yelled like Indians as they perpetrated these attacks, again pointing to the way that contact with Native peoples shaped agrarian violence. Connecticut claimant John McDonner recalled how he and twenty-eight companions painted themselves like Indians and "abused & Robbed" Amos Ogden and those who leased land from him in April 1770. In his own testimony concerning the attack on his farmstead, Ogden mentioned that the rioters advanced "with Drum beating and Indian shouts." Likewise, in one of the more self-conscious associations between agrarian conflict and the region's history of Indian-white violence, Yankee settler Chester Pearce threatened Pennsylvania claimant Jonathan Marsh that "the woods shall be as full of White Indians this Summer as ever they were of Black ones" and that the Yankees intended "to lay in the woods" and "shoot the Heads of the Pennsylvanians."[48]

Revolutionary Violence

In 1776 the Revolutionary War overshadowed conflict between Pennamites and Yankees. Though America's struggle for independence from Britain never managed to fully divert Wyoming's inhabitants from their local struggles, the conflict did refuel Indian-white contention along the frontier and revive the connection between racialized violence and agrarian unrest.

46. SCP 3: xxix; Harvey and Smith, *History of Wilkes-Barre*, 2:626–27, 669–71; Extract from the Connecticut Courant, Oct. 5, 1770, and Eliphalet Dyer to William Samuel Johnson, Dec. 15, 1770, SCP 4:129, 142.
47. John Thompson to Charles Stewart, July 5, 1771; Minutes of the Pennsylvania Council, July 16, 1771; James Hamilton and Others to Edmund Physick, July 17, 1771; and Affidavit of Asher Clayton, Aug. 22, 1771, SCP 4:219, 223, 225, 252–54.
48. Eliphalet Dyer and Others to Jonathan Trumbull, March 27, 1771, SCP 4:194–95 n. 36; Deposition of Jonathan Marsh, Aug. 10, 1784, PA1 10:641.

The Revolutionary War in the upper Susquehanna Valley was very much an Indian war and, as such, it was a racially polarized conflict where combatants and noncombatants alike became victims. The hundreds of Indians and Loyalists who swept down on Wyoming in the summer of 1778 killed or captured hundreds of Connecticut claimants, burned their homes, destroyed their crops, and drove off their livestock. Among the slain was Lazarus Stewart; he thus became a victim of the violence that he had very much helped to create. Among the Indians who joined in the raid were a number of Delaware who looked on the campaign as an opportunity to take their revenge on the New Englanders who had invaded their territory. North of Wyoming, in November 1778, Indians and Loyalists destroyed the settlement of Cherry Valley in New York killing more than forty women and children.[49] The thousands of Continental army soldiers and militiamen who invaded Iroquois territory in 1779 under the command of General John Sullivan responded in kind. Time and time again, Sullivan's men entered Iroquois towns, marveled at the sturdiness of Iroquois cabins and the fruitfulness of Iroquois orchards and fields, and then burned them. Tioguanda, an Onondaga chief, recounted how the revolutionaries killed women and children when they raided his village.[50] For all of its destructiveness, Sullivan's expedition failed to secure the New York–Pennsylvania frontier. Indians allied with Great Britain continued to raid Northeast Pennsylvania, spreading death and destruction in their wake. Indians and Tories killed or captured hundreds of settlers and forced hundreds more to flee. Between 1778 and 1780, the number of taxables counted by Connecticut authorities in the Wyoming Valley dropped from more than five hundred to about a hundred. Over the same period of time, the region's Connecticut claimants suffered £38,308 in damages.[51]

America's war for independence introduced the next generation of Wyoming inhabitants to the brutalizing effects of frontier conflict. John Franklin, John Jenkins, John Swift, Elisha Satterlee, Elisha Mathewson, and other Connecticut claimants who would lead the fight against Pennsylvania following independence gained firsthand experience of the bitter violence that characterized the Revolutionary War in the backcountry. All of these men served stints in the Continen-

---

49. Charles Miner, *History of Wyoming* (Philadelphia, 1845), 219–28, 242–44; Mancall, *Valley of Opportunity*, 137–38.

50. For an account of Sullivan's expedition, see Joseph R. Fischer, *A Well-Executed Failure: The Sullivan Campaign Against the Iroquois, July–September, 1779* (Columbia, SC, 1997). The brutal nature of the Revolution along the frontier is described in Mancall, *Valley of Opportunity*, 130–59 (Tioguanda's account on 151–52); Gregory T. Knouff, "'An Arduous Service': The Pennsylvania Backcountry Soldiers' Revolution," *Pennsylvania History* 61 (Jan. 1994): 45–74; and Colin G. Calloway, *The American Revolution in Indian Country* (New York, 1995).

51. Harvey and Smith, *History of Wilkes-Barre*, 2:951–52; 3:1254–55, 1277–79, 1280–82.

tal line or militia during the war; more important, all of them took part in the brutal frontier struggle waged between Indians and whites during the conflict. Jenkins (who had recently returned from Montreal after being captured by Indians), Franklin, Swift, and Mathewson were all present in the valley during the Battle of Wyoming or its immediate aftermath and saw the burnt homes, destroyed crops, and mutilated bodies the Indians and Loyalists left in their wake. Moreover, all of these men took part in Sullivan's expedition in which they participated in the destruction of Iroquois homes, fields, and orchards and, when they encountered them, engaged Indians in battles in which no quarter was offered. John Franklin was seriously wounded by Indians in one of these fights and John Jenkins took part in the Battle of Newtown after which several American officers made leggings from the skin of dead Indian warriors.[52]

After the Revolutionary War, Pennsylvania and Connecticut claimants resumed their struggle for the Wyoming Valley, producing a level of bloodshed surpassing that of Pennamite-Yankee conflict in the 1760s and 1770s as well as contemporary episodes of agrarian unrest, including Shays's Rebellion and the Whiskey Rebellion. Armed conflict between the two sides erupted in the fall of 1783 and raged through the following year.[53] In July 1784, patrols of Pennamites and Yankees exchanged shots after they stumbled into one another. Two Pennsylvania claimants, Henry Brink and Wilhelmus Van Gordon, were wounded and two Connecticut claimants, Elisha Garret and Chester Paine, killed.[54] Four days later, Yankee settler Benjamin Blanchard received a gunshot wound in the thigh and, the following day, a rifle shot killed another Connecticut man. Later that week Pennamites shot John Franklin through the wrist and killed New Englander Nathan Stevens. On October 19 a party of Pennamites "lying in ambush" along a road near Abraham's Creek wounded Joshua Terry in the shoulder. Likewise, on October 28 and November 4, Pennamites opened fire on Yankee settlers, setting off another pair of skirmishes. Connecticut claimants met Pennamite violence with their own acts of murder and mayhem. In July 1784 Connecticut claimants subjected Pennamites in Wilkes-Barre's fort to a nine-day siege.[55] The following month, Yankees killed one

---

52. For information on the Revolutionary War experience of these men, see Harvey and Smith, *History of Wilkes-Barre*, vol. 2, chaps. 13, 15, 16, and 18; and Clement F. Heverly, *Patriot and Pioneer Families of Bradford County, Pennsylvania, 1770–1800* (Towanda, PA, 1915), 1:154–55.

53. *SCP* 7:xxxiii–xxxix; *SCP* 8:xvi–xxii.

54. Deposition of William Brink, July 27, 1784, *SCP* 8:7–8; Depositions of Henry Brink and Wilhelmus Van Gordon, Aug. 15, 1784; and Deposition of Catherine Cortright, Aug. 11, 1784, *PA1* 10:651, 652, 642; John Franklin to William Samuel Johnson, Eliphalet Dyer, and Jesse Root, Oct. 11, 1784, *SCP* 8:109–10.

55. John Franklin's Diary, July 3–Dec. 7, 1784 and John Franklin to Frederick Antes, Oct. 23, 1784, *SCP* 8:155–56, 131; Deposition of John Armstrong, Jr., July 28, 1784, *PA1* 10:623–24.

Pennsylvania militiamen and wounded three others in a skirmish at Locust Hill, and several weeks later they shot and killed Lieutenants Andrew Henderson and Samuel Reed during a raid on Wilkes-Barre.[56] Finally, in October, half-a-dozen Pennamites and Pennsylvania militiamen became casualties during an intense gun battle with Connecticut claimants near Abraham's Creek.[57]

Once again, the region's history of racialized conflict provides a critical context for understanding this surge in agrarian violence. By the end of the Revolutionary War, many Connecticut claimants drew a close association between Pennamites, Tories, and Indians. During the 1770s scores of dispossessed Pennsylvania claimants fled north into the waiting arms of the British. Many of these refugees returned to the Wyoming Valley as members of the Loyalist military unit, Butler's Rangers, and engaged with Indian allies in the destruction of Wyoming's Connecticut settlements and the killing of its inhabitants. The war in the valley produced several stories, some possibly apocryphal, of one-time Wyoming inhabitants who became Tories and returned to Northeast Pennsylvania only to murder (and often scalp and mutilate) former friends and family members who fought with Patriot forces. What is most important about these stories is how they portrayed Tories as people who possessed the same savagery, mercilessness, and brutality that supposedly characterized Indians. Indeed, as Gregory Knouff reminds us, frontier Patriots saw Tories "not only to be traitors to their country but also traitors to their race." By extension, Wyoming's Yankee settlers, who considered their Pennamite opponents as little more than thinly disguised Tories, found it easy to apply the same brutal treatment to them as they had to Indian adversaries.[58]

The experience of Wyoming's Tories reveals something else about the relationship between agrarian unrest and Indian-European relations in early America. White settlers' struggles for land and independence did not invariably put them at odds with Indians and their sovereignty and soil rights. Pennsylvania claimants joined the British not so much out of any deep-felt loyalty to the crown, but in hopes that casting their allegiance with the empire would ultimately enable

---

56. Deposition of James Moore, Sept. 14, 1784; Deposition of John Stickafoos, Sept. 24, 1784; and Deposition of Harmon Brink, Sept. 22, 1784, *PA1* 10:656–57, 667–68, 661; Alexander Patterson to John Armstrong, Jr., Sept. 28, 1784, *SCP* 8:85; Deposition of Henry Shoemaker, Sept. 28, 1784 in Harvey and Smith, *History of Wilkes-Barre*, 3:1438–39.

57. John Franklin to Frederick Antes, Daniel Montgomery, and William Bonam, Oct. 23, 1784 and John Armstrong, Jr., to John Dickinson, Oct. 25, 1784, *SCP* 8:130–31,135; Deposition of John Armstrong, Jr., July 28, 1784, *PA1* 10:623–24.

58. Stories concerning Tory atrocities in the Wyoming Valley, and their deeper meanings, are discussed in Gregory T. Knouff, *The Soldiers' Revolution: Pennsylvanians in Arms and the Forging of Early American Identity* (University Park, PA, 2004), 195–96, 218–19; and Knouff, " 'An Arduous Service' ": 68.

them to regain the property and prospect of independence that had been taken from them by their Patriot foes. In taking sides with the crown, Wyoming's Tories sided, by extension, with Britain's Indian allies. In sum, the logic of independence drove Wyoming's Tories to join the British and not the revolutionaries and, more to the point, to fight beside Indians striving to defend their homelands rather than against them. Hence, to a certain degree, the revolutionaries' critique of frontier Tories was accurate. They were men who betrayed their nation and their race insofar as they contravened the vision of an America cleared of its Native peoples and solely occupied by whites. This is not to say that frontier Tories were free of the racial hostility that was turning many white settlers against Indians but that, it certain times and places, the pursuit of independence could trump a legacy of Indian-white mistrust, if only temporarily.[59]

The violence that plagued the revolutionary-era Wyoming Valley was shaped by decades of conflict between Indians and whites; however, the similarities between Pennamite-Yankee and Indian-white violence only go so deep. First, contention between Pennamites and Yankees may have been colored by racialized frontier conflict, but it never took on the racially motivated savagery of struggles between whites and Indians. Connecticut and Pennsylvania claimants may have come from different regional and ethnic backgrounds, but they did not perceive each other as different races nor did they dehumanize each other as they did Indians. Moreover, Pennamites and Yankees may have attacked and even killed each other, but they did not engage in the scalpings and mutilations that marked violence between Indians and whites. Even Lazarus Stewart, who contributed to his violent reputation when he killed Nathan Ogden, did not repeat the sort of butchery that made his attacks on the Indians at Conestoga and Lancaster so infamous. Finally, Pennamites and Yankees may have dispossessed and terrified women and children but they did not indiscriminately slaughter them.

The final act of Indian dispossession related to the Wyoming controversy came at the end of the Revolutionary War and more than a decade after Native people had been driven from Northeast Pennsylvania. Late in 1782, lawyers

---

59. For two essays that explore how Indians and white settlers found common ground (at least temporarily) in their efforts to secure their survival and land along the frontier, see David L. Preston, "Squatters, Indians, Proprietary Government, and Land in the Susquehanna Valley," in *Friends and Enemies*, 180–200; and Stephen Aron, "Pigs and Hunters: 'Rights in the Woods' on the Trans-Appalachian Frontier," in *Contact Points: American Frontiers from the Mohawk Valley to the Mississippi, 1750–1830*, ed. Andrew R. L. Cayton and Fredrika J. Teute (Chapel Hill, NC, 1998), 175–204.

hired by Pennsylvania and Connecticut dueled over the legal merits of each state's jurisdictional claims before a national court convened at Trenton, New Jersey.[60] Arguing the case for Connecticut were Jesse Root and William Samuel Johnson. Faced with imperfections in the Indian deeds acquired by the Susquehannah and Delaware companies in 1754, they decided to abandon Indian deeds as a basis for the Connecticut claim. Moreover, in order to undercut Pennsylvania's contention that their territorial rights were reinforced by a series of legitimate Indian purchases, Root and Johnson called into question the legality of all rights in property acquired through Indians. Holding that occupancy and cultivation of the soil represented the ultimate sources of possession, the two asserted that Indians never truly owned the land they lived on. Deploying a well-worn argument, Root and Johnson contended that Indian populations were too scattered and mobile to truly occupy the land and that Indian farming was too haphazard and primitive to be considered true cultivation. Connecticut's legal council, in short, denied that Indians *ever* possessed Northeast Pennsylvania, challenging the legitimacy and memory of hundreds of years of Indian habitation.[61]

This legal wrangling between Pennsylvania and Connecticut again illustrates that the Wyoming dispute was intertwined with the question of Native soil rights and, in the end, became an instrument of Indian dispossession. The battle for land and autonomy fought by Indians against European colonists was foundational to future conflict along the revolutionary frontier, for in the defeat and dispossession of Native peoples were sown the seeds for future disputes among whites. The bitter struggle colonists waged against Indians in the Wyoming region was only the first round in a much longer fight for land and independence, which would eventually bring white backcountry inhabitants into conflict with powerful speculators, government authorities, and other settlers. This new contest was, in turn, marked by a culture of violence born of decades of Indian-European conflict that took root among the region's white frontier inhabitants.

---

60. For a thorough examination of the Trenton trial, see Robert J. Taylor, "Trial at Trenton," *WMQ* 26 (Oct. 1969): 521–47; and *SCP* 7:xxii–xxxiii, 144–249.

61. Taylor, "Trial at Trenton," 531–33. William Cronon charts how these arguments became instruments of Indian dispossession in seventeenth-century New England in *Changes in the Land*, 55–57.

CHAPTER 2

"A GREAT MANY WRANGLING DISPUTES"

Authority, Allegiance, Property, and the Frontier War for Independence

In the summer of 1785, Pennsylvania claimant and Northumberland County magistrate David Mead found himself under siege. His troubles began in the winter when Connecticut claimants started to harass Pennsylvania settlers and force them from their lands. In the spring, this trickle of dispossessions became a flood as Yankees systematically cleared the Wyoming Valley of Pennamite settlers. Mead gathered evidence against the rioters and sent reports to Philadelphia describing the growing crisis but found that he could do little to stop it. In July Mead himself became a target of violence when a group of Connecticut claimants attacked his farmstead. The rioters "beat and abused" his farmhands, knocked down his fences, plundered his crops, and drove off his livestock to the sound of their "Indian yell." Holed up in his house while this assault was underway, Mead penned a plea for help to Pennsylvania's president, John Dickinson, in which he chronicled the progressive collapse of state authority in the Wyoming Valley. As if to punctuate what he described as the "deplorable situation of this part of the state," Mead closed his letter by mentioning that the rioters had just shot down his dog as it stood at his door.[1]

Mead's ordeal was an episode in one of several waves of agrarian violence that swept the Wyoming Valley between 1770 and the mid 1780s. These "Pennamite-Yankee wars" illustrate three overlapping struggles that constituted the

---

1. David Mead to John Bayard, June 10, 1785, *SCP* 8:244–45; David Mead to President Dickinson, Mar. 30, 1785 (with attached depositions of Charles Manrow, Mar. 24, 1785, Samuel Karr and Daniel Swart, March 25, 1785, and John Cartright, March 30, 1785), *PA1* 10:707–10; David Mead to President Dickinson, July 6, 1785, *PA1* 11:454–55.

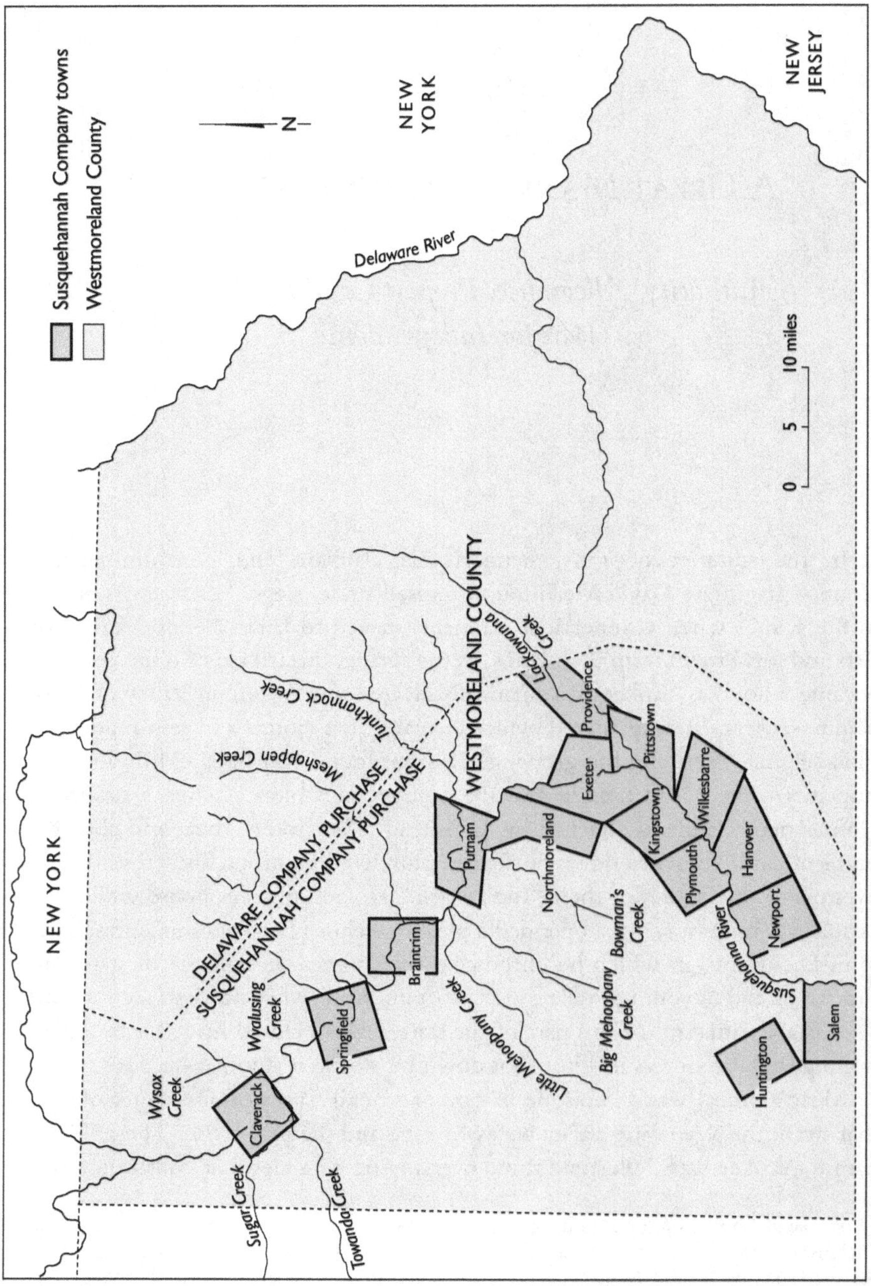

Map 2. The Wyoming Valley, 1760–85

revolutionary frontier's war for independence. First and foremost, it demonstrates the importance of property to agrarian contention. Pennamites and Yankees fought for land and, as occupants of a war-torn frontier where food and other basic necessities were often in short supply, over the very means of subsistence. Backcountry inhabitants also quarreled over the nature and possession of authority because these issues directly impinged on their efforts to acquire land.[2] This power struggle ultimately hinged on a battle over allegiance. Pennsylvania, Connecticut, or Connecticut's land companies could not long hold sway over the Wyoming region without first winning the support of its inhabitants. The contest over allegiance was also tied to the struggle over property in the sense that settlers cast their loyalties with reference to how such decisions would affect their ability to obtain land.

Authority

Pennsylvania's Pennamite-Yankee wars were the product of a contest over political authority—over who would wield power in the Wyoming region and under what terms. Similar battles occurred across the revolutionary frontier. The ability of settlers to secure frontier freeholds and achieve independence rested, in part, on their ability to acquire land and defend their claims in court actions that required government institutions amicable to their efforts to obtain and hold property. The possession of legitimate political authority could also go a long way toward validating (and strengthening) backcountry inhabitants' extralegal pursuit of property, for with it mobs could become militias and illegal dispossessions, legal ejectments. Besides being central to the Wyoming controversy, the contest over authority was complex and multidimensional. On the one hand, the struggle for power in Northeast Pennsylvania was framed by a straightforward jurisdictional dispute between Pennsylvania and Connecticut. On the other, it was fueled by contention between backcountry inhabitants who wished to exercise power locally and outside officials who attempted to direct affairs along the frontier.

The jurisdictional struggle that paralleled Pennsylvania's Pennamite-Yankee wars unfolded in several distinct phases. The first of these spanned the period between 1770 when Connecticut claimants established a foothold in the

---

2. For other studies that chart the connection between disputes over property and jurisdictional authority, see Charles D. Dutrizac, "Local Identity and Authority in a Disputed Hinterland: The Pennsylvania-Maryland Border in the 1730s," *PMHB* III (Jan. 1991): 35–61; and Michael A. Bellesiles, *Revolutionary Outlaws: Ethan Allan and the Struggle for Independence on the Early American Frontier* (Charlottesville, VA, 1993).

Susquehanna Valley and Connecticut's decision to annex the Wyoming region in 1774. These years can be characterized as a jurisdictional conflict by proxy. The contestants for power in Northeast Pennsylvania were not two colonies but one colony and a set of Connecticut-based land companies whose pretense to authority rested more on presumption than the law. This situation placed Yankee settlers at a distinct disadvantage. While Pennsylvania claimants could avail themselves of an array of provincial institutions in their struggle for property, the New Englanders had to rely on extralegal methods. Connecticut claimants confronted sheriff's posses and militia units raised under the authority of Pennsylvania and faced prosecution in Pennsylvania courts. To meet these challenges, Yankees could only turn to violence and threats such as when Connecticut settlers along the Delaware declared that "if any Sheriff came to molest them they wou'd tie a Stone about his Neck, & send him down to his Governor."[3]

Connecticut's decision to officially extend its authority over the contested region was precipitated by the aggressive politicking of the Susquehannah and Delaware companies and the growing size and stability of their settlements west of the Delaware. The Susquehannah Company repeatedly petitioned the Connecticut legislature to assert the colony's western claims and made sure that a special agent representing its interests attended almost every legislative session in the colony between 1769 and 1774. Not satisfied with such measures, the companies gained leverage by liberally awarding shares in the Connecticut claim to persons with power and influence within the colony, including Connecticut's governor, Jonathan Trumbull. The companies also waged an energetic public relations campaign through the colony's newspapers. Descriptions of the Wyoming region's rich soils and bountiful woodlands appeared in print as did impassioned defenses of the colony's western claims.[4] Moreover, in the years that followed the decisive defeat of Wyoming's Pennamite settlers in 1771, Connecticut claimants flooded into the region. Northeast Pennsylvania's Yankee population, which probably numbered only a couple of hundred in 1771, reached two thousand in 1774 and three thousand two years later.[5] In light of these developments, the Connecticut legislature finally recognized the Susque-

---

3. Examples of legal action taken against Connecticut claimants by Pennsylvania includes: Warrant for the Arrest of Isaac Tripp and Others, Mar. 15, 1769; Presentment of Isaac Trip and Others by the Northampton Country Grand Jury, Apr. 1 1769; and Depositions of John Jennings and Joseph Morris, June 1, 1769, *SCP* 3:91–923, 130–35. Quote taken from the Deposition of John Williamson, June 18, 1762, *SCP* 2:137.

4. *SCP* 4: xviii–xix; Julian P. Boyd, "Connecticut's Experiment in Expansion: The Susquehannah Company, 1753–1803," *Journal of Economic and Business History* 27 (1931): 52, 55–62.

5. Boyd, "Connecticut's Experiment in Expansion," 62; Oscar Jewell Harvey and Ernst G. Smith, *History of Wilkes-Barre, Luzerne County, Pennsylvania*, 6 vols. (Wilkes-Barre, PA, 1927–30), 2:876–78.

hannah and Delaware company purchases as the town of Westmoreland in 1774 and attached it to Litchfield County. Two years later it converted the town into Westmoreland County.[6]

Connecticut's annexation of the disputed region initiated a second phase of the Wyoming dispute. Now, in addition to contending with ambitious land companies and unruly Yankee settlers, Pennsylvania had to compete with their home colony. In the spring of 1774, Governor John Penn brought Pennsylvania's case before Britain's Board of Trade. His initiative, however, met with disappointing results, for the board, preoccupied with the growing rebellion in Britain's North American colonies, decided to put off any decision on the matter.[7] Pennsylvania claimants took their own measures against Connecticut. A group of leading state landholders formed an association in 1775 that provided funds for the use of armed force against Connecticut settlers—a policy that culminated in Plunket's failed expedition against Wyoming's Yankee settlements.[8] Amidst this acrimony, the Continental Congress, which by 1775 was rapidly taking over matters of intercolony relations from the British crown, waded into the Wyoming dispute. Hoping to avoid an open break between Pennsylvania and Connecticut that would divide the colonies in the face of their common British foe, Congress searched for a solution to the crisis. In December it finally came to a decision and awarded Connecticut jurisdiction over the area till a more permanent settlement was achieved.[9] This decision ushered in an eight-year period of Connecticut rule over the Wyoming region.

The final phase of the Wyoming controversy's jurisdictional struggle saw the restoration of Pennsylvania's authority over its Northeast frontier. In 1779 Pennsylvania, hoping to find a final solution to the quarrel over the Wyoming region, requested that Connecticut join it in submitting their dispute to the national government under the terms of the Articles of Confederation. In 1782, after an extended period of foot-dragging, Connecticut finally agreed. By November both sides were ready to try their case before a special five-judge tribunal convened at Trenton, New Jersey. On December 30, after more than a

---

6. Resolution of the Connecticut Legislature Concerning the Western Claim, May 1771, *SCP* 4:215; Act of the Connecticut General Assembly Erecting the Town of Westmoreland, Jan. 1774, *SCP* 5:268–69; Act of the Connecticut General Assembly, May 1775, *SCP* 6:319–20; An Act Making Westmoreland a County, Oct 1776, *SCP* 7:23–24. For a more complete examination of the rise of Connecticut's rule west of Delaware, see Richard T. Warfle, *Connecticut's Western Colony: The Susquehannah Affair* (Hartford, CT, 1979).

7. *SCP* 5: xxvii–xxviii, xliii–xliv; Henry Wilmot to William Baker, Jan. 16, 1776, *SCP* 7:2.

8. Subscriptions of Pennsylvania Claimants to Lands on the West Branch, Nov. 11, 1775, and Joseph Shippen, Jr., and Others to William Plunket and Others, Oct. 13, 1775, *SCP* 6:366, 371; Boyd, "Connecticut's Experiment in Expansion," 63.

9. *SCP* 5:xlviii–lii.

month of testimony, the judges announced their verdict, ruling that "the Jurisdiction and Pre-emption of all the Territory lying within the Charter boundary of Pennsylvania, and now claimed by the State of Connecticut, do of right belong to the State of Pennsylvania." With this decision, Connecticut lost its western colony.[10]

The Trenton Decree did not bring the contest over authority in Northeast Pennsylvania to an end. Though it gave Pennsylvania power over the Wyoming Valley on paper, the court's ruling did little to dampen unrest among the region's inhabitants. At this point, the struggle for power in Northeast Pennsylvania shifted from a relatively clear-cut jurisdictional fight between colonies and states to a far more complex battle for political legitimacy. The question now was not what state would have authority over the Wyoming region but how that authority would be constructed and exercised. Specifically, the Wyoming Valley became the scene of a struggle in which state authorities squared off against settlers—both Yankees and Pennamites alike—who desired to exercise power locally and who resisted all efforts to limit this autonomy.

This contest over the legitimacy and locus of power pitted the state of Pennsylvania against Wyoming's Connecticut claimants. Although there were some overtures toward reconciliation between Yankee settlers and the state after the Trenton Decree, hopes for a quick and bloodless resolution of the Wyoming controversy rapidly dimmed. The state took the first step toward conflict when it ordered two companies of Pennsylvania troops to occupy the Wyoming Valley. Connecticut claimants opposed this move fearing that the troops would be used to force them from their lands.[11] The prospect for peace grew even more distant when negotiations between Connecticut claimants and a committee appointed by the Pennsylvania Assembly in February 1783 to negotiate a settlement on the question of private soil rights collapsed in April. The New Englanders contributed to this when they sought to secure not only the lands they had occupied and improved but also those that were claimed by the nonresident shareholders of the Susquehannah and Delaware companies. Pennsylvania was willing to discuss compensation for actual settlers but found this larger demand unacceptable. The state also undermined the negotiations by exhibiting blatant favoritism toward Pennamites. Indeed, the only plan for reconciliation proposed by the commissioners—which required Connecticut claimants to vacate their

---

10. Judgment of the Court Convened at Trenton, Dec. 30, 1782, *SCP* 7:245–46. For an account of the Trenton Trial, see: *SCP* 7:xx–xxxiii, 144–246; and Robert J. Taylor, "Trial at Trenton," *WMQ* 26 (Oct. 1969): 521–47.

11. Extract from the Minutes of the Pennsylvania Council, Feb. 1, 1783; Instructions to Captains Shrawder and Robinson, Mar. 4, 1783; Thomas Robinson to John Dickinson, Mar. 26, 1783; and Philip Shrawder to John Dickinson, Mar. 29, 1783, *SCP* 7:261, 268, 271–73.

farms within one year in order to obtain state lands further west—was merely forwarded to Connecticut claimants on behalf of an association of prominent Pennsylvania landholders. Needless to say, Yankees who had invested years of labor in their farms and harbored a deep animosity toward their old Pennamite adversaries rejected this plan.[12]

Having failed to resolve the conflict through negotiation, Pennsylvania moved toward more forceful means. In September the state assembly voted to reinforce its Wyoming Valley garrison and repealed an act passed in March 1783 staying ejectment suits against Connecticut claimants.[13] It also divided the Wyoming Valley into townships and appointed local magistrates without the consent of Connecticut claimants. These decisions benefited Pennamite landholders. Among the men appointed as Wyoming justices was Alexander Patterson, the leading agent of the Pennsylvania land claimants' association and a veteran of the Pennamite-Yankee wars. As one Connecticut claimant put it, the state provided the means by which a "whole herd of Pennsylvania landjobbers were set loose upon the Inhabitants to Exercise their wonted avaritious and hellish Practices."[14]

Concerns over the shift in jurisdiction from Connecticut to Pennsylvania were certainly a major source of anxiety among Yankee settlers. Pennsylvania's accession to power challenged the New Englanders' basic understandings of political authority. The Yankees who settled in Northeast Pennsylvania came out of a regional culture where a considerable amount of power was vested locally in face-to-face communities.[15] From the early seventeenth century, New England's central institution of local government was the town rather than, as was the case in the rest of Britain's North American colonies, the county. In addition, between their arrival in Northeast Pennsylvania and Connecticut's annexation of the region, Yankee settlers had, out of necessity, largely run their own affairs. They established communities, distributed land, and selected local officials who did everything from levying taxes and regulating the sale of

---

12. Pennsylvania Claimants to the Pennsylvania Commissioners, Apr. 22, 1783; The Pennsylvania Commissioners to the Connecticut Claimants, Apr. 22, 1783; and The Connecticut Claimants to the Pennsylvania Commissioners, Apr. 23, 1783, *SCP* 7:282–86.

13. Repeal of the Act Staying Suits of Ejectment against Connecticut Settlers, Sept. 9, 1783, and Extract from the Minutes of the Pennsylvania Council, Sept. 25, 1783, *SCP* 7:304–5, 306–7.

14. Repeal of the Act Staying Suits of Ejectment Against Conn. Settlers, Sept. 9, 1783; The Pennsylvania Claimants to the Pennsylvania Commissioners, Apr. 17, 1783; John Franklin to the Governor of Connecticut, May 10, 1784; and Obadiah Gore to William Judd, Nov. 21, 1783, *SCP* 7:305 n.3; 276, 413, 331.

15. T. H. Breen explores the origins of New England's localist political institution in "Persistent Localism: English Social Change and the Shaping of New England Institutions" *WMQ* 32 (Jan. 1975): 3–28.

alcohol to maintaining law and order.[16] Connecticut claimants also had to fend for themselves in the face of threats posed by Indians and Pennamites, and between 1769 and 1772 Yankee settlements resembled military camps more than agricultural communities: guard duty was strictly regulated and enforced, food was rationed, and to enhance security, all field work was done communally.[17]

In light of their cultural background and more immediate historical experience, Yankee resistance to Pennsylvania's authority takes on new meaning. Besides the threat it posed to Yankee soil rights, the advent of state rule foreboded the end of more than a decade of local autonomy and the dissolution of familiar New England institutions. Some reacted to this prospect by stubbornly maintaining their allegiance to Connecticut and its New England–style institutions of local government. They continued to refer to the region as Westmoreland County and maintained a host of local offices, including representatives to the Connecticut legislature, town selectmen, and a sheriff in direct defiance of Pennsylvania's jurisdictional claims.[18] Other Connecticut claimants more forcefully challenged state authority. In 1784, John Okely and Major John Boyd, two members of a four-man committee appointed by the Pennsylvania Council to investigate the unrest that continued to plague the Wyoming region, came face to face with the violent side of Yankee resistance. On September 20, Connecticut claimants Phinehas Stevens and Waterman Baldwin accosted Okely and Boyd as they walked through Wilkes-Barre. Baldwin asked Major Boyd, "An't you, one of the Commissioners that Pull'd off your hat to us when we laid down our arms." Here, Baldwin referred to an event that occurred a month earlier during which Yankees submitted to Pennsylvania officials, only to be double-crossed, imprisoned, and delivered into the hands of their Pennamite foes. When Boyd answered that he was, Baldwin yelled, "Pull off your hat for me now," and struck Major Boyd in the head with a stick "with great Violence."[19]

Yankees rejected Pennsylvania's authority when it threatened their interests but were not above using it when it served their needs. For instance, Yankee

---

16. *SCP* 5:xxii–xxvii; Minutes of a Meeting of the Proprietors and Settlers in Wilkes-Barre, June 29, 1772; Minutes of a Meeting of the Proprietors and Settlers in Wilkes-Barre, Dec. 28, 1772; Report of Committee of Connecticut Settlers on Rules and Regulations, Mar. 8, 1773; and Minutes of a Meeting of the Susquehannah Company, June 2, 1773, *SCP* 5:6–7, 62–63, 72, 138–45.

17. *SCP* 4:xxiv; Minutes of a Meeting of the Inhabitants of Wyoming, Aug. 22, 1771, and Minutes of a Meeting of the Inhabitants of Wilkes-Barre, Sept. 30, 1771, *SCP* 4:264–65, 271–72.

18. John Seely to Alexander Patterson, Jan. 31, 1784, *SCP* 7:353.

19. Resolution of the Pennsylvania General Assembly Concerning Connecticut Claimants, Sept. 7, 1784, and Extract from the Minutes of the Pennsylvania Council, Sept. 9, 1784, *SCP* 8:47–48, 52; Depositions of John Okely and James Reed, Sept. 22, 1784, *PA1* 10:659.

stalwarts John Swift and Lawrence Meyers obtained appointments as deputy sheriffs from Northumberland County sheriff Henry Antes and then employed their position to harass Pennamites. Pennsylvania claimant Garret Shoemaker testified that in June 1784 Connecticut claimants took him prisoner and brought him before a Yankee mob led by Swift and Meyers. On the two deputies' orders, the mob flogged Shoemaker with "their iron Ramrods" and "knock'd him down with their Guns" before carrying him off to the county jail at Sunbury.[20] Later that summer, Pennsylvania authorized Connecticut claimants who had been illegally dispossessed to reoccupy their lands. The New Englanders used the state's decision as a weapon against Pennamite settlers, ejecting Pennsylvania claimants who had taken their property by force as well as those who had occupied lands without displacing Yankees. Even as they paid lip service to Pennsylvania's laws, Connecticut claimants sought to undermine the soil rights of its citizens.[21]

Instead of a two-way battle, with Yankees on one side and Pennsylvanians on the other, the years following the Trenton Decree saw the emergence of a three-way struggle between Connecticut claimants, Pennsylvania claimants, and the state of Pennsylvania. Both Yankees and Pennamites placed their immediate interests ahead of their obligations to outside authorities. John Armstrong, Jr., one of the state officials tasked with restoring order in the Wyoming region, encountered both the outright opposition of Yankees and the more subtle dissent of Pennamites. Venting his frustration in a letter to President Dickinson, Armstrong observed that when he tried to enforce the law he was "not only attacked by one, but in a great degree deserted by the other."[22] Pennsylvanians shared their Yankee opponents' localism and single-minded focus on their land and livelihood. This is reflected in a letter that Northampton County magistrate Lewis Gordon sent to Edmund Physick, a member of Pennsylvania's Board of Property, in 1769. Gordon reported that Pennsylvania farmers interested in taking up lands in the Wyoming Valley were more apprehensive about their colony's land policies than intruding Connecticut claimants. In particular, he detailed Northampton County residents' complaints regarding how proprietary agents and New Jersey natives Charles Stewart and Amos Ogden ignored their applications for land while funneling property into the hands of their fellow Jerseymen.[23] To the Pennsylvanians, the Jersey settlers, like the New Englanders, were outsiders and potential competitors. The fact that the Jerseymens' soil

20. Deposition of Garret Shoemaker, Aug. 10, 1784, PA1 10:643.
21. Act of the Pennsylvania General Assembly, Sept. 15, 1784, and Deposition of Lena Tillbury, Jan. 14, 1785, SCP 8:71–72, 196–97; Deposition of Thomas Brink, Aug. 12, 1784; Deposition of Barnabas Cary, Aug. 14, 1784, PA1 10:649, 651.
22. John Armstrong, Jr., to John Dickinson, Oct. 25, 1784, SCP 8:135.
23. Lewis Gordon to Edmund Physick, Aug. 7, 1769, and Lewis Gordon to Edmund Physick, Aug. 14, 1769, SCP 3:157–58, 163–65.

rights ultimately rested on the authority of Pennsylvania's proprietors was irrelevant, for, like the Connecticut claim, proprietary policy ultimately threatened their access to land.

Pennamites challenged Pennsylvania's authority insomuch as they were unwilling to subordinate their interests to those of the state. On the one hand, this was a consequence of the Pennsylvania claimants' preoccupation with property. On the other, it was the product of a dangerous conflict of interest the state allowed to take root among the men it appointed to keep the peace at Wyoming after the Trenton Decree. These officials did not serve as impartial umpires in disputes between Pennamites and Yankees but became embroiled in the contest for property and power. Alexander Patterson, John Seely, Henry Shoemaker, and David Mead—four of the Wyoming justices appointed by the state in 1783—all claimed land in the Wyoming Valley under Pennsylvania, possessed close ties to Pennamite interests, and according to Yankees, "were pointed out as tools" for their dispossession. Connecticut claimant Christopher Hurlbut characterized Patterson as "a man of considerable abilities, but bold, daring and completly unprincipled" and described Mead as an "insinuating, plausible and flattering" individual who covered his enmity toward Yankees with "pretended friendship." Hurlbut saved his most damning words for Seely, whom he judged had just enough sense "to act out the villian without disguise." Hurlbut's characterization of Seely might be passed off as partisan rhetoric were it not for the fact that even his fellow magistrate David Mead had to admit that Seely was too deeply involved in efforts to eject Yankee settlers to be an effective justice. Nothing better illustrates Seely's willingness to put his own interests before the law than his residence on a farm forcibly taken from a Connecticut claimant.[24]

Alexander Patterson, who became the undisputed leader of Pennamite settlers after the Trenton Decree, exemplifies how Pennsylvania claimants subordinated the law and loyalty to the state to the pursuit of property. Patterson orchestrated a campaign of harassment aimed at forcing Yankees off the land. Acting as an agent for prominent Pennsylvania landholders, he intimidated weak-willed Yankees into relinquishing their Connecticut deeds and signing lease agreements with state landholders. Meanwhile, he used his power as a county justice to prosecute and dispossess Connecticut claimants who resisted his ploys. Indeed, the systematic dispossession of Yankee settlers formed a visible subtext to the activities of Wyoming's Pennamite justices. Connecticut claimant Benjamin Harvey, on returning to his farm after being imprisoned in Wilkes-Barre under false pretenses, found that a Pennamite family had occu-

---

24. Obadiah Gore to William Judd, Nov. 21, 1783, *SCP* 7:331; Harvey and Smith, *History of Wilkes-Barre*, 3:1391; David Mead to John Dickinson, Oct. 22, 1784, *SCP* 8:128.

pied his home. Likewise, Pennsylvania soldiers under the direction of local magistrates placed Samuel Ransom under arrest in the fall of 1783 then took advantage of his absence to eject his family from their home.[25]

Pennamites further undercut the state's ability to control events by gaining the cooperation of the officers who commanded Wyoming's garrison of state troops. By the fall of 1783, Major James Moore; Captains James Christy and Philip Shrawder; and Lieutenants Blackall William Ball, Andrew Henderson, Samuel Reed, and John Armstrong commanded the troops stationed at Wilkes-Barre.[26] Instead of maintaining order, these officers enmeshed themselves in a Pennamite land grab. Alexander Patterson issued sizable grants to Moore, Henderson, and the other garrison officers.[27] In return, they provided Patterson with the armed force he needed to intimidate Yankees. Captain Christy came up with his own methods of vexing Connecticut claimants. Instead of finding room for his men in Wilkes-Barre's fort or public buildings, he billeted them in Yankee households. Christy singled out the leading Connecticut claimant Zebulon Butler by crowding his home with soldiers. In addition, state troops made a general nuisance of themselves by assaulting and throwing Yankees in jail, tearing down their fences, and killing their livestock.[28]

Thus Pennsylvania had to deal with the outright resistance of Connecticut claimants as well as the more subtle, but equally pernicious, manipulation of state power by Pennamites. Officials outside of the Wyoming region found themselves in a situation where they did not know whom to trust. Nothing illustrates this point better than the fate of state efforts to restore peace to the Wyoming Valley in September 1784. In that month the Pennsylvania Assembly resolved to send a four-man committee to the valley to identify Connecticut claimants who had settled before the Trenton Decree and defended the region during the Revolutionary War, to negotiate some form of settlement with these deserving inhabitants.[29] From the start, however, the commission ran into problems. Yankee settlers voiced their mistrust of two of the four commissioners,

---

25. Harvey and Smith, *History of Wilkes-Barre* 3:1352, 1354–55, and Alexander Patterson to John Dickinson, Apr. 29, 1784 on 1377–78.

26. Harvey and Smith, *History of Wilkes-Barre*, 3:1345–47, 1351; Extract of the Minutes of the Pennsylvania Council, Sept. 25, 1783, *SCP* 7:306–7.

27. Harvey and Smith, *History of Wilkes-Barre*, 3:1392 and Alexander Patterson to John Dickinson, April 29, 1784 on pgs.1377–78.

28. Harvey and Smith, *History of Wilkes-Barre*, 3:1351–53; Zebulon Butler to James Christy, Oct. 22, 1783, and Petition of Zebulon Butler and Others to the Continental Congress, May 1, 1784, *SCP* 7:310, 401–5.

29. Resolution of the Pennsylvania General Assembly Concerning the Connecticut Claimants, Sept. 7, 1784, and Extract from the Minutes of the Pennsylvania Council, Sept. 9, 1784, *SCP* 8:47–48, 52.

Colonel John Armstrong and John Boyd, because of their previous association with Pennamites.[30] What ultimately caused the commissioners to fail in their mission was not this dissent, but violence. On the night of September 26, the homes in which the committee members lodged came under fire; fearing for their lives, the commissioners beat a hasty retreat and made their way back to Philadelphia. Armstrong, writing on behalf of the committee, blamed the attack on the Yankees. John Franklin and other leading Connecticut claimants had a different story to tell. They declared that their people "knew nothing of the affair, Directly or Indirectly" and asserted that Armstrong and Patterson had staged the assault to provide an excuse for the committeemen to abandon their mission.[31] Either version of events was plausible and state authorities found themselves standing alone in a region beset by violence and populated by settlers who placed their struggles for property and power before the law.

It is no small irony that when the state of Pennsylvania finally did take effective steps to quell unrest in the Wyoming Valley, it moved against the region's Pennamites rather than its Connecticut claimants. The valley's Pennsylvania claimants discovered that their close association with government authority cut both ways. It gave them ready access to state institutions that aided their pursuit of property, but it also made them more dependent on, and ultimately more vulnerable to, the exercise of state power. After years of bending Pennsylvania's authority and institutions to their own ends, Pennamites finally managed to raise the ire of state officials. In May 1784, a number of Northumberland County officials penned an alarming letter to President Dickinson in which they reported the "outrageous conduct" of the Wilkes-Barre garrison, recounting how the troops had "intimidated and confined under a close Military Guard" county officials who had gone to the valley to restore order. They ended the letter by informing the president that, "instead of aiding the Civil Authority," Wyoming's magistrates, Pennsylvania claimants, and garrison had "set it at defiance, and place[d] themselves above the Laws." President Dickinson responded to this report and others of its kind by ordering the Wyoming garrison to evacuate the valley by the first of June.[32]

Friction with state- and county-level officials eventually undermined the position of Wyoming's Pennamites. In the spring and summer of 1784, Northumberland officials gathered evidence against and indicted forty-five Pennsylvania

30. Address of the Connecticut Settlers to Commissioners Read and Okely, Sept. 25, 1784, and John Dickinson to the Commissioners, Sept. 28, 1784, *SCP* 8:80–82, 84.
31. The Commissioners to John Dickinson, Oct. 1, 1784, and John Franklin, Ebenezer Johnson, and Phineas Peirce to John Dickinson, Oct. 5, 1784, *SCP* 8:87, 98–101.
32. John Buyers and Others to John Dickinson, May 17, 1784, and John Dickinson to James Moore, April 20, 1784, *SCP* 7:410–11, 393.

claimants on charges of riot, assault, robbery, and false imprisonment. Among the accused were country magistrates Alexander Patterson and Henry Shoemaker and the officers of Wyoming's garrison. In November, Northumberland's county court found forty-two of the accused guilty, punishing them with hefty fines and levying substantial bonds to guarantee their future good behavior. The convictions broke the Pennamites' hold on power in the Wyoming Valley; Alexander Patterson resigned as a county magistrate and left the valley on his indictment and the state stripped Henry Shoemaker of his post as a justice of the peace. With this loss of leadership and armed force, Wyoming's Pennamites began to lose ground in the valley.[33]

Alexander Patterson effectively summed up the outlook that contributed to Wyoming's contest over authority in a letter he wrote to Pennsylvania's Supreme Court before his trial. Defending himself against the charges he faced, Patterson admitted that the measures he took against Connecticut claimants were "not strictly consonant with the Letter of the Law." Nevertheless, he justified them, arguing that they had been "dictated solely by the principles of self preservation." Like Patterson, Pennamites and Yankees acted with reference to their own interests, placing the pursuit of property and power before the law or loyalty to the state.[34]

Allegiance

A contest over allegiance closely paralleled the struggle over authority in the Wyoming Valley, for it was difficult to translate authority, no matter its legal merits, into effective power without the support and loyalty of the region's settlers. Northeast Pennsylvania's landscape of allegiance was a complex one where loyalties were not fixed but flexible, and where both self-interest and collective identity shaped how settlers chose sides. The region's inhabitants cast their allegiance with regard to how such decisions affected their ability to obtain land. The pursuit of property cut across and undermined loyalties based on identification with a provincial or state government, ethnic group, or regional culture. Indeed, it overwhelmed all but the strongest interpersonal ties rooted in family, kin, and locale.

Loyalty to provincial or state governments was only lukewarm among backcountry inhabitants. Dr. Hugh Williamson, an emissary of Pennsylvania's

33. Thomas McKean, William Atlee, and Jacob Rush to John Dickinson, June 7, 1784, *SCP* 7:431–32, 432 n. 4; Minutes of the Court at Sunbury, Nov. 8, 1784, *SCP* 8:145–46; Harvey and Smith, *History of Wilkes-Barre*, 3:1382, 1453–55.

34. Alexander Patterson to Thomas McKean and Other Judges of the Supreme Court, May 30, 1784, *SCP* 7:427–28.

proprietors who circulated among the colony's disaffected frontier populace before the Revolutionary War, encountered this firsthand. In March 1770, Williamson journeyed from Philadelphia to western Lancaster County to try to stem the flow of men and provisions from there to Yankees in the Wyoming Valley. In a self-congratulatory letter he sent to Governor John Penn, the doctor noted that "in this I effectually succeeded, & perceive they have not made any Recruits except among the Germans." Later, Williamson traveled to Wyoming where he found that Pennamites had captured a number of would-be Connecticut claimants, including three "German lads" from Lancaster County. After meeting with these prisoners, the doctor obtained their pledge to renounce the Connecticut claim and support Pennsylvania. Williamson had the men released and allowed them to go to a fort held by Connecticut claimants from both New England and Pennsylvania in an attempt to dissuade the latter "from their Design of keeping Possession of the Ground." When the three failed to return from their mission, Williamson assumed that they were being held against their will. He later learned that the Pennsylvanians had once again shifted sides and "declared themselves in favor of the Rioters."[35]

Such disregard for government authority frequently bedeviled officials' attempts to impose order over the Wyoming region. For example, Northampton County militiamen resisted efforts to muster and march them on the Wyoming Valley in 1771 and again 1784. In the first instance, a paltry twenty-five men responded to the province's attempt to raise a force to relieve a besieged Pennamite fort. In the second, less than a third of the troops called out to restore order in the valley responded. Of those who did, many arrived unarmed and unwilling to obey orders. As in 1771, the source of the militiamen's foot-dragging was the belief that what was going on in the Wyoming Valley was none of their concern—"that it was Quarrell of a Sett of Landjobbers that ... was not worth the life of a single Man, or the labor of the many who were now called out."[36]

The region's settlers similarly ignored or manipulated their allegiance to larger political entities (in this case the United States and the British Empire) during the Revolution.[37] The Yankees who held power over the Wyoming

35. John Penn to Thomas Penn, March 10, 1770, and Dr. Hugh Williamson to John Penn, Mar. 24, 1770, *SCP* 4:43, 46–48.
36. Lewis Gordon to James Tilghman, Aug. 11, 1771, and James Hamilton and Others to Thomas Penn and John Penn, Aug. 20, 1771, *SCP* 4:238–39, 249; John Boyd and John Armstrong, Jr., to John Dickinson, Aug. 7, 1784, *SCP* 8:20–21.
37. For studies that highlight how local disputes and ethnic divisions intertwined with the Revolution in the backcountry, see Gregory T. Knouff, *The Soldier's Revolution: Pennsylvanians in Arms and the Forging of Early American Identity* (University Park, PA, 2004), chaps. 5 and 6; and Knouff, "'An Arduous Service': The Pennsylvania Backcountry Soldiers' Revolution,"

region during the Revolutionary War used their authority to label Pennsylvania claimants as Tories, and persecute them as such, regardless of their attitudes toward American independence. Westmoreland County's revolutionary Committee of Inspection took the lead in harassing Pennamites. It required all inhabitants, regardless of what province they held land under, to sign an oath promising to "conform to the laws of the Colony of Connecticut" and considered all who refused as counterrevolutionaries.[38] Yet what these "Tories" had in common was not their ties to Britain, but Pennsylvania. For example, Westmoreland's Committee of Inspection informed Adonijah Stansbury that he was "suspected of Toryism" in January 1777 because of his ties with the leading Pennamite and Pennsylvania surveyor, Charles Stewart. Frederick Vanderlip also paid for his support of Pennsylvania soil rights when Yankees branded him as a Tory and expelled him from his land.[39] Such treatment forced many Pennsylvania claimants to become what Yankees accused them of being. Frederick Vanderlip and dozens of settlers like him fled the upper Susquehanna Valley and moved north into the waiting arms of Loyalists in central and western New York. About thirty Pennamite refugees ended up serving in Loyalist military units. Many of them later returned to the Wyoming Valley as Tory raiders and took their revenge.[40]

Ethnicity and regional culture constituted more essential building blocks of identity and played a more prominent role in determining how settlers' chose sides than did loyalty to a colony, state, empire, or nation. Whatever else they may have signified, the labels of "Patriot" and "Loyalist" reflected ethnic and regional distinctions among Wyoming settlers. The people accused of being Tories were ethnically and culturally distinct from those who did the accusing. Many alleged Loyalists—men like Philip Buck, Abraham Wortman, Casper Hover, and Frederick Vanderlip—were German and Dutch colonists who had migrated to the Susquehanna Valley from settlements along the Mohawk River

---

Pennsylvania History 61 (Jan. 1994): 45–74; Ann M. Ousterhout, "Frontier Vengeance: Connecticut Yankees vs. Pennamites in the Wyoming Valley," *Pennsylvania History* 62 (1995): 330–63; Ousterhout, *A State Divided: Opposition in Pennsylvania to the American Revolution* (New York, 1987); Albert H. Tillson, Jr., "The Localist Roots of Backcountry Loyalism: An Examination of Popular Political Culture in Virginia's New River Valley," *Journal of Southern History* 54 (Aug. 1988): 387–404; and Ronald Hoffman, Thad W. Tate, and Peter J. Albert, eds., *An Uncivil War: The Southern Backcountry during the American Revolution* (Charlottesville, VA, 1985).

38. Ousterhout, *A State Divided*, 231–40; Meeting of the Inhabitants of Westmoreland, Jan. 6, 1776, *SCP* 7:1.

39. Committee of Inspection to Adonijah Stanburrough and Others, Jan. 1, 1777, *SCP* 7:33; Charles Stewart to Adonijah Stansbury, Dec. 9, 1775, and Minutes of a Meeting of the Proprietors and Settlers in Wilkes-Barre, Nov. 22, 1774, *SCP* 6:401–2, 292–93.

40. Ousterhout, *A State Divided*, 240, 234–35, 272–73n; Nathan Denison to Oliver Wolcott, Sept. 20, 1777, *SCP* 7:36; Harvey and Smith, *History of Wilkes-Barre*, 2:944–45.

in the 1770s. They were people distinct from Yankees in terms of their language, religion, and culture.[41] Such divisions had separated Pennamites from Yankees before the Revolution and continued to do so long after. The New Englanders who upheld the Connecticut claim were mainly English in ethnicity, Congregationalists (or at least Calvinists) in faith, and possessed a common regional background rooted in New England's distinct religious, political, and social institutions. The Pennamites who opposed them were far more ethnically and religiously diverse and drew on a regional culture that was quite different from that of New England.[42]

Ethnicity and regional culture did not just separate Pennamites from Yankees; they also formed the basis for divisions among Connecticut claimants. One episode of factionalism within the ranks of Wyoming's Connecticut claimants pitted New Englanders against Pennsylvania's Paxton settlers. In 1771, just two years after the Paxton men joined forces with the Yankees to wrest control of the Wyoming region from Pennsylvania, tensions emerged between the two groups. In October, reports reached Pennsylvania's proprietors that "a disagreement between the New England Men and Stewarts Party" had arisen. The informants did not specify the source of the trouble, but the dispute undoubtedly concerned the Susquehannah Company's agreement to bestow a town grant on the Paxton settlers as a reward for their services. In 1772 it laid out a separate township for the Pennsylvanians along Fishing Creek, "in Lieu of Nantecock which ye Paxton took in Lieu of ye six mile township." Apparently a disagreement arose when the Paxton settlers demanded Nanticoke, one of the five original townships laid out by the Susquehannah Company, instead of waiting to have new town located and surveyed for them. Seven months later, the company resolved the dispute when they reversed their earlier decision and allowed the Paxton settlers to occupy Nanticoke Township—which they promptly renamed Hanover.[43] Besides disputes over land, tensions between Connecticut claimants from Pennsylvania and New England took on

41. Ousterhout, *A State Divided*, 245, 272–73 n; Harvey and Smith, *History of Wilkes-Barre*, 2:867, 1049–50.
42. For works that consider how constructs of ethnicity and regional culture shaped backcountry land and jurisdictional disputes, see Dutrizac, "Local Identity and Authority in a Disputed Hinterland"; Ousterhout, "Frontier Vengeance"; Brendan McConville, *These Daring Disturbers of the Public Peace: The Struggle for Property and Power in Early New Jersey* (Ithaca, NY, 1999), 47–66; and Edward Countryman, " 'Out of the Bounds of the Law': Northern Land Rioters in the Eighteenth Century," in *The American Revolution: Explorations in the History of American Radicalism*, ed. Alfred F. Young (DeKalb, IL, 1976), 50–56.
43. James Hamilton and Others to Thomas and John Penn, Oct. 8, 1771, and Minutes of a Meeting in Wilkes-Barre, Mar. 11, 1772, *SCP* 4:274, 308; Minutes of a Meeting of the Proprietors in Wilkes-Barre, Oct. 19, 1772, *SCP* 5:51–52.

more serious dimensions. In July 1772 Zebulon Butler received an anonymous letter warning him that Pennsylvania had offered to pardon Lazarus Stewart and his followers if they turned against their Yankee allies. Butler did not show any signs that this report made him doubt the Paxton settlers' loyalty to the Connecticut claim, but other New Englanders were clearly suspicious of the Pennsylvanians. Ezekiel Pierce, a leading Connecticut claimant, attempted to betray Lazarus Stewart and his followers and deliver them into the hands of Pennsylvania officials. In the end, Pierce's plot against the Paxton settlers came to naught as the leadership of the Susquehannah Company repudiated his plan.[44]

Though they certainly shaped the contours of factionalism in the Wyoming region, ethnicity and regional culture did not trump settlers' paramount concern: the pursuit of property. Indeed, the valley's inhabitants repeatedly made common cause with people of different backgrounds in order to better their chances of obtaining land and maintaining their hold on it. Both before and after the Trenton Decree, the ranks of Connecticut claimants included both Yankees from New England and German and Scots-Irish settlers from Pennsylvania. Likewise, within Pennamite ranks could be found settlers of various ethnicities as well as several New Englanders who abandoned the Connecticut claim and took up land under Pennsylvania. Preserved Cooley, John Borlen, Jacob Tillbury, Obadiah Walker, Isaac Van Norman, and other Connecticut claimants who had fought against Pennamites, Indians, and Tories before the Trenton Decree dropped their allegiance to Connecticut, abandoned their former comrades, and took up land under Pennsylvania after it won jurisdiction over the Wyoming region. For his part, Cooley not only relinquished his ties to the Connecticut claim, but became a prominent and aggressive Pennamite.[45] The Paxton settlers also illustrate how lines of allegiance cut across ethnicity and regional culture. They were not ethnically homogeneous but included settlers of various ethnic backgrounds: besides Lazarus Stewart, Robert Kidd, Robert Young and other Scots-Irish settlers stood Baltzer Stager, George Espy, Adolph Diehl, and a number of Germans. These Pennsylvanians also demonstrated their willingness to transcend ethnic and regional differences when they joined forces with New Englanders to challenge Pennsylvania's territorial and jurisdictional claims.[46]

---

44. "A Good Friend" to Zebulon Butler, July 17, 1772; Amos Ogden to E.P. (Ezekiel Pierce), July 1772; and Eliphalet Dyer and Committee to Ezekiel Pierce, Sept. 14, 1772, *SCP* 5:9, 12–13, 31–32.
45. Harvey and Smith, *History of Wilkes-Barre*, 2:980–81, 1096, 1225–30, 3:1416; Petition of Westmoreland Militia, Jan. 23, 1781, *SCP* 7:79–80.
46. William H. Egle, "The House of Lancaster to the Rescue," *Proceedings and Collections of the Wyoming Historical and Geological Society* 6 (1901): 97–105.

It was settlers' determination to obtain frontier freeholds that most powerfully shaped how they cast their allegiance. The timing of Preserved Cooley's defection from the Connecticut claim highlights how the desire to secure property lay at the bottom of his transfer of loyalties. He became a Pennamite at about the same time negotiations over soil rights unraveled between Pennsylvania officials and Connecticut claimants. Up until this point, he could retain his Connecticut deed without risking his property. However, after talks collapsed and Pennsylvania began to take measures against settlers who held Connecticut titles, Yankees had to decide between their loyalty to the Connecticut claim and their own self-interest. In the end, Cooley decided that repudiating the Connecticut claim held fewer risks than opposing the power of Pennsylvania.[47] David Mead's involvement in the Wyoming dispute also illustrates backcountry inhabitants' willingness to transfer their allegiance, not only once, but multiple times in order to gain advantage in the struggle for property and power. Mead, a native of Hudson, New York, first came to the Wyoming Valley in 1769 when the Susquehannah Company engaged him as a surveyor. He obtained land in return for his services and returned to the valley in 1773 to occupy his claim. With the outbreak of the Revolutionary War, Mead moved to the relative safety of Sunbury. No doubt believing that the Trenton Decree had given Pennsylvania the upper hand in the Wyoming dispute, he returned to the valley in 1783, not as a Connecticut claimant, but as a Pennsylvania landholder and justice of the peace. Mead attempted yet another change in allegiance when Pennamite fortunes in the Wyoming Valley began to decline in 1784. As the year came to a close, Mead increasingly distanced himself from Pennsylvania and its land claimants—a change of heart reflected in Pennsylvania claimants' numerous complaints concerning his unwillingness to prosecute Yankee rioters and his efforts to curry favor with Connecticut settlers.[48]

That settlers placed their desire for land before loyalty to the state, ethnic affiliation, or a shared regional culture does not necessarily mean that they were aggressive individualists who placed personal gain before any considerations of group loyalty. There were other more foundational building blocks of settler identity—ones anchored in family, kin, and locale—that, far from being trumped by the pursuit of independence, were central to it. The Paxton settlers

---

47. A List of Wyoming Settlers Divided According to Political Outlook, Apr. 1783, and Petition of Dissident from the Inhabitants of Wyoming, Dec. 29, 1783, *SCP* 7:290–91, 340–42; Harvey and Smith, *History of Wilkes-Barre*, 3:1416.
48. Harvey and Smith, *History of Wilkes-Barre*, 3:1463; Deposition of Henry Brink, Jan. 14, 1785, *SCP* 7:200; Depositions of Obadiah Walker and Joseph Montawney, Jan. 14, 1785 and Alexander Patterson and Others to John Boyd and John Armstrong, Jr., Aug. 1784, *SCP* 8:192–93, 45–46.

are an example of how kinship and locale stood at the center of backcountry inhabitants' collective identities and allegiance. A network of personal ties held together Lazarus Stewart and his followers in their struggles against Indians, state officials, and Pennamites. Many of the men who joined Stewart in his move to the Wyoming Valley were close kin: his brother, William, and his sons, William, James, and Lazarus Stewart, Jr., all journeyed with him to Northeast Pennsylvania in 1770. They were joined there by kinsmen Robert and Peter Kidd and William, Lazarus, and Robert Young. In addition to these family ties, a common place of origin bound Stewart to his Wyoming Valley neighbors. John Laird, George Mease, John Stiller, and George Espy all hailed from Stewart's Pennsylvania birthplace, Hanover. Many of these men had served under Lazarus Stewart during the Seven Years' War and later followed him as frontier outlaws.[49]

In sum, the Wyoming Valley's contest for allegiance was far more akin to a feud between two contending networks of kin, neighbors, and friends brought together by the common pursuit of property than to an ethnic conflict or a clash of regional cultures. The Inmans, Slocums, and Satterlees were some of the interrelated families who formed the backbone of Wyoming's Yankee faction and who contended against a cohort of Pennamite households that included the Shoemakers, Brinks, Van Normans, Cortrights, and Tillburys. Though fidelity to Pennsylvania and Connecticut or any sense of ethnic affiliation took a back seat to efforts to secure property, the struggle for land did not sunder the face-to-face ties that circumscribed the lives of backcountry inhabitants.

Interpersonal relationships and identities rooted in family, kin, and locale endured among Wyoming's settlers because they were foundational to agrarian independence. Male frontier settlers certainly strove after independence for the personal rewards—the social status, political empowerment, economic security, and sense of masculinity—its attainment brought. Nevertheless, they also pursued it for the benefits it would convey to their children and their children's children. Independence was the concern of households and generations, not simply individuals. Moreover, for backcountry settlers, independence did not mean individualism. Attaining and securing independence was, as the day-to-day rounds of rural life taught them, the work of families, friends, and neighbors striving together. In the final calculation, the ethos of independence was a vision of an ideal *society*—of a society populated by neighbors, not landlords

---

49. William H. Egle, *History of the Counties of Dauphin and Lebanon in the Commonwealth of Pennsylvania: Biographical and Genealogical* (Philadelphia, 1883), 71; Egle, "The House of Lancaster to the Rescue," 103.

and tenants, and of a society where reciprocity and mutuality, not patronage and obligation, formed the foundation of interpersonal relationships.[50]

Property

The conflicts over authority and allegiance that beset the Wyoming region were ultimately rooted in settlers' efforts to secure frontier property. Pennamites and Yankees fought over land and, in the wake of the destruction wrought by the Revolutionary War, the resources essential to their survival. Captain Thomas Robinson, who commanded one of the two companies of Pennsylvania state troops sent to occupy the Wyoming Valley in 1783, touched on this discord when he noted that the valley's inhabitants, "Imajining no Law was to take Hold of them," became involved in "a great Many Wrangling Disputes" over land, crops, and livestock. Here, Captain Robinson hit on one element that converted competition over property into frontier warfare—the absence of unified, effective authority. On a deeper level, conflict between Pennsylvania and Connecticut claimants was a product of tensions that existed beneath the surface of rural communities throughout early America. In a world of limited resources and a growing population, the pursuit of household independence often led to competition and contention between farm families.[51]

This contest over property only intensified after the Revolutionary War. The Trenton Decree failed to imbue state institutions with the legitimacy they needed to adjudicate settlers' land disputes and, thus, served only to transform the Wyoming dispute into a face-to-face quarrel over property. Between 1783 and 1785 the valley once again became the scene of mass dispossessions during which armed bands of Pennsylvania and Connecticut claimants stripped scores of families of their land, food, and shelter. Pennsylvania never sanctioned the unlawful ejection of settlers, yet Pennamites often took matters into their own hands. In May 1784, Alexander Patterson, with the help of Wilkes-Barre's garrison, forced more than 150 Yankee families from their farms, "tumbled their

---

50. For two works that echo my assessment of backcountry settlers' social vision, see Alan Taylor, *Liberty Men and Great Proprietors: The Revolutionary Settlement of the Maine Frontier, 1760–1820* (Chapel Hill, NC, 1990) and Gordon S. Wood, *The Radicalism of the American Revolution* (New York, 1991).

51. Captain Robinson to Governor Dickinson, June 8, 1783, in Harvey and Smith, *History of Wilkes-Barre*, 3:1338. For a study that explores the sources of tension and conflict in rural communities throughout early America, see Daniel Vickers, "Competency and Competition: Economic Culture in Early America," *WMQ* 47 (Jan. 1990): 3–29.

Goods and Every thing out of doors," and burned their homes. Once they were out of the way, Pennsylvania claimants occupied the land.[52] Yankees struck back in the summer of 1784 after Pennsylvania recalled its troops from the valley. They drove "off every Pennsylvania Settler, Men, Women, and Children . . . plundered every house, stolen their horses, and killed their Cattle." One inhabitant estimated that by January 1785 Yankees had forced more than six hundred Pennamite men, women, and children from the land.[53]

As was the case before the Revolution, much of the violence perpetrated by Pennsylvania and Connecticut claimants was simply aimed at driving their opponents off the land. On October 20, 1784, a gang of Pennamites led by Henry Shoemaker entered the dwelling of Connecticut claimant Dorcas Stewart, threw her belongings out of the cabin, and then "knocked the Logs out of the House till the loft Fell Down." Abigail Jameson received similar treatment from a party of Pennsylvanians led by Alexander Patterson. The Pennamites forced her, her ailing mother-in-law, and her two-year-old daughter out of their cabin, threw their household goods out on the ground, and then nailed up the cabin door. Patterson then threatened Jameson that the cabin "would be demolished over her head in case she went into it & lived there again." Pennsylvania claimants also suffered at the hands of Yankee rioters. Connecticut settlers "armed with Rifles & Pistolls" plundered the farm of Henry Brink, then ordered him to "quit the Country," threatening that if he did not go, "they would drive him before the Muzzle of their guns." Likewise, after forcing James Johnston from his home and plundering his property, Yankee rioters warned that "if he ever returned to his house they would sweep him to hell."[54] In all of these cases, rioters threatened their victims and stripped them of their homes, crops, and livestock in order to undermine their resolve and ability to remain in the valley.

What distinguishes Pennamite-Yankee conflict after the Trenton Decree, however, is the degree to which Wyoming's inhabitants quarreled, not just over land, but over possessions critical to the survival of frontier families. The battle

---

52. Harvey and Smith, *History of Wilkes-Barre*, 3:1380; Obadiah Gore to William Judd, Nov. 21, 1783, and John Franklin's Diary, May 2–July 3, 1784, *SCP* 7:334, 436–37; John Franklin to William Samuel Johnson, Eliphalet Dyer, and Jesse Root, Oct. 11, 1784, *SCP* 8:106–7.

53. Harvey and Smith, *History of Wilkes-Barre*, 3:1397–99; Alexander Patterson and Others to John Boyd and John Armstrong, Jr., Aug. 1784; John Franklin to William Samuel Johnson, Eliphalet Dyer, and Jesse Root, Oct. 20, 1784; and Deposition of Preserved Cooley, Jan. 14, 1785, *SCP* 8:43, 120–21, 198.

54. Deposition of Dorcas Stewart, Nov. 10, 1784, and Deposition of Abigail Jameson, Nov. 10, 1784, *PA1* 10:693, 689; Deposition of Henry Brink, Jan. 14, 1785 and Deposition of Lena Tillbury, Jan. 14, 1785, *SCP* 8:200, 196.

for property in Northeast Pennsylvania became a struggle over the means of subsistence where crops and livestock became contested commodities over which settlers fought and died.

The Revolutionary War had much to do with this subtle shift in the nature of agrarian unrest. The conflict had devastated the region, creating an atmosphere of material insecurity and want that sparked competition over scarce resources.[55] In November 1784, Griffith Evans journeyed down the north branch of the Susquehanna River after representing Pennsylvania at treaty negotiations with the Iroquois at Fort Stanwix, New York. Along the way, he described a landscape wasted by years of warfare. Evans noted that whites had settled the region before the Revolution but added that Indians had driven them off and destroyed their farms during the war. In particular, he observed that Wilkes-Barre, though it lay on a "beautiful rich plane," had "suffered from every quarter" during the war and had "been little improved" since then. Raw numbers can do little to capture the emotional cost of warfare but they do suggest the material dimension of the setbacks experienced by Wyoming's inhabitants. In 1778 Connecticut rated Westmoreland County's taxable estates at £20,322. In 1780, two years after the disastrous Battle of Wyoming, officials valued county assets at £2,353—a little more than a tenth of their value three years earlier. By 1781 this situation had improved slightly (the county contained about 150 taxable males who possessed property worth approximately £4,500), but the county's population and wealth remained far below prewar levels.[56]

In addition to the man-made devastation wrought by the Revolution, Wyoming's inhabitants had to contend with the unpredictability and destructive force of nature. This reality was brought home to the region's settlers when a devastating flood swept the valley on March 15, 1784. A spell of warm weather triggered the "freshet" when it caused the sudden collapse of an ice dam that had blocked the upper reaches of the Susquehanna River during the winter. Pennsylvania president John Dickinson received a report from the commander of Wyoming's garrison stating that the flood carried away trees, over a hundred and fifty houses, and a large number of livestock. Another account of the flood by several Connecticut claimants detailed its "extraordinary effects": flood waters mixed with boulder-sized chunks of ice carried settlers' cabins as far as seven miles down river; one settlement lost ninety cattle, twenty-seven horses, sixty-five sheep, and over a hundred swine. Even though only one person died in

---

55. For a description of the destruction wrought on the Upper Susquehannah River Valley during the Revolution, see Peter C. Mancall, *Valley of Opportunity: Economic Culture along the Upper Susquehanna, 1700–1800* (Ithaca, NY, 1991), 130–59.

56. Hallock F. Raup, ed., "Journal of Griffith Evans, 1784–1788," *PMHB* 65 (Apr. 1941): 223–24; Harvey and Smith, *History of Wilkes-Barre*, 2:951–52, 3:1254–55, 1277–79.

the flood, the survivors were left homeless and destitute. Adding to their troubles, the flood had left the riverside flats on which they had hoped to plant their crops buried in mud, ice, and debris.[57]

With much of the Wyoming Valley in ruins, houses, cleared fields, crops, and livestock became items of contention between Yankees and Pennamites. In September 1784, state commissioners John Okely, John Boyd, John Armstrong Jr., and James Read reported on how the immediate needs of frontier people, not abstract questions of what constituted rightful possession, came to dominate contests over property. They feared that disputes over unharvested grain would spark a new round of armed conflict, observing that contention over crops and livestock often lay at the center of violence in the valley.[58] The commissioners probably had in mind a deadly confrontation over ripening fields of grain between armed bands of Yankees and Pennamites that left two Pennsylvanians wounded and two New Englanders killed just two months before.[59] The testimony of Pennsylvania claimants backs up the committee's conclusions. William Lantarman deposed that Waterman Baldwin accosted him as he was harvesting grain in a field and threatened "that if he caught him taking any corn out of that field, he . . . would scalp him." Seeing that Baldwin carried a rifle and two pistols, Lantarman asked if he would shoot him for taking corn. Baldwin answered that he would. When Lantarman responded "that such conduct was contrary to the law," Baldwin retorted that "there was no law here." Nicodemus Travis reported that Daniel Gore, armed with a club, confronted him over a wagon-load of oats. Gore declared that Pennamites would "have none of his Crops" and warned that he would "sacrifice" Travis if he did not hand over the grain (which he promptly did). In January 1785, Enos Randel recounted how a Yankee mob tore down his house, plundered his crops, and "destroyed" his cattle. Afterward, Randal went to the New Englanders and begged for "a little of his corn for the subsistence of a numerous family thro' the winter." But the Yankees denied him any support, saying that "they would want it all the next summer for the supply of the Troops." In her deposition, Catherine Bowerlane testified that after fleeing their home in the face of Yankee violence, her husband returned "to gather Corn when they [the Yankees] killed him" and "took all his grain of every Sort."[60]

57. James Moore to John Dickinson, Mar. 20, 1784 and Rev. Jacob Johnson, et. al to John Franklin, Mar. 24, 1784, SCP 7:377, 383–84.
58. Commissioners to President Dickinson, Sept. 24, 1784, PA1 10:564.
59. Deposition of William Brink, July 27, 1784, and John Franklin to William Samuel Johnson, Eliphalet Dyer, and Jesse Root, Oct. 11, 1784, SCP 8:7–8, 209–10; Depositions of Henry Brink and Wilhelmus Van Gordon, Aug. 15, 1784, and Deposition of Catherine Cortright, Aug. 11, 1784, PA1 10:651–52, 642.
60. Depositions of William Lantarman and Nicodemus Travis, Sept. 22, 1784, PA1 10:660–62; Depositions of Catherine Bowerlane and Enos Randal, Jan. 14, 1785, SCP 8:195, 199.

Besides crops and livestock, Pennamites and Yankees robbed each other of guns, tools, and other essentials of frontier life. In a region beset by violence, it is not surprising that firearms became an object of plunder. Abraham Gooden, James Landon, Obadiah Walker, and other settlers complained of being robbed of their guns, shot, and powder. All told, John Franklin estimated (and perhaps exaggerated) that Pennsylvanians robbed Connecticut claimants of "at least 300 good Rifles and fire arms" between May and October 1784. Pennamite and Yankee gangs also stripped their victims of clothing, tools, and salt—the latter item being critical to the preservation of food and, thus, vital for survival.[61]

The struggle over property in Northeast Pennsylvania involved not only men, but also women and children. It left entire families destitute of food, clothing, and shelter and became as much an obstacle to household subsistence as natural disasters or the destruction wrought by the Revolutionary War. Yankees and Pennsylvanians alike spoke of being "Stript and Plundered" and "Turned almost naked out of doors" and of "Women and Children naked and Destitute of the Necessaries of life." One Pennamite refugee testified to having survived along with fifteen other men, women, and children "upon a small quantity of bread and bran, and the berries which the Woods afforded."[62] Griffith Evans also recorded seeing "large families of women and young children flying . . . to unimproved wilds" without a "single atom to support them" during his journey down the Susquehanna in 1784. However, he makes it clear that women were not just victims of, but participants in, the Wyoming controversy. Stopping at a cabin near the juncture of the Susquehanna and Lackawanna rivers in search of lodging, Evans found the women who occupied it to be "amazing warm yankees and inveterate to an extreme against the Pennamites." They caused "some high scenes" for reasons he never made clear; perhaps the women's prejudice against Pennsylvania made tempers flare when they learned of his connections to the state. Clearly, partisanship could not be claimed as the exclusive property of men.[63]

Women became enmeshed in the revolutionary frontiers' contest over property because it disrupted household economies involving women's productive labors. Society may have recognized adult men as heads of households, but farm families required the cooperation of husbands, wives, and children to

61. Depositions of James Landon and Abraham Gooden, Aug. 11, 1784 and Deposition of Charles Manrow, Mar. 24, 1784, *PA1* 10:635, 639, 708; Deposition of Obadiah Walker, Jan. 14, 1785, and John Franklin to William Samuel Johnson, Eliphalet Dyer, and Jesse Root, Oct. 20, 1784, *SCP* 8:192, 121.
62. John Franklin to Ebenezer Gray, Nov. 10, 1784, and Deposition of John Tilbury, Jan. 14, 1785, *SCP* 8:149, 195; Deposition of Samuel Karr, Charles Manrow, and Daniel Swart, Mar. 25, 1785, *PA1* 10:708–9.
63. Raup, "Journal of Griffith Evans," 223–24.

make ends meet. In preindustrial America, women retained responsibility for critical aspects of household production: they spun thread, wove cloth, and made numerous other household goods both for home consumption and trade. They also tended the gardens that lay close to their homes, saw to the feeding of chickens and pigs, milked cows, and prepared or preserved the family's food.[64]

Women's domestic responsibilities put them on the front lines of agrarian conflict. They came face-to-face with bands of male settlers who uprooted gardens, knocked down fences, and robbed families of their food, livestock, and domestic goods. Catherine Sims's description of her dispossession by Yankee settlers illustrates how agrarian violence touched the lives of women and how women experienced and perceived it differently than men. Sims, in contrast to men's concerns with grain crops, oxen, and horses, focused on her fight with three Yankees over her family's pair of milk cows. Drawing a line between her and her husband's spheres of activity, she took care to record how her assailants "plundered" *her* household goods and "destroyed" *her* garden. Lois King, another Pennamite women, also made distinctions between property that belonged to her husband and that which belonged to her. In her description of an attack on her family's farm, King distinguished between Yankees tearing off the roof of "her husband's house, in which she lived" and rioters plundering her domestic possessions.[65]

In a region beset by bloodshed and murder, male settlers who feared for their lives often left to their wives the difficult task of holding property against marauding bands of land rioters. After Yankees threatened to "make a corpse" of him, Charles Manrow, "not thinking himself safe to stay in his house," fled but left his family behind to occupy their land. A number of depositions collected from both Pennamites and Yankees contain references to women confronting hostile mobs. While men risked severe beatings or even death if they attempted to protect their farms, women were able to maintain possession without running the same level of risk. Hannah Schoonhover's description of her encounter with a band of Yankee rioters led by Waterman Baldwin makes clear the fine line Wyoming's women trod in their efforts to retain their families' property. Hannah recounted how she and her sister-in-law barred the door of their cabin when they saw the Yankees approaching. Baldwin, perhaps wanting to know what level of resistance he could expect to meet, asked Hannah

---

64. For an exploration of women's activities in early America's rural households, see Laruel Thatcher Ulrich, *A Midwife's Tale: The Life of Martha Ballard Based on Her Diary, 1785–1812* (New York, 1991); and Ulrich, "Martha Ballard and Her Girls: Women's Work in Eighteenth-Century Maine," in *Work and Labor in Early America*, ed. Stephen Innes (Chapel Hill, NC, 1988), 70–105.

65. Depositions of Catherine Sims and Lois King, Aug. 10, 1784, *PA1* 10:644–45.

"if there was any men in the house." After she replied that there were not, the rioters proceeded to break down the door and plunder her house. The Yankees then ordered Hannah to join her husband at Wilkes-Barre's fort. When she refused, her assailants told her that she would "be abus'd" if she did not abandon her farm. In the end, Hannah Schoonhover lost her family's property but managed to escape her encounter alive and unharmed—something many men in similar circumstances failed to do.[66]

Yet women were not immune to the violence that claimed the lives of their husbands, fathers, sons, and brothers. Threading its way through the letters and depositions of Wyoming's inhabitants is a litany of threats against women and children. Abraham Gooden reported that Yankee rioters declared that they would put captured Pennamites "to Death, [and] the Children they would Tawmehack."[67] There was far more bark to such threats than bite, but women and children did become targets of violence. In August 1784, state commissioners Boyd and Armstrong reported that "some women and one Child" had been wounded in fighting between Pennamites and Yankees. In the same year, Elizabeth Van Norman testified that Yankee rioters had sought permission to shoot women and children from their "captain," John Swift, and that, three days later, Yankees opened fire on her when she went to fetch a pail of water. Lois King deposed that Waterman Baldwin shot her dog as it walked by her side, expressing her strong belief that the bullet was meant for her. Yankees were not the only ones guilty of violence against women and children. John Franklin claimed that a party of Pennsylvania claimants "beat and abused" two Yankee women "in a Shameful Disgraceful and Cruel Manner," and that a six-month-old child "received a slighty wound in the forehead" from a Pennamite musket ball while the infants' mother held him "at her breast."[68]

That women's domestic responsibilities bound them up in the Wyoming Valley's contest over property and subsistence explains why they became victims of agrarian violence. Nonetheless, it is also worth considering how deeper, gendered tensions may have contributed to attacks against women. Although it is scant, there is evidence of the rape (or at least attempted rape) of women by Wyoming's land rioters. The only solid (but certainly not unbiased) testimony concerning sexual assault is found in a letter penned by John

---

66. Deposition of Hannah Schoonhover, Aug. 10, 1784, *PA1* 10:646.
67. Depositions of Abraham Gooden (quoted) and William Hartman, Aug. 11, 1784, *PA1* 10:639, 647.
68. John Boyd and John Armstrong, Jr., to John Dickinson, Aug. 2, 1784, *SCP* 8:17; Deposition of Elizabeth Van Norman, Aug. 11, 1784, and Deposition of Lois King, Aug. 10, 1784, *PA1* 10:643, 645; John Franklin to Frederick Antes, Daniel Montgomery, and William Bonam, Oct. 23, 1784, *SCP* 8:131, 132.

Franklin. In it he asserts that Pennamites "attempted to ravish" two Yankee women "at Lackawana, after Plundering them of their all." There are several explanations for the scarcity of reports concerning rape. On the one hand, the dearth of such testimony might simply reflect that rape was rarely committed by agrarian rioters; on the other, it might reflect the fact that then, as now, women were reluctant to admit to being victims. But it is not unlikely that in a dispute marked by murder, robbery, and brutal violence that men raped women. There are repeated references in court depositions to women being "abused." These might very well be references to sexual assault.[69]

Men embroiled in an aggressive struggle over land and authority may have used rape as a way of expressing their manliness and power. The revolutionary frontiers' struggle for independence was also closely bound to male settlers' efforts to attain and protect a masculine ideal. The ethos of male independence was predicated on property ownership *and* on the dependence of women and children: the true man was one who had the land to support, and the authority to command, a household. With this gendered understanding of independence in mind, violence against women takes on greater meaning. From the perspective of male land rioters, women who stayed behind to protect their homes challenged conventional gender norms. They held and defended property (the supposed prerogative of men) and directly challenged men's efforts to appropriate that property for themselves. Rape and other acts of violence against women may have been attempts by men to restore the proper gender hierarchy and to highlight women's dependent, subjective status. Agrarian rioters may have also used sexual assault to strike at their male opponents: by raping one man's wife or daughter another man was, in effect, challenging his authority over his household. In this sense, rape was just as much an attack on a man's independence as robbing him of his property.[70]

Together, material insecurity and a lack of an effective, unified authority transformed the Wyoming Valley into a more turbulent image of agrarian society. Under normal circumstances, encounters among rural inhabitants revolved around exchanges of news, tools, and labor. But conditions were anything but normal in Northeast Pennsylvania, and interpersonal relations there often

---

69. Sharon Block, "Bringing Rapes to Court," *Common Place* 3 (Apr. 2003) <www.common-place.org>; John Franklin to Frederick Antes, Daniel Montgomery, and William Bonam, Oct. 23, 1784, *SCP* 8:131, 132.

70. My discussion of the relationship between rape and agrarian violence has been informed by the following works: Michael Kaplan, "New York City Tavern Violence and the Creation of a Working-Class Made Identity," *Journal of the Early Republic* 15 (winter 1995): 609–15; Sharon Block, "Rape without Women: Print Culture and the Politicization of Rape, 1765–1815," *Journal of American History* 89:3 (2002): 849–68; and Sean Moore, "'Justifiable Provocation': Violence against Women in Essex County, New York, 1799–1860," *Journal of Social History* 35:4 (2002): 889–918.

exhibited a darker side of rural life. Violence between Pennamites and Yankees mirrored (in amplified form) the discord that inevitably arose when families came into competition for the land and resources that were foundational to independence. Typically, rural inhabitants controlled these tensions through communal rituals, a cultivated spirit of neighborliness, and persistent litigation through mutually recognized judicial institutions. But in places like the Wyoming Valley, where there was no unified community and where authority was in dispute, such everyday conflicts easily spun out of control.[71]

In the end, David Mead failed to maintain his power or his property. The events that led to his downfall unfolded in the summer of 1785. After Yankee rioters sacked his farm on July 6, Mead fortified his home and hired dozens of men to garrison the makeshift fort. This move provoked the valley's Connecticut claimants, and by August they had mustered a sufficient force to surround Mead's farm. When the Yankees "paraded" a cannon before his homestead, Mead and his men fled the valley.[72] Mead's defeat reflects larger dimensions of the Pennamite-Yankee wars that convulsed Northeast Pennsylvania between 1769 and 1785. Mead ultimately became a victim of a conflict that grew out of settlers' unchecked competition for land and resources. He discovered that his authority as a justice of the peace, though rooted in Pennsylvania's jurisdictional rights, meant very little in a region rent by property disputes and where fidelity to family, kin, and neighbors overwhelmed notions of allegiance to the state.

David Mead's flight from the Susquehanna Valley was both an ending and a beginning. One the one hand, it signified the conclusion of a decade-and-a-half struggle between Pennamites and Yankees over possession of the Wyoming Valley. Never again would large numbers of Pennsylvania settlers contest Connecticut claimants' hold on the state's Northeast frontier. On the other, it marked the emergence of new dynamics of unrest in the region. Even as Mead braced himself for his final showdown with Yankee rioters, the Susquehannah Company's shareholders reaffirmed their determination to defend the Connecticut claim.[73] Soon, new agendas and new faces appeared in the Wyoming region that would broaden and deepen the insurgency Pennsylvania faced.

---

71. For works that discuss the social dynamics of rural conflict, see Lucy Jayne Botscharow-Kamau, "Neighbors: Harmony and Conflict on the Indiana Frontier," *Journal of the Early Republic* 11 (winter 1991): 507–29; and Vickers, "Competency and Competition."

72. John Franklin's Diary, July 1–Nov. 15, 1785, and John Franklin to William Samuel Johnson, July 19, 1785, *SCP* 8:275–76, 251–52; Harvey and Smith, *History of Wilkes-Barre*, 3:1476.

73. Minutes of a Meeting of the Susquehannah Company, July 13, 1785, *SCP* 8:247–50.

CHAPTER 3

"A Dangerous Combination of Villains"

The Social Context of Agrarian Resistance

On the night of June 26, 1788, a band of Yankee insurgents crept into Wilkes-Barre, Pennsylvania, broke into the home of Luzerne county clerk Timothy Pickering, and entered the room where he, his wife Rebecca, and their nine-month-old son slept. Startled awake, Pickering asked who was there, to which he received the curt reply, "get up." Pickering got out of bed and started to dress; Rebecca left the room and returned with a lit candle. In its dim glow, Pickering saw that the room was "filled with men, armed with guns and hatchets, having their faces blacked and handkerchiefs tied round their heads." Once Pickering had dressed, the intruders bound his arms and spirited him out into the night. After a brief stop for a drink at a tavern ten miles above Wilkes-Barre, Pickering's kidnappers carried him up the Susquehanna River into the sparsely inhabited forests of northern Pennsylvania.[1]

Settler resistance in Northeast Pennsylvania was not an isolated event, but joined a broad current of agrarian unrest in the 1780s. In central and western Massachusetts, farmers angered by the state's unwillingness to grant them tax or debt relief took up arms during Shays's Rebellion. In Vermont, settlers and speculators fought for land and independent statehood against New York. Meanwhile, in Maine, squatters and powerful landlords engaged in a contentious battle over frontier property. Vermont's agrarian rebels were known as

---

1. Charles W. Upham, *The Life of Timothy Pickering*, 4 vols. (Boston, 1873), 2:381–82.

"Green Mountain Boys" and Maine's as "Liberty Men."[2] By 1787, Pennsylvania's disaffected Connecticut claimants, described by the *Connecticut Courant* as "a dangerous combination of villains, composed of runaway debtors, criminals, [and] adherents of Shays," had earned the appellation "Wild Yankees." Like their counterparts in New England, Pennsylvania's Yankee settlers fought for land and independence and forged a long-term resistance movement.[3]

Timothy Pickering's abduction brings us face to face with early America's agrarian insurgents. The events surrounding the kidnapping provide an opportunity to reexamine the social context of agrarian resistance. Historians have portrayed rural rebels and their movements in one of three ways. For some, the disturbances are clear indications of class conflict. Under this paradigm, unrest was the product of farmers' efforts to resist exploitation at the hands of wealthy land speculators, government officials, and backcountry merchants.[4] Other historians portray rebellious rural inhabitants as being motivated, not by class enmity, but by a simple desire for property. Under this formulation, agrarian insurgents possessed the same acquisitiveness and drive for personal advantage that characterized the landlords and speculators they fought against.[5] A third group has more

---

2. David P. Szatmary, *Shays' Rebellion: The Making of an Agrarian Insurrection* (Amherst, MA, 1980); Michael Bellesiles, *Revolutionary Outlaws: Ethan Allen and the Struggle for Independence on the Early American Frontier* (Charlottesville, VA, 1993), 80–111; Alan Taylor, *Liberty Men and Great Proprietors: The Revolutionary Settlement of the Maine Frontier, 1760–1820* (Chapel Hill, NC, 1990), 89–122, 181–208.

3. William Hooker Smith to Timothy Pickering, Oct. 1787 and Extract from the *Connecticut Courant*, Sept. 10, 1787, SCP 9:254, 188.

4. The class-conflict model of agrarian unrest has been around for a long time and finds its roots in the scholarship of progressive historians such as Irving Mark, *Agrarian Conflicts in Colonial New York, 1711–1775* (New York, 1940). This perspective has been revived by neoprogressives such Michael Kay, "The North Carolina Regulation, 1766–1776: A Class Conflict" in *The American Revolution: Explorations in the History of American Radicalism*, ed. Alfred F. Young (DeKalb, IL, 1976), 71–123; Staughton Lynd, "Who Should Rule at Home? Dutchess County, New York, in the American Revolution" and "The Tenant Rising at Livingston Manor, May 1777," in *Class Conflict, Slavery, and the United States Constitution*, ed. Staughton Lynd (Indianapolis, 1967), 63–77; and Edward Countryman, " 'Out of the Bounds of the Law: Northern Land Rioters in the Eighteenth Century," in *The American Revolution: Explorations in the History of American Radicalism*, edited by Alfred F. Young (DeKalb, IL, 1976), 37–69. Some more recent studies emphasize cultural conflict over class enmity but still tend to portray agrarian disturbances as confrontations between communitarian farmers and wealthy gentlemen who represented a new, more commercialized social order: Szatmary, *Shays' Rebellion*, esp. 1, 18, and Marjoline Kars, *Breaking Loose Together: The Regulator Rebellion in Pre-Revolutionary North Carolina* (Chapel Hill, NC, 2002), esp. 6, 215–16.

5. For this perspective on early America's agrarian insurgencies, see Thomas L. Purvis, "Origins and Patterns of Agrarian Unrest in New Jersey, 1735–1754," *WMQ* 39 (Oct. 1982): 600–627, esp. 615; Sung Bok Kim, "The Impact of Class Relations and Warfare in the American Revolution: The New York Experience," *Journal of American History* 69 (Sept. 1982): 326–46, esp. 332, 345; and Kim, *Landlord and Tenant in Colonial New York: Manorial Society, 1604–1775* (Chapel Hill, NC, 1978) chaps. 7 and 8, esp. 415.

recently forwarded a vision of early America's agrarian rebels that bridges some of the gaps between the first two and that strikes out in new directions. Denying that rural dissidents were solely motivated by class, they contend that deep disagreements between them and their opponents over the nature of property and how it could be rightfully acquired, over theology and religious practice, and over the meaning of the American Revolution fueled agrarian disturbances.[6]

The story of Pickering's kidnapping challenges existing views of agrarian insurgents in two respects. First, it demonstrates that contests over property did not invariably pit farmers against land speculators. Although Wild Yankees bitterly resisted the claims of some of Pennsylvania's most powerful land developers, they cooperated with speculators who supported the Connecticut claim. Indeed, the region's "dangerous combination of villains" included ordinary settlers who struggled to defend their frontier freeholds *and* land speculators from New England and New York who sought to secure far more extensive claims.[7] This fact belies the notion that agrarian unrest was simply an expression of class enmity. Though agrarian disturbances commonly pitted the few against the many, rural folk only came into conflict with the wealthy gentlemen when the latter stood in the way of their achieving independence. Put another way, the relationship between class conflict and rural discord was more circumstantial than systemic.

Second, the events surrounding the abduction reveal that settler resistance emerged out of, and was intertwined with, the aspirations, day-to-day activities, and face-to-face relationships that circumscribed the lives of ordinary farm families. This observation places the social origins of agrarian conflict in a broader, and ultimately more meaningful, context. Besides being agrarian

---

6. These studies, mostly published in the last decade and a half, take somewhat of a middle ground between the two previous schools of thought: on the one hand, they shy away from blunt class-conflict explanations of rural contention but, on the other, argue that there were serious conflicts of interest and ideology between farmers and elites: Alan Taylor, "Agrarian Independence: Northern Land Rioters after the Revolution," in *Beyond the American Revolution: Explorations in the History of American Radicalism*, ed. Alfred F. Young (DeKalb, IL, 1993), 224–26; Taylor, *Liberty Men*, esp. 5–9; James P. Whittenburg, "Planters, Merchants, and Lawyers: Social Change and the Origins of the North Carolina Regulation," *WMQ* 34 (Apr. 1977): 215–38, esp. 220; Brendan McConville, *These Daring Disturbers of the Public Peace: The Struggle for Property and Power in Early New Jersey* (Ithaca, NY, 1999), esp. 2–3, 174–76; Charles E. Brooks, *Frontier Settlement and Market Revolution: The Holland Land Purchase* (Ithaca, NY, 1996), esp. 11–12; and Paul Douglas Newman, *Fries's Rebellion: The Enduring Struggle for the American Revolution* (Philadelphia, 2004), chap. 1.

7. For another study that finds settlers and land speculators working in cooperation in the context of agrarian resistance in Northeast Pennsylvania and elsewhere, see Alan Taylor, " 'To Man Their Rights': The Frontier Revolution," in *The Transforming Hand of Revolution: Reconsidering the American Revolution as a Social Movement*, ed. Ronald Hoffman and Peter J. Albert (Charlottesville, VA, 1995), 231–57.

insurgents, Pennsylvania's Wild Yankees were rural people enmeshed in local relationships and motivated by a powerful aspiration: the desire to secure a freehold sizeable enough to support a household and free it from dependency on, and subordination to, others. It was this pursuit of independence that stood at the center of agrarian unrest in early America. Those historians who portray rural rebels as rambunctious petty capitalists are right in focusing on their determined efforts to acquire land, but largely fail to recognize that the pursuit of property intersected with deep social tensions and could, in itself, generate popular movements with radical potential. Farmers did not have to draw inspiration from the American Revolution or evangelical Christianity in order to mount campaigns of agrarian resistance. The sources of and motivations for conflict were intrinsic to rural society itself.

The Kidnapping

Pennsylvania's efforts to quiet Yankee resistance set in motion the events that led to Timothy Pickering's kidnapping. In March 1787 the state passed the Confirming Act—a piece of legislation that sought to end conflict in Northeast Pennsylvania by recognizing the tenure of Connecticut claimants who had obtained and occupied lands *before* the Trenton Decree. However, the law made no provision for settlers who took up lands *after* the court's decision or for nonresident proprietors. The Confirming Act, not accidentally, served to divide Connecticut claimants into two parties: more established settlers who could take advantage of the state's offer versus those holding newly issued deeds that were excluded from the legislation's provisions. The state further inflamed Yankee factionalism when it set off the upper Susquehanna Valley (an area mostly inhabited by Connecticut claimants) from Northumberland County and established the separate county of Luzerne. Some Connecticut claimants reacted positively toward the state's initiative, seeing in it an opportunity to gain greater control over local affairs. However, Yankee hardliners opposed the move, fearing that it would bring state authority closer to their doorsteps and reacted angrily toward those who supported the formation of the new county. Solomon Strong, a die-hard supporter of the Connecticut claim, warned William Hooker Smith that if he did not withdraw his support for the state's plan, Yankee insurgents, or "Mad Boys" as he called them, would "Destroye him."[8]

---

8. The Confirming Act, March 28, 1787, *SCP* 9:82–86; *SCP* 8:xxxv–xxxix; Resolution of the Pennsylvania General Assembly, Apr. 3, 1786, and Solomon Strong to Zebulon Butler and Paul Schott, May 22, 1786, *SCP* 8:313–14, 314 n. 4, 338.

The factionalism produced by the Confirming Act and the creation of Luzerne County reshaped the geography of resistance in Northeast Pennsylvania. The Wyoming Valley, once the heartland of support for the Connecticut claim, became a stronghold of moderate settlers who wished to negotiate a settlement with Pennsylvania. Meanwhile, Wild Yankees came to dominate the region north of Tunkhannock Creek. When arranged by township, the names of settlers who signed petitions in support of county elections or took oaths of allegiance to the state reveal this transformation. Settlements south of Tunkhannock Creek overwhelmingly favored elections and provided the lion's share of inhabitants who took the loyalty oath. In contrast, settlers who dwelt north of the creek rarely took the loyalty oath or signed petitions that favored county elections.[9] The territory between Tioga Point and Tunkhannock Creek became the crucible of Wild Yankee resistance, and this region would supply all of the men who participated in Pickering's kidnapping.

A wave of popular discontent and backcountry rebellion outside of Pennsylvania also contributed to tensions between state officials and Connecticut settlers. In the 1780s settlers in Vermont expanded their resistance to New York landlords into a drive for statehood.[10] This separatist movement provided a compelling precedent for Connecticut claimants who sought to establish their autonomy from Pennsylvania. Indeed, one Yankee dissident expressed his desire to turn Northeast Pennsylvania into a "New Vermont."[11] Shays's Rebellion also cast its shadow over the Wyoming controversy. Early in 1787, reports began to filter into Pennsylvania describing how discord in Massachusetts had grown into a "Serious War" and predicting that the rebellion would spread across New England. Connecticut claimants paid close attention to the Massachusetts Regulation because they believed that, no matter what turn events took, they would be buffeted by the consequences. Joseph Sprague, an inhabitant of Wilkes-Barre, argued that "if the moob Suceeds the Consequenc will be the disalution of Feaderal government" and claimed that if the regulators failed, thousands of rebels would flee Massachusetts and "Take Aselum" in Pennsylvania. Like Sprague, many Yankee settlers reckoned that if the rebels lost, then large numbers of Shaysite refugees would immigrate to Pennsylvania and support their cause and that, if they won, the resulting political upheaval would

---

9. Declarations in Support of the Laws of Pennsylvania, April 21, 1787; Oaths of Allegiance of Timothy Pickering and Others, April 26, 1787; and Oaths of Allegiance before Timothy Pickering and Others, Jan.–Feb. 1787, *SCP* 9:106–10, 111–15, 13–17.

10. Peter S. Onuf, *The Origins of the Federal Republic: Jurisdictional Controversies in the United States, 1775–1787* (Philadelphia, 1983), 70–71, 152, 177–78; Thomas P. Slaughter, *The Whiskey Rebellion: Frontier Epilogue to the American Revolution* (New York, 1986), 21–38.

11. Deposition of Preserved Cooley, Jan. 14, 1785, *SCP* 8:197.

allow Connecticut claimants to establish their autonomy. William Judd echoed these expectations when he observed that the nation was "upon its last Leggs" and predicted that Connecticut settlers would "stand an Equal Chance with the rest of mankind" to establish their independence after the collapse of the federal government.[12]

Like Connecticut claimants, Pennsylvania officials closely followed events outside of the state; however, unlike the Yankees, news from New England produced unease rather than hope. This apprehension ultimately evolved into the belief that Yankees planned to form an independent state out of portions of Pennsylvania and New York. Starting in 1786 rumors of a separatist plot began to reach the ears of state authorities. In May 1786, William Montgomery, a member of Pennsylvania's Council of Censors, informed Chief Justice Thomas McKean that there existed "the greatest & most imminent danger of a dismemberment of the State" by Yankee insurgents and assured McKean that "the most limited claim of the Schemers" was to hold all of Pennsylvania north of the forks of the Susquehanna River. Days before Montgomery delivered his report he had received word that James Finn, a Baptist preacher and Connecticut claimant, had gone to the West Branch of the Susquehanna "to preach about amongst The people Thare, and feale out Thare minds, In Reguard To a New State." On another occasion, an anonymous informant told Timothy Pickering that Yankees were planning an uprising and had placed arms and ammunition "in convenient places" for that purpose.[13] Pennsylvania authorities eventually accused William Judd and other prominent Connecticut claimants of having drawn up a constitution for a planned breakaway state. Timothy Pickering, who believed that such a document existed, asserted that its authors "lived in the states of Connecticut & New York" and claimed that "Westmoreland" was to be the name of the new state.[14]

It was in the midst of this deepening factionalism among Yankee settlers and growing anxiety among state officials that Timothy Pickering entered the Wyoming dispute. Officially, he came to help organize the new county government; unofficially, his task was to take the lead in state efforts to pro-

---

12. Timothy Hosmer to John Paul Schott, Feb. 2, 1787; Dr. Joseph Sprague to Timothy Pickering, Feb. 20, 1787; and William Judd to Zebulon Butler, Jan. 11, 1787, *SCP* 9:21–22, 64, 6.

13. William Hooker Smith, Samuel Hover, and Abraham Westbrook to William Montgomery, May 14, 1786, *SCP* 8:326–27; Timothy Pickering to Samuel Hodgdon, Aug. 12, 1787, and Information Regarding the Designs of John Franklin, April 22, 1787, *SCP* 9:161, 110.

14. Obadiah Gore to Timothy Pickering, Nov. 12, 1787; Mathias Hollenback to John Nicholson, Nov. 13, 1787; and Timothy Pickering to John Pickering, Nov. 17, 1787, *SCP* 9:266–67, 272, 285. The most comprehensive discussion of this alleged separatist plot can be found in Julian P. Boyd, "Attempts to Form New States in New York and Pennsylvania, 1786–96," *New York State Historical Association Quarterly Journal* 12 (July 1931): 257–70.

Figure 1. *Portrait of Timothy Pickering*. By Charles Balthazar Julian Févret de Saint Memin, American (born in France), 1770–1852. Black chalk heightened with white on pink prepared paper. 56.8×41.6 cm (22 ⅜× 16 ⅜ in.) Museum of Fine Arts, Boston. Frederick Brown Fund, 33.578. Photograph © 2007 Museum of Fine Arts, Boston.

mote the Confirming Act and divide and conquer Yankee resistance. Like the insurgents he faced, Pickering was a New Englander. Born in 1745 to one of the leading families of Salem, Massachusetts, Pickering graduated from Harvard in 1763 and then returned home to practice law. During the Revolution he sided with the Patriot cause and served in the Massachusetts militia before joining the Continental Army in 1776 where he rose to the post of adjutant general and, later, quartermaster-general. After the war, Pickering moved to Philadelphia with hopes of entering into business. However, instead of becoming a merchant, he used his political connections to become a leading figure in Pennsylvania's efforts to resolve the Wyoming controversy. Pickering and his family took up residence in Wilkes-Barre early in 1787. He spent the rest of the period up to his abduction convincing Connecticut claimants to accept state authority and keeping state officials abreast of Yankee activities.[15]

John Franklin, who would emerge as Pickering's most inveterate opponent, consolidated his position as the Wild Yankees' leading man in the years following the Trenton Decree. Franklin, whose father had been an early shareholder in the Susquehannah Company, moved from Connecticut to the Wyoming Valley in 1772. Once there, he slowly rose through the ranks of local officeholders and earned the rank of captain in the militia by the Revolutionary War. After the war Franklin emerged as an important figure among Yankee settlers and gained prominence within the Susquehannah Company.[16] In September 1787, Franklin made the fateful decision to disrupt the formation of Luzerne County's militia, believing that the creation of an armed force controlled by the state would shift the balance of power solidly against his Wild Yankees. On September 29, Franklin ordered his followers to gather together on the morning of October 9 "Completely Armed & equiped" in order to prevent the "Pennsylvania Loyalists" from forming a militia.[17] State officials quickly got wind of Franklin's scheme and set in motion plans to rid themselves of this persistent troublemaker. On October 2, six deputies arrived at Wilkes-Barre to arrest Franklin. Posing as prospective settlers, they entered the settlement and accosted Franklin in the street. After a sharp struggle, in which Timothy Pickering intervened on the side of the deputies, the Pennsylvanians bound Franklin to a horse and whisked him away to Philadelphia. Charged with treason (mainly for the role he reportedly played in Northeast Pennsylvania's alleged separatist

15. SCP 9:xv–xvi; Dictionary of American Biography, 31 vols. (New York, 1928), 14:565–66; Upham, Life of Timothy Pickering, vols. 1–2.
16. James Edward Brady, "Wyoming: A Study of John Franklin and the Connecticut Settlement into Pennsylvania" (Ph.D. diss., Syracuse University, 1973), 20–22, 88, 146–52, 190.
17. Nathan Kingsley to Zebulon Butler, Sept. 29, 1787, and John Franklin to Jehiel Franklin, Sept. 29, 1787, SCP 9:209–10.

Figure 2. John Franklin. From Robert J. Taylor, ed. *The Susquehannah Company Papers*, vol. 8 (Ithaca, NY, 1969).

plot), Franklin languished in a miserable Philadelphia jail cell where his hopes and health quickly declined.[18]

In the wake of Franklin's arrest, Yankee insurgents struck back at pro-Pennsylvania settlers and symbols of state authority. Timothy Pickering nearly

---

18. Proclamation for the Arrest of John Franklin and Others, Sept. 25, 1787, and Instructions to John Craig, Sept. 26, 1787, *SCP* 9:204–5, 207; Stewart Pearce, *Annals of Luzerne County* (Philadelphia, 1866), 93–95.

became a victim of mob action when irate settlers surrounded his home in hopes of catching the man they blamed for Franklin's capture. Pickering escaped into the woods and fled to Philadelphia, where he stayed till tempers cooled.[19] Obadiah Gore, whose activities as a state informant, election inspector, and a leading moderate had vexed Yankee hardliners on many occasions, did not fare so well. Wild Yankees "abused Esqr Gore in a shameful manner" and forced him to flee from his home at Tioga Point.[20] Connecticut claimants also continued their resistance through nonviolent means. In Luzerne County's lower district, disgruntled settlers opposed Yankee moderates and the state by forwarding John Swift and Elisha Mathewson, two prominent supporters of the Connecticut claim, as candidates for colonel and major of Luzerne's first militia battalion. In the county's upper district, where Wild Yankees held sway, voters elected John Jenkins as colonel of Luzerne's second battalion. In the same election, Martin Dudley, who would later take an active role in Pickering's abduction, won the post of militia captain.[21]

Outraged by the protracted imprisonment of their leader, Wild Yankees decided to take Pickering hostage and to use him to bargain for Franklin's freedom. This plan culminated in the June 26 raid that resulted in Pickering's capture. After being taken, Pickering spent the next twenty days in the comfortless care of Yankee insurgents—an experience he documented in a diary he kept during his captivity. Pickering occupied his time by recording bits of homespun knowledge he gleaned from his guards on topics that ranged from the feeding of pigs and the proper handling of oxen, to the most effective ways to clear trees from the land. On one occasion, he even learned of a backcountry substitute for coffee: a well-toasted crust of bread boiled in water. Pickering found the beverage "very tolerable."[22]

Although the settlers' scheme got off to a promising start, the kidnapping plot ended in disaster. Instead of forcing Pennsylvania to release Franklin, Pickering's abduction gave state officials an excuse to use military force. Within days of the abduction, the kidnappers found themselves hunted by numerous parties of militia. This backwoods chase led to the death of one kidnapper and the near mortal wounding of a militia officer. Locally, the kidnapping exacerbated divisions between Yankees instead of removing them. Many settlers north

19. Oscar Jewell Harvey and Ernst G. Smith, *History of Wilkes-Barre, Luzerne County, Pennsylvania*, 6 vols. (Wilkes-Barre, P.A., 1927–30), 3:1587–88.
20. Ebenezer Bowman to Timothy Pickering, Oct. 17, 1787, and Timothy Pickering to Samuel Hodgdon, Oct. 19, 1787, SCP 9:242, 245.
21. Ebenezer Bowman to Timothy Pickering, Oct. 21, 1787, and William Hooker Smith to Timothy Pickering, Dec. 7, 1787, SCP 9:248, 308.
22. Journal Kept by Timothy Pickering during His Captivity, June 26–July 15, 1788, SCP 9:406–9; Upham, *The Life of Timothy Pickering*, 2:381–90.

of Tunkhannock Creek aided the kidnappers. In contrast, Connecticut claimants south of the creek withheld their support while others, believing that resistance to Pennsylvania was doomed to failure, took part in efforts to bring the kidnappers to justice. Gideon Church, who had been one of John Franklin's trusted lieutenants, turned against his fellow Wild Yankees and led a posse in pursuit of the kidnappers.[23] In the end, the kidnappers decided to release their prisoner. Before freeing him, they sought Pickering's forgiveness and offered to turn themselves in to state officials if he agreed to intercede on their behalf (Pickering declined to make any such promise). In a strange turn of events, these Wild Yankees switched from frontier rebels into deferential farmers and attempted to transform Pickering from captive to patron.[24]

Settlers and Speculators

One key to understanding the kidnapping plot's failure lies in recognizing that settler resistance in Northeast Pennsylvania was abetted by nonresident land speculators who held thousands of acres in the region under the Connecticut claim. The Susquehannah Company, which had taken a leading role in promoting the Connecticut claim before the Revolutionary War, again became a major player in the Wyoming controversy when aggressive land developers resurrected the company and offered their support to Yankee insurgents.[25] Yankee resistance was not predicated on a class enmity between settlers and land speculators. Instead, the rebellious New Englanders drew distinctions between land developers who aligned themselves with Pennsylvania and threatened their freeholds, and those who supported the Connecticut claim and by connection the soil rights of Connecticut settlers.[26]

Both Pickering and his captors firmly believed that land speculators associated with the Connecticut claim supported, if not instigated, the kidnapping

---

23. Timothy Pickering to Benjamin Franklin, Sept. 24, 1788; Zebulon Butler and Others to Benjamin Franklin, July 9, 1788; and Zebulon Butler to Peter Muhlenberg, July 29, 1788, *SCP* 9:497, 399–400, 438–40.

24. John Hyde, Jr., and Others to Timothy Pickering, July 15, 1788, and Timothy Pickering to Benjamin Franklin, July 19, 1788, *SCP* 9:409–10, 415–17.

25. For an overview of the history of the Susquehannah Company, see Julian P. Boyd, "Connecticut's Experiment in Expansion: The Susquehannah Company, 1753–1803," *Journal of Economic and Business History* 27 (1931): 38–69.

26. Alan Taylor makes a similar distinction in " 'To Man Their Rights,' " 232–38. Taylor also provides a sensitive analysis of relations between settlers and various types of land speculators along the revolutionary-era frontier in *William Cooper's Town: Power and Persuasion on the Frontier of the Early American Republic* (New York, 1996), 70–75, 87–110.

plot. During his captivity, Pickering heard his guards make allusions to the "great men" who directed their actions. More tellingly, he recalled that several months before his abduction, John Jenkins, who served as the Susquehannah Company's chief surveyor and as a liaison between Yankee settlers and the company's leading proprietors, had "menacingly" threatened that Wild Yankees would carry him off. It is clear that Jenkins and his brother, Stephen, took a hand in recruiting and encouraging the kidnappers. One of Pickering's captors later claimed that John Jenkins offered him land at Tioga Point in return for taking part in the kidnapping and promised to give fifty dollars to the "boys" who captured Pickering so that they would "have the money among them to make a frolic." Another kidnapper testified that the Jenkins brothers had "at sundry times" "urged" him and others to "make a party & sieze Colo Pickering" and, once the kidnappers had assembled, supplied them with gunpowder.[27] The insurgents also believed that prominent figures in the company planned to support their insurrection by marching into Pennsylvania at the head of five hundred men.[28] Such rumors, though they proved to be based more on fantasy than fact, demonstrate that Wild Yankees expected leadership and aid from the Susquehannah Company's chief proprietors.

The plan to win John Franklin's freedom began to unravel as the gap widened between the backing Wild Yankees expected from the company and the aid they actually received. John and Stephen Jenkins backpedaled on the promises they had made to the kidnappers and slipped out of Pennsylvania to take refuge in New York.[29] Eleven of the kidnappers made their way to Susquehannah Company's frontier headquarters at Tioga Point to see for themselves if its proprietors and agents would match their pledges of assistance with action. They must not have received much satisfaction. On their return, the insurgents freed Pickering and either returned to their farms or fled the state. Daniel Earl complained that the "persons who had advised them in this affair, had now fallen back" and expressed his desire that "the whole matter should now be brought out, that the worst should come to the worst" and that, as he put it, "every shoe should bear its own weight." John Hyde pinned the blame on Stephen Jenkins, exclaiming, "Dam that Villain! If it had not been

27. Deposition of Daniel Earl, Sept. 13, 1788; Deposition of Benjamin Earl, July 19, 1788; and Deposition of Noah Phelps, Aug. 26, 1788, *SCP* 9:488–98, 418–20, 477–78.

28. Timothy Pickering to Benjamin Franklin, July 19, 1788, *SCP* 9:416–17; Upham, *Life of Timothy Pickering*, 2:381, 385; Deposition of William Carney, July 29, 1788, and Deposition of Garret Smith, Aug. 7, 1788, *SCP* 9:432, 454.

29. Deposition of Daniel Earl, Sept. 13, 1788, *SCP* 9:489–90; Deposition of Isaac Blackmer, Aug. 1, 1788, TPP 58:75.

for him I should never have gone into this scrape. . . . It will never do for him to show his head again where I am, for I [would] cudgel him."[30]

Whether it illustrates cooperation or conflict between settlers and speculators, the kidnapping plot demonstrates that a relationship existed between the two groups. Even the anger Wild Yankees exhibited toward their speculator allies in the wake of Pickering's release was an animosity based on intimacy. The kidnapping plot was a disappointing reversal to what had been a productive relationship between Yankee insurgents and leading members of the Susquehannah Company. Although the company failed to support its settler allies in the wake of Pickering's kidnapping, they had aided in the creation of a coherent resistance movement in the years preceding it.

This settler-speculator alliance first came into focus in 1785. Encouraged by the bold resistance of Connecticut claimants immediately following the Trenton Decree and tempted by the rising value of frontier lands, speculators from New England and New York revived the Susquehannah Company and its claims. These men, who based their claims on the company's old Indian purchase, coveted a massive tract of land. Their claim stretched from the Delaware River to the headwaters of the Allegheny River, and from the New York state line to a point just north of where the Susquehanna River split into its western and northern branches. This territory was many times larger than the area actually held by Connecticut claimants. However, the company's new directors hoped that by helping Yankee settlers win possession of their farms, they would win title to the entire Connecticut claim and gain the profits that would come from its sale and development.

The leaders of the Susquehannah Company initiated a process whereby they transformed unrest in Northeast Pennsylvania from a contest between the state and Yankee settlers into a struggle that would spread beyond the Wyoming Valley and involve the energies and fortunes of settlers and speculators throughout the Northeast. But before the Susquehannah Company could change Yankee resistance, it first had to change itself. At a meeting held on July 13, 1785, company shareholders decided "to dispose of Six Hundred Rights" totaling some 360,000 acres of land to those willing to promote the settlement of Northeast Pennsylvania under the Connecticut claim.[31] The offer of six hundred full-share rights drew new men to the Susquehannah Company and rekindled the ambitions of many of its long-standing proprietors. John Franklin and other individuals who had led Yankee settlers against Pennsylvania and its land

---

30. Deposition of Isaac Blackmer, Aug. 1, 1788, TPP 58:75; Deposition of Noah Phelps, Aug. 26, 1788, and Deposition of William Griffith, Aug. 18, 1788, SCP 9:477–78, 469.
31. Minutes of a Meeting of the Susquehannah Company, July 13, 1785, SCP 8:249.

claimants obtained a number of full shares. By handing land rights to these men, the Susquehannah Company hoped to regain the loyalty of Wyoming's chief Connecticut claimants and thereby gain influence over Yankee settlers in Pennsylvania.[32]

More strikingly, the company awarded twelve shares to the architect of agrarian insurgency in Vermont, Ethan Allen, in order to win his support.[33] In August the company asked him to recruit "hardy Vermonters" willing to journey to the Susquehanna Valley and join the fight against Pennsylvania. Allen took up the challenge. Agreeing "to spedily repair to Wyoming with a small detachment of green Mountain Boys," he lived up to his promise and crossed into Pennsylvania to tour its Yankee settlements in 1786. At one point in his travels, Allen declared that "he had formed one new State and with one hundred Green Mountain Boys and [with] two hundred Riffle men" he could make another "in defiance of Pennsya." Yet the promise of an alliance between backcountry insurgents in Pennsylvania and Vermont never bore fruit. Allen stayed in Pennsylvania only long enough to administer a dose of the belligerent rhetoric for which he was famous and then made his way back to Vermont, never to return.[34] In New York, however, the Susquehannah Company found more determined adherents.

Many of the six hundred full-share rights issued by the company ended up in the hands of John Jay AcModer, Captain Peter Loop, Captain John Bortle, and other individuals who inhabited New York's eastern frontier. A swath of territory lying between the Hudson River and the borders of New England, the region had become home to a large number of New England immigrants during the second half of the eighteenth century.[35] For decades the New York–New England borderlands had experienced the sorts of jurisdictional conflicts, land disputes, and popular disturbances that troubled northeastern

---

32. Whole shares nos. 77, 79, 80 granted to John Franklin, May 1 and June 28, 1786, SCA Liber I:58.

33. Letter to Ethan Allen, Aug. 4, 1785; Ethan Allen to William Samuel Johnson, Aug. 15, 1785; and Ethan Allen's Receipt for Susquehannah Company Shares, Aug. 19, 1785, SCP 8:254–56. For insights into Ethan Allen's relationship to the Susquehannah Company and his past speculating efforts in Vermont, see J. Kevin Graffagnino, " 'The Country My Soul Dlights In': The Onion River Land Company and the Vermont Frontier," *New England Quarterly* 65 (March 1992): 24–60.

34. William Shaw to Benjamin Franklin and the Pennsylvania Council, May 18, 1786, SCP 8:332.

35. Whole shares nos. 43, 44, and 38 issued to Capt. John Bortle, Nov. 24, 1786; Whole share no. 82 issued to Capt. Peter Loop, Nov. 24, 1786; and Whole share no. 32 issued to John Jay AcModer, Sept. 28, 1786, SCA Liber I: 28, 168; David J. Goodall, "New Light on the Border: New England Squatter Settlements in New York During the American Revolution" (Ph.D. diss., State University of New York at Albany, 1984).

Pennsylvania. Thus, with its offer of shares, the Susquehannah Company recruited new members from a region whose own turbulent history of agrarian unrest had taught them that conflict could translate into an opportunity for land acquisition.[36]

A triumvirate of New England–born Hudson Valley speculators stood at the center of the revival of the Susquehannah Company and the resurrection of the Connecticut claim. Caleb Benton of Hillsdale, Joseph Hamilton of Hudson, and Zerah Beach of Amenia won positions of authority within the company and obtained rights entitling them to tens of thousands of acres in the Connecticut claim.[37] Some of the most pressing calls for violent resistance came from these men, and their names repeatedly crop up in connection with episodes of Yankee resistance as well as the rumored new state plot.[38] Less than a month before his arrest, John Franklin received a letter from Joseph Hamilton warning him that "principle & leading characters" in New York did not believe that he would be able "to klink up a Bubbery" (cause a disturbance) sufficient to overturn state rule. On another occasion, Hamilton chided Franklin and his followers for being "jockeyed" and "trucked" out of their lands without the "flash of a single Gun rifle or any of the least resistance."[39]

Under the guidance of Hamilton, Beach, and Benton, the Susquehannah Company converted itself from an institution modeled after New England's seventeenth-century town corporations to an organization geared toward frontier insurgency and land speculation. These men rearranged the company's internal structure, turning away from democratic decision making and embracing a more efficient, top-down system that placed power in the hands of a small group of powerful shareholders. During a May 1786 meeting, company shareholders empowered John Franklin, Ethan Allen, John Jenkins, and Zebulon Butler to locate new townships within the company purchase and to resolve land conflicts between Connecticut claimants. Before this decision, only a general meeting of company shareholders could wield such power. Those attending

---

36. Oscar Handlin, "The Eastern Frontier of New York," *New York History* 18 (Jan. 1937): 50–75; David M. Ellis, "Yankee-Dutch Confrontation in the Albany Area," *New England Quarterly* 45 (June 1972): 262–70. For an analysis of the political dimension of jurisdictional disputes along the New York-Massachusetts border, refer to Philip J. Schwartz, *The Jarring Interests: New York's Boundary Makers, 1664–1776* (Albany, NY, 1979), chaps. 6, 7, and 12.

37. Newton Reed, *Early History of Amenia* (Amenia, NY, 1875), 81, 120. For shares held by the New Yorkers see "600 Whole Share Proprietors," SCA Liber A; John Franklin to Joseph Hamilton, Nov. 25, 1786; John Franklin to Joseph Hamilton, June 8, 1786; and Minutes of a Meeting of the Susquehannah Company, Dec. 26, 1786, *SCP* 8:421,358, 426.

38. For a discussion of the new state plot, see Julian P. Boyd, "Attempts to Form New States in New York and Pennsylvania," and the introduction to *SCP* vol. 8.

39. Joseph Hamilton to John Franklin, Sept. 10, 1787, *SCP* 9:185, 187.

also voted to make John Franklin the company's clerk, giving him control over all its records and access to all of its business.[40] These moves reflected a trend whereby power within the Susquehannah Company slipped away from its shareholders in Connecticut and came into the hands of Yankee hard-liners in Pennsylvania and New York. At a second company meeting in December, shareholders created a powerful twenty-two-member commission that took charge of granting new towns, issuing rights, and judging the legitimacy of shareholders' claims. Prominent Yankee settlers who upheld the Connecticut claim and leading Susquehannah Company proprietors from New York dominated this commission. John Franklin, Simon Spalding, John Jenkins, Zebulon Butler, and John Paul Schott numbered among the former, and Joseph Hamilton, Zerah Beach, John Bortle, and Peter Loop among the latter.[41]

In addition to lobbying for the support of prominent men from across New England and New York, the company's new leadership also offered free land to individuals who were willing to settle Northeast Pennsylvania under the Connecticut claim. At a meeting of the Susquehannah Company held in Hartford on July 13, 1785, shareholders voted to award three hundred acres to "every Able bodied and effective Man" who would "Submit himself to the Orders" of the company. Since three hundred acres was half the size of a standard company share, or "right," those who took up this offer became known as "half-share men." In return for land and the prospect of legal title, settlers who took up half-share rights had to fulfill a number of obligations. First and foremost, the Susquehannah Company demanded loyalty from its half-share men and expected them to defend the Connecticut claim. Moreover, half-share settlers had to remain on the ground for three years in order to have their rights confirmed. Finally, settlement had to be immediate: the company specified that it would revoke the rights of half-share men who did not occupy their lands by October 1, 1786.[42]

Through the half-share initiative the company promoted the development of a coherent Yankee resistance movement. Timothy Pickering claimed that the Susquehannah Company "principally depended" on the support of its half-share men and asserted that they had "been the instruments of all the outrages" committed against Pennsylvania.[43] A careful examination of who obtained half-shares bears out Pickering's assessment. Two months after the company's July 1785 meeting, John Franklin brought together the first contingent of settlers who had agreed to take up half-share grants and issued them their deeds. A search through the Susquehannah Company's account books reveals that

40. Minutes of a Meeting of the Susquehannah Company, May 17, 1786, *SCP* 9:331, 331 n. 4.
41. Minutes of a Meeting of the Susquehannah Company, Dec. 26, 1786, *SCP* 8:426–28.
42. Minutes of a Meeting of the Susquehannah Company, July 13, 1785, *SCP* 8:249.
43. Timothy Pickering to John Pickering, Aug. 4, 1788, *SCP* 9:446–49.

several of the men who took part in Pickering's abduction obtained half-share rights at this meeting. Other future kidnappers received half-share grants in the months that followed.[44]

In sum, Wild Yankee resistance was born of settlers' determination to secure frontier freeholds *and* nonresident speculators' efforts to acquire, and profit from, large tracts of frontier land. On July 20, 1786, Yankee settlers (mostly half-share men) and representatives of the Susquehannah Company—including John Franklin, John Jenkins, and Zerah Beach—gathered together and articulated the principles that framed their commitment to the Connecticut claim. Those attending described themselves as "joint-tenants" of the land and declared that they would stand together in the defense of their property. They argued that legitimate possession of the land could only be obtained through a combination of "purchase and occupancy" and asserted that "the labours bestowed in subduing a rugged wilderness" could not be wrested from frontier inhabitants without "infringing [upon] the eternal rules of right."[45]

These statements blended two images of property. On the one hand, Connecticut claimants' talk of "purchase" as a means of acquiring land evoked a commercial conception of property in which land was a commodity that could only be acquired through a strict adherence to legal procedure. On the other, their mention of "occupancy" and "subduing a rugged wilderness" alludes to a more leveling vision of property rights that emphasized how occupation and the application of labor, not money or legal right, provided the ultimate title to unsettled lands. The former perspective was more hierarchical and formal—it was the perspective of wealthy, well-connected land speculators and government authorities—the latter was the more egalitarian perspective of backcountry farmers.[46] The juxtaposition of these divergent views reflects the extent to which these speculators and frontier yeomen managed to bring themselves together and highlights the distance that still separated them. Indeed, these competing definitions of property would remain compatible only for as long as Yankee settlers and Susquehannah Company speculators found common ground in their struggle for land.

The alliance between Connecticut settlers and Susquehannah Company proprietors undermines the claim that relations between farmers and gentlemen

---

44. John Franklin's Diary, Sept. 10, 1785, *SCP* 8:277. Joseph Kinny, Zebulon Cady, Daniel Earl all obtained half-shares on Sept. 10, 1785. Another kidnapper, Benjamin Earl, received his half-share on Oct. 1, 1785. See SCA Liber I:12, 32, 33, 98. For half-share grants to other kidnappers, see "Of the 400 Half Shares I issued to settlers," SCA Liber C.

45. Minutes of a Meeting Held in Wyoming, July 20, 1786, *SCP* 8:371–72.

46. For a more extensive exploration of these competing visions of property, see Taylor, *Liberty Men*, 24–29; and Brooks, *Frontier Settlement and Market Revolution* 31, 121, 124, 130–32.

were innately and invariably antagonistic. The willingness of Wild Yankees' to cooperate with speculators demonstrates that distinctions of wealth and status between settlers and land developers could be mitigated by a common foe, a common set of interests, and perhaps even a common ethnic and regional background.[47] Thus any attempt to comprehend what motivated Pennsylvania's Wild Yankees needs to move away from explanations that focus solely on class conflict and toward ones that envision the social context of rural unrest in broader terms.

Half-share Men

Soon after his capture, Timothy Pickering discovered that beneath the blacking that covered his assailants' faces were the familiar visages of Gideon and Joseph Dudley, sons of Martin Dudley, who had once been a "near neighbor" to Pickering in Wilkes-Barre.[48] This moment of recognition reflects how interpersonal relationships intersected with agrarian unrest—how settlers blended their activities as backcountry rebels with their roles as members of households and communities.

Understanding just who Pennsylvania's Yankee insurgents were is the first step in gaining a deeper appreciation of how agrarian unrest merged with everyday life. For their part, Pennsylvania officials routinely portrayed Wild Yankees as outside agitators of little wealth and fewer morals who, having failed to make ends meet in older, eastern settlements, became willing recruits of the Susquehannah Company. In 1786 Timothy Pickering estimated that the vast majority of the 250 families who supported the Confirming Act were "old" settlers (Connecticut claimants who had settled their rights before the Trenton Decree) and reckoned that an equal number of "New Comers" (the half-share settlers who had taken up land after the decree) provided the bulk of the Wild Yankees' rank and file.[49] Such characterizations, however, rested more on prejudice than fact. Indeed, Pickering stopped drawing sharp distinctions between troublesome "New-Comers" and more orderly "old settlers," after he realized

---

47. Taylor, " 'To Man Their Rights,' " 233–36. The concept of "ethno-deference" that Brendan McConville forwards in *These Daring Disturbers of the Public Peace* (47–50) provides a model for understanding the complex relationships that developed between Yankee settlers and land speculators in Northeast Pennsylvania.

48. Upham, *Life of Pickering*, 2:384.

49. Extracts from Timothy Pickering's Journal, Aug. 1786, *SCP* 8:385–86.

that "*one half* of the old settlers & their sons" held half-share rights. In other words, the majority of Wild Yankees, far from being footloose outsiders, were settlers who had migrated to Pennsylvania before the Susquehannah Company adopted the half-share resolves. They had eagerly accepted new lands from the company in return for their promise to hold it through "craft and violence."[50] Other evidence backs this conclusion. Susquehannah Company proprietor Zerah Beach cautioned his associates not "to have much dependence" on new immigrants lending their support to the cause and recommended that company agents concentrate on issuing half-share grants to Connecticut claimants who already resided in Pennsylvania. In addition, John Jenkins claimed that only thirty of the half-share rights issued by the company had been given to people who did not already reside in the Wyoming region.[51]

Pennsylvania's Wild Yankees were not mercenaries drawn to the Wyoming region by the Susquehannah Company's offer of free land but members of backcountry households and communities who saw in the half-share grants an opportunity to further their pursuit of property and independence. A handful of settlements tied together by kinship, the collective endeavor of frontier settlement, and mutual opposition to Pennsylvania's rule provided the bulk of active Wild Yankees and nearly all the individuals who took part in Pickering's abduction. Kidnappers Ira Manville; Benjamin, Daniel, and Solomon Earl; Zebulon Cady; Daniel Taylor; and Frederick Budd all resided in the neighborhood of Tunkhannock Creek. Allensburgh, a settlement on the banks of Wyalusing Creek, contributed John Hyde, Gideon and Joseph Dudley, Aaron and Timothy Kilborn, David Woodward, and William Carney to the party that took Pickering. Finally, kidnappers Benjamin and Nathan Abbot, Garret Smith, and John Tyler hailed from Whitehaven, a Yankee enclave just south of Meshoppen Creek.[52]

Like communities across the early American countryside, Pennsylvania's Yankee settlements rested on a hierarchy in which a few leading men maintained links with the wider world and provided leadership to a larger number

---

50. Timothy Pickering to Peter Muhlenberg, Aug. 9, 1788, and Timothy Pickering to Benjamin Franklin, July 28, 1788, *SCP* 9:460–61, 429.

51. Zerah Beach to Zebulon Butler, Sept. 21, 1785, *SCP* 8:262; Timothy Pickering to Peter Muhlenberg, Aug. 9, 1788, *SCP* 9:460. For a listing of half-share grants issued by John Franklin, see SCA Liber I.

52. "Of the 400 Half Shares I issued to settlers," SCA Liber C; "Proceedings of Committee of Claims Respecting the Claimants of Putnam," Nov. 27, 1786, SCA Liber I, 31. It is important to note that the term *town* refers to a New England town (a distinct area of land and a unit of local jurisdiction comparable to a Pennsylvania township) rather than an urban center.

of humble but independent householders who, in turn, held authority over an even larger group of dependent sons waiting to obtain their own freeholds. In such communities, age, family ties, and local reputation, not just wealth, helped to establish male social rank.[53] A petition drawn up by Connecticut claimants protesting their treatment by the state of Pennsylvania illustrates this social structure. Among the names included on the document were those of John Jenkins, Elisha Satterlee, and John Swift. These individuals represented a veteran cadre of leading men who had lived in the Wyoming Valley since before the Revolutionary War. Next, men like Joseph Earl, Nathan Abbot, Ephraim Tyler, and Martin Dudley signed the petition. These individuals were older household heads who advised and supported the efforts of younger, rank-and-file Wild Yankees. Among this latter group were Ira Manville, John Hyde, Daniel Earl, Benjamin Earl, Gideon Dudley, and other signatories who actually perpetrated Pickering's kidnapping.[54]

Agrarian resistance grew out of this rural social order. In the case of Northeast Pennsylvania, it provided Wild Yankees with a chain of command and a system of recruitment. Leading men like John Swift and Elisha Mathewson served both as local resistance leaders and as intermediaries between their neighbors and the Susquehannah Company. Older heads of households like Nathan Abbot and Joseph Earl provided the insurgents with material support; more important, they supplied the resistance with recruits. Many of the settlers who kidnapped Timothy Pickering were the sons of established freeholders, and it is likely that younger men represented a good portion of the Wild Yankees' rank and file.[55] During a tour of Pennsylvania's Northeast frontier in 1787, Timothy Pickering commented that only "rash young men" openly supported the Susquehannah Company and engaged in acts of resistance. Likewise, the

---

53. Robert Gross describes this age- and kin-based status structure throughout his book, *The Minutemen and Their World* (New York, 1976), 10–11, 62–63, 70–71. Also see Christopher M. Jedry, *The World of John Cleaveland: Family and Community in Eighteenth-Century New England* (New York, 1979).

54. Remonstrance of Luzerne Inhabitants against William Montgomery, Sept. 18, 1787, SCP 9:195–98.

55. Alan Taylor and Michael Bellesiles have put together age profiles for agrarian insurgents in Maine and Vermont that seem to contradict this assertion. Both authors find that individuals under the age of 26 are actually underrepresented in the ranks of the insurgents and that those over the age of 26 are dramatically overrepresented (Taylor, *Liberty Men*, 260–62; Bellesiles, *Revolutionary Outlaws*, 285–86). Nonetheless, the samples (108 individuals for Bellesiles and 127 for Taylor) on which both authors base their findings only represent a small proportion (less than 10 percent in the case of Bellesiles) of insurgents in Vermont and Maine. Moreover, as Bellesiles points out, those backcountry insurgents for whom biographical information exists might well represent more prominent members of their respective resistance movements who were perhaps older than the norm and thus may skew the insurgent's age profile.

word *boys* repeatedly cropped up in descriptions of the kidnappers. This characterization was accurate: one of Nathan Abbot's sons was seventeen years old when he helped to abduct Pickering; Aaron Kilborn, who also played a supporting role in the kidnapping, was only fifteen.[56] Moreover, most of the settlers who kidnapped Pickering do not appear in lists of Connecticut settlers before the late 1780s because of their youth and propertylessness. In many cases the names and identity of these young men were subsumed beneath those of their fathers. Martin Dudley turns up in a 1783 list of Connecticut claimants as a carpenter residing in Wilkes-Barre while his two sons, Gideon and Joseph, do not. Likewise, Darius Parks's signature appears on a petition from 1783 but William Carney, Parks's grandson and another one of Pickering's kidnappers, does not.[57]

Dependency, not poverty, was the essential characteristic of most of Pickering's kidnappers. The Yankee insurgents were household dependents. They were young, aspiring farmers separated from property and independence, not by static social barriers, but by a dynamic social process whereby one generation passed on property to the next. This pattern was well established in the northern countryside where a household economy that rested on the productive capacity of families reinforced generational ties between parents who depended on their progeny for labor and children who looked to inherit property from their elders.[58]

Wild Yankees tapped into a familiar framework of household relationships—particularly those that bound fathers and sons together—to bridge the gap between agrarian insurgency and their lives as backcountry farmers. The roles young men played in early America's rural communities made them ideal Wild Yankee recruits. They formed a household-based labor force that lent a hand on the family farm or were hired out by their fathers to work for others. This practice rested on a long-standing tradition whereby sons labored for fathers who, in return, promised to supply them with the land, tools, and livestock they would need to set up their own farms when they came of age. An example of this labor

---

56. Journal of Timothy Pickering's Visit to Wyoming, Jan. 26 and 31, 1787; Timothy Pickering to Peter Muhlenberg, Aug. 9, 1788; and Timothy Pickering to Thomas Mifflin, Nov. 15, 1788, SCP 9:52, 56, 458, 518; Upton, *Life of Pickering*, 2:386.

57. Harvey and Smith, *History of Wilkes-Barre*, 3:1312–14, 1332–33.

58. For more on the relationship between age, wealth, and social standing in New England, see Philip J. Greven, Jr., "Family Structure in Seventeenth-Century Andover, Massachusetts," *WMQ* 23 (April 1966): 234–56; Daniel Vickers, *Farmers and Fishermen: Two Centuries of Work in Essex County, Massachusetts, 1630–1850* (Chapel Hill, NC, 1994), 64–77, 219–29; Fred Anderson, *A People's Army: Massachusetts Soldiers and Society in the Seven Years' War* (Chapel Hill, NC, 1984), 28–39; Jedry, *The World of John Cleaveland*, 63–64; James A. Henretta, "Families and Farms: *Mentalité* in Pre-Industrial America," *WMQ* 35 (Jan. 1978): 6–8.

system appears in testimony collected after the kidnapping. A few days after Pickering was taken, Stephen Jenkins hired Calvin Adams to accompany him on a journey down the Susquehanna River. Jenkins negotiated the arrangement, not with Calvin, but with his father.[59] This same arrangement furnished Yankee settlers with a method for obtaining men to carry out Pickering's kidnapping and other acts of insurgency. For instance, a few weeks before the abduction, Darius Parks told John Jenkins that, in addition to donating money and provisions to the kidnappers, he "would turn out one man." Daniel Earl shed light on Parks's statement when he later testified that "William Carney was encouraged to join us by Darius Parks his grandfather who fixed him out for the purpose." Like Mr. Adams, Mr. Parks used his patriarchal authority to engage the services of his grandson "Billy"; however, unlike Calvin Adams, William Carney was employed not as a laborer, but as a kidnapper.[60]

The investigation that followed Pickering's abduction revealed the importance of local networks to Yankee resistance. State authorities discovered that the kidnappers' kin and neighbors had provided them with provisions, shelter, and information on the whereabouts of state troops. Once state officials fully realized the extent of this community-based support network, they arrested the kidnappers' fathers and other close relations. Joseph Earl, Martin Dudley, and Joseph Kilborn ended up before Pennsylvania magistrates for the auxiliary role they played in the abduction. They all claimed that they had no foreknowledge of any plans to take Pickering, yet the testimony of their fellow conspirators did not support their story.[61] Garret Smith testified that when he asked Martin Dudley if he knew anything of the plot, Dudley answered that he did and added that he did not want both of his sons to participate in the kidnapping. When Smith asked him why, Dudley replied, "For fear they should be found out, for if one was at home, people would think the other was somewhere at work." In the end, Martin decided that Gideon would go and that Joseph would stay, "lest it should be found out that his sons were in the Scrape."[62]

---

59. For a discussion of household labor systems in early America, see Daniel Vickers, "Working the Fields in a Developing Economy: Essex County, Massachusetts, 1630–1675," in *Work and Labor in Early America*, ed. Stephen Innes (Chapel Hill, NC, 1988), 49–69; and Vickers, *Farmers and Fishermen*, 64–77, 219–29. Deposition of Calvin Adams, Aug. 19, 1788, TPP 58:109.

60. Deposition of Anna Dudley, Aug. 20, 1788; Deposition of Daniel Earl, Sept. 13, 1788; and Deposition of William Carney, July 29, 1788, SCP 9:473, 490, 431.

61. Evidence against Thomas Kinney, Elijah Reynolds, Joseph Earl, Ephraim Tyler, Martin Dudley, and Joseph Kilborn, July 5, 1788, TPP 58:111.

62. Deposition of Garret Smith, Aug. 7, 1788, SCP 9:452–53. For additional evidence of Martin Dudley's prior knowledge of the kidnapping, see the deposition of William Carney, July 29, 1788, SCP 9:431.

This marriage of household relationships and backcountry insurgency did not operate without tension, both between the Susquehanna Company and Yankee insurgents and within settler households. Opposition to the state of Pennsylvania held many risks and imposed many burdens that struggling farm families could ill afford. Some parents willingly sent their sons to help kidnap Pickering, others did so only grudgingly. Anna Dudley defied the directives of the Susquehannah Company and leading Wild Yankees when she opposed her family's involvement in the plot. When Darius Parks asked Anna to tell her husband to "turn out provisions" for the kidnappers, she refused and told Parks that she would speak against anyone who "should attempt to persuade him to it." Anna Dudley never specified why she opposed the plot to take Pickering, but it is likely that she was loath to risk her sons in such a desperate venture. As a woman in a society that provided few if any opportunities for females to own land, Anna may not have been as invested as husband and sons in Northeast Pennsylvania's battle for property.[63]

Besides dividing men and women, the kidnapping plot generated friction between parents and children. Rather than invariably enhancing parental authority and domestic harmony, Yankee resistance could also undermine it. Joseph Earl was one father whose protests of ignorance about his sons' involvement in the kidnapping may have been genuine. Joseph claimed that he only learned of their part in the plot when he returned home one day to find his wife crying because Daniel, Solomon, and Benjamin had gone off to take Pickering. Likewise, Joseph Dudley, despite his fathers' decision that he stay at home, defied his parents and went with his brother, Gideon, to join the party that kidnapped Pickering.[64]

Wild Yankees and other rural rebels were not all young men whose activities as insurgents were an adjunct to their roles as household dependents. What is important is not the particulars of the above analysis but its broader implications. The close intertwining of face-to-face relationships and Yankee insurgency indicates that the real impetus behind agrarian unrest lay in the aspirations and experience of ordinary farm folk.

Independence and Dependency

If the relationships that tied early America's rural inhabitants together into households and neighborhoods structured Yankee resistance, then it was the attitudes and aspirations of ordinary rural folk that motivated Yankee insurgents

---

63. Testimony Concerning the Capture of Timothy Pickering, July 5, 1788, *SCP* 9:394.
64. Ibid.

and determined their goals. Agrarian resistance, first and foremost, was tied to the pursuit of agrarian independence. In Northeast Pennsylvania, and across the early American countryside, farmers translated the ethos of independence into social action by building farms, raising families, and on occasion, taking up arms against those who threatened their property and autonomy. This reality sheds additional light on the relationship between rural society and agrarian resistance as well as on the ties, and the tensions, that developed between Yankee settlers and the Susquehannah Company.

On the day of Pickering's abduction, an encounter took place that illustrates the central role that the pursuit of independence played in motivating agrarian resistance. The episode started when Joseph Kilborn accosted Minor York as the latter was clearing land along Mehoopany Creek. York, hoping to secure rightful possession of the property, had recently replaced his Connecticut deed with a Pennsylvania patent obtained through Timothy Pickering. In doing so, he made himself the enemy of settlers such as Kilborn, who exclusively supported the Connecticut claim. Kilborn told York that those who accepted Pennsylvania titles would not be allowed to hold land and that the property he was clearing had been awarded to John Hyde and Martin Dudley—two staunch supporters of the Connecticut claim. Before leaving, Kilborn informed York that if he did not quit the land within a week he would receive a "threshing." The day after this confrontation, York returned to the contested tract and squared off against Kilborn and another Wild Yankee, Thomas Kinney. The two men warned York to abandon the land. York responded by informing them that Timothy Pickering had accepted the legitimacy of his claims and issued him a Pennsylvania deed. To this Kilborn responded, "If Pickering & his laws are any thing, I am nothing, and hold no lands: but if I am any thing, & hold land, then Pickering & his laws are nothing."[65] To Kilborn, land did not just represent a material object but the key to individual self worth—to him, the struggle for the Connecticut claim was both a matter of possession and identity.

Wild Yankees like Joseph Kilborn had to contend not only with compromise-minded settlers like Minor York but with the paradox of a resistance movement that on one level promoted their property rights and independence, but on another required them to subordinate themselves to the dictates of a land company dominated by nonresident speculators. They had to reconcile their interests, which were anchored in households and local communities, with the more far-reaching aspirations of their speculator allies and mesh their struggle

---

65. Deposition of Elizabeth Wigton, Aug. 1, 1788; Deposition of Minor York, Aug. 18, 1788, *SCP* 9:444–45, 470–71.

for property with a larger defense of the Connecticut claim. For Wild Yankees, the conditions of occupancy and obedience the company attached to its half-share grants contradicted a central tenant of agrarian independence: the right of every man to attend to his own affairs without outside interference. Simply put, fealty to the company was, at best, a potential infringement on a settler's autonomy and, at worst, a dependent relationship that would undermine his independence.[66] The Susquehannah Company hoped that its half-share men would serve as obedient pawns in its land-grabbing schemes. Events, however, proved that Yankee insurgents remained conscious of, and committed to, their own goals.

Wild Yankees overcame these inconsistencies by turning to a larger paradox that stood at the center of rural society: that the independence of male household heads rested on the subordination of their wives and children. In particular, they looked to a familiar domestic hierarchy that structured relations between parents and children to help legitimize their relationship with the company. Adult male property holders wielded power over dependent sons who lacked the resources they needed to establish their own independent households. Moreover, when yeomen fathers participated in economic exchanges that infringed on their status as autonomous householders—ones that required them to sell their labor or involved commercial relationships beyond their immediate control—they relegated such duties, when possible, to their dependents. For instance, in order to make ends meet, parents might arrange for their children to work as wage laborers for a wealthy neighbor or to participate in craft production for local merchants.[67] In other words, only dependent people were fit for dependent labor. Seen in this light, the fact that many of Pickering's kidnappers were young men takes on additional significance. To avoid the dependant relationship that came with the acceptance of half-share grants, at least some Yankee fathers turned to their sons to carry out the most onerous of their obligations to the Susquehannah Company. Half-share man Nathan Abbot sent his two sons, Benjamin and Nathan, Jr., to abduct Pickering instead of taking part in the kidnapping himself. Likewise, Solomon Earl did not hold a half-share right but he may have joined the kidnapping party in the place of his father and half-share holder, Joseph Earl.[68]

---

66. For an in-depth discussion of independence and dependency, see Vickers, *Farmers and Fishermen*, esp. pages 14–16, 19; Vickers, "Competency and Competition": 7; and Richard L. Bushman, " 'This New Man': Dependence and Independence, 1776" in *Uprooted Americans: Essays in Honor of Oscar Handlin*, ed. Richard L. Bushman et al. (Boston, 1979), 77–96, esp. 81.

67. Vickers, "Competency and Competition": 9–10.

68. For the half-shares (no. 101 and 104) issued to Nathan Abbot and Joseph Earl: see "Of the 400 Half Shares I issued to settlers," SCA Liber C.

The kidnapping of Timothy Pickering was bound up in the tensions that simmered between fathers who wished to exercise their patriarchal authority and sons on the cusp of adult independence who bridled at their continued subordination.[69] To young men, half-share grants represented both an entrance to landed independence and an exit from parental dependence. This helps to explain the glimpses of generational conflict that appear in the court depositions collected in the aftermath of the kidnapping. Joseph Dudley's defiance of his father's wish that he not join the kidnapping party reflects how the plot to take Pickering forced young half-share men to choose between obedience to their fathers and loyalty to the Susquehannah Company. Joseph may have participated in the kidnapping against his father's will fearing that, if he did not, the company would revoke the half-share right he held. Daniel and Benjamin Earl's obligations to the Susquehannah Company also seem to have trumped obedience to their father. If, as Joseph Earl alleged, the two brothers joined the kidnappers without his knowledge or permission, they probably did so in order to secure half-share grants that would have offered them passage into the ranks of independent landholders.[70] In the end, a settler's choice to accept a half-share grant should be seen in this light—as an effort by older settlers to secure property and independence, or as a decision made by their sons to accelerate their passage from adolescent dependence to adult autonomy.

Besides backcountry inhabitants' efforts to secure their independence, the other factor that framed agrarian resistance in Northeast Pennsylvania was Yankee settlers' deep-dyed localism. An emphasis on personal autonomy, the importance of kin and neighborhood networks, and the primacy of a household economy all engendered localism among rural inhabitants.[71] This localism, like

---

69. Gross, *Minutemen and Their World*, 75–76, 81–83, 88–89; Vickers, "Competency and Competition": 23; Vickers, *Farmers and Fishermen*, 219–29; Jedry, *The World of John Cleaveland*, 73–74.

70. For the half-share grants (nos. 80, 103, 203, and 204) issued to Daniel and Benjamin Earl and Gideon and Joseph Dudley, see: "Of the 400 Half Shares I issued to settlers," SCA Liber C; Testimony Concerning the Capture of Timothy Pickering, July 5, 1788, and Deposition of Garret Smith, Aug. 7, 1788, *SCP* 9:394, 452–53.

71. A good exploration into the theme of localism in early American can be found in Darrett B. Rutman, "Assessing the Little Communities of Early America," *WMQ* 43 (Apr. 1986): 166–67, 178. In contrast to Rutman's broad overview of localism, other historians have focused on how such parochialism manifested itself in the backcountry: Albert H. Tillson, Jr., "The Localist Roots of Backcountry Loyalism: An Examination of Popular Political Culture in Virginia's New River Valley," *Journal of Southern History* 54 (Aug. 1988): 387–88; and Charles Desmond Dutrizac, "Local Identity and Authority in a Disputed Hinterland: The Pennsylvania-Maryland Border in the 1730s," *PMHB* 115 (Jan. 1991): 35–61. For insights into New England's localist culture see Michael Zuckerman, *Peaceable Kingdoms: New England Towns in the Eighteenth Century* (New York, 1970), 15–16, 46, 254; and T.H. Breen, "Persistent Localism: English Social Changes and the Shaping of New England Institutions," *WMQ* 32 (1975): 3–28.

the household hierarchy that enabled yeoman fathers to mobilize the labor of their dependant sons, helped half-share men fuse their aspirations with the goals of Susquehannah Company speculators.

Kidnapper Garret Smith described how he and his compatriots effortlessly blended their attempt to win John Franklin's release with more parochial concerns. Smith believed that in return for Pickering's capture he would receive land and crops confiscated from Yankee turncoats who had turned their backs on the Connecticut claim and transferred their allegiance to Pennsylvania. In particular, he claimed that the kidnappers planned to take possession of a mill owned by Wilkes-Barre merchant John Hollenback. Smith recalled that when he asked Gideon Dudley what they would do if they captured Hollenback, Dudley replied that they would "tomahawk him." That Hollenback, a one time shareholder in the Susquehannah Company, had recently turned in his Connecticut deeds for title under Pennsylvania would explain why he became a focus of Wild Yankee ire. However, the kidnappers' animosity was more directly rooted in an incident that took place the preceding summer when Hollenback had a writ served against Joseph Earl for debts he owed to him. What galled Earl and other Wild Yankees was not so much that Hollenback wanted his money back, but that, instead of seeking redress locally, he prosecuted Earl under Pennsylvania law.[72]

The tensions that emerged when settlers' local ambitions came into conflict with the wider goals of the Susquehannah Company can be seen throughout the kidnapping crisis. A week after Pickering's abduction, Wild Yankees from Tunkhannock Creek "assembled in a riotous manner about the House of a Mr. [Zebulon] Marcey" and tore down his cabin. Though a Connecticut claimant, Marcy had angered his predominantly half-share neighbors on two counts: he challenged their property rights before the Susquehannah Company's executive committee in 1786 and later came out in support of Pennsylvania's authority. Thus the attack on Marcy's home in 1788 was, at least in part, the product of an old grudge. Soon after the riot, Pickering's captors came out of hiding with the intent of killing Zebulon Marcey's oxen; only with some difficulty did Stephen Jenkins, who feared that they would be apprehended by the numerous parties of militia scouring the woods for them, divert the kidnappers from their plan. Here, and elsewhere, Yankee insurgents' goals intertwined and, at times, interfered with the larger objective of winning John Franklin's release.[73]

72. Deposition of Garret Smith, Aug. 7, 1788, and Timothy Pickering to Samuel Hodgdon, Aug. 9, 1787, *SCP* 9:454, 156.
73. Deposition of Andrew Ellicott, June 8, 1788, *SCP* 9:394–95; Proceedings of Committee of Claims Respecting the Claimants of Putnam, Nov. 7, 1786, SCA Liber I, 31; Deposition of Isaac Blackmer, Aug. 1, 1788, TPP, 58:75.

In the end, the deconstruction of Timothy Pickering's kidnapping illustrates that ordinary farmers' vigorous pursuit of land formed the mainspring of Yankee resistance and that the battle for independence was complex and multifaceted. On one level, it was a contest over land that divided people along lines of jurisdictional affiliation and class, pitting ordinary Connecticut settlers against Pennsylvania and its most powerful land speculators. On another—and one that followed and *crossed* class lines—the struggle generated tensions between Yankee settlers, their speculator allies, and the different and, at times, contradictory visions of property they held. Finally, the battle was waged within the confines of rural households. Here the contest mainly involved yeoman fathers who attempted to gain land in order to secure their status as autonomous householders and sons who perhaps saw agrarian resistance as an avenue to acquire property and escape subordination to their fathers.

By the fall of 1788, the furor produced by Pickering's kidnapping had died down and Northeast Pennsylvania returned to a tense and temporary calm. Pickering continued to preside as one of Luzerne County's leading officials until he accepted the post of United States postmaster general and moved his family back to Philadelphia in 1791. Pickering would later become secretary of war in 1795 and, less than a year later, secretary of state—a post he held till 1800. A staunch Federalist, Pickering returned to his native Massachusetts, which he represented in Congress till he retired from public life in 1820.[74] John Franklin finally returned home after being released on bail in March 1789 (he was never brought to trial). His seventeen-month jail term may have subdued Franklin's opposition to the state, but it certainly did not extinguish it. Shortly after his return, Franklin moved from Wilkes-Barre upriver to Tioga Point where he continued to lead efforts to vindicate the Connecticut claim.[75]

Compared to Pickering and Franklin, the kidnappers, their accomplices, and families did not fare so well. Most of those involved in the abduction plot ended up before Pennsylvania magistrates. In an effort to avoid any more disturbances, state officials reduced the charges the kidnappers faced from treason (which carried the death penalty) to riot and assault. Young Aaron Kilborn, "who had particularly insulted" Pickering, spent a month in jail. Zebulon Cady, described as "an atrocious villain," avoided a fine because of his poverty but spent three months in prison. The rest of the "young men" who had been "misled by the old men" received lesser sentences. Of the kidnappers' elders, the court acquitted Martin Dudley, Ephraim Taylor, and Nathan Abbot. Darius

74. *Dictionary of American Biography*, 14:566–67.
75. Pearce, *Annals of Luzerne*, 524; Brady, "Wyoming: A Study of John Franklin," 275–76, 288, 301.

Parks received a fifty-dollar fine, while Thomas Kinney received a one-hundred-dollar fine and a six-month prison term.[76] John Hyde, Frederick Budd, and others connected to the plot escaped justice by fleeing to New York. Joseph Dudley, who received a mortal gunshot wound during a skirmish with militiamen, became the only fatality associated with the kidnapping.[77] For the Dudley family, the gamble they took in accepting half-share grants ended in disaster. Instead of strengthening their family's economic standing, Martin and Anna Dudley lost their son. His death, more than anything else, symbolizes how the needs of settler households, the interests of land speculators, and the demands of agrarian resistance did not always exist in harmony.

The debacle sparked by the kidnapping did not undo the settler-speculators alliance that had catalyzed Yankee resistance. Opposition to Pennsylvania's authority and soil rights, as well as membership in the Susquehannah Company, created a common ground for backcountry settlers and nonresident land developers. Besides this simple congruence of interests, the ability of backcountry inhabitants to integrate agrarian insurgency into familiar patterns of daily life and link it to their struggles for personal independence assured the survival and effectiveness of this settler-speculator union. Cooperation between settlers and speculators ultimately rested on the Susquehannah Company's ability to provide the former with freeholds and the latter with commercial opportunity. Both, in turn, rested on the expansion of company settlements in Pennsylvania. This alliance of yeomen and land developers, which had helped to catalyze resistance in the latter 1780s, would also provide the blueprint by which Wild Yankees would expand their challenge to the state of Pennsylvania in the following decade.

---

76. Indictment of Ira Manville and Thirteen Others, Sept. 2, 1788 and Timothy Pickering to Samuel Hodgdon, Nov. 9, 1788, *SCP* 9:480–82, 516–17.

77. Timothy Pickering to Benjamin Franklin, July 29, 1788; Timothy Pickering's Memorandum on His Abductors, Aug. 7, 1788; and Timothy Pickering to Thomas Mifflin, Nov. 15, 1788, *SCP* 9:432–38, 517–19.

CHAPTER 4

"ALL THE DIFFICULTIES OF FORMING A NEW SETTLEMENT"

Frontier Migration, Land Speculation, and Settler Insurgency

In October 1792, frontier entrepreneur and Pennsylvania land speculator Samuel Wallis led a group of men up Tunkhannock Creek to survey lands claimed by Samuel Meredith and other Philadelphia merchants. Wallis's survey was interrupted when Wild Yankees lying in ambush fired on his workmen. No one was injured but a musket ball smacked into a tree, narrowly missing two men. Fearing for their lives, the Pennsylvanians retreated to their camp. But their ordeal was not over. After dark, a "party of Armed men with their faces black'd" surrounded the surveyors and "order[ed] themselves as they were about to Attack." The insurgents held the Pennsylvanians at gunpoint and only released them after they promised that they would abandon their work. In accordance with their pledge, Wallis and his men struck camp and marched away the next morning.[1]

Wallis's encounter is proof that Yankee resistance survived the debacle that followed the kidnapping of Timothy Pickering and reflects the forces that transformed it at the turn of the century. That the confrontation was brought on by the act of surveying—an act inextricably tied to gaining possession of, and profit from, the land—reflects how agrarian unrest in Northeast Pennsylvania was linked to the settlement of, and the market in, frontier land. Starting in the 1790s, thousands of settlers flooded into the region in search of home-

---

1. Linda Fossler, "Samuel Wallis: Colonial Merchant, Secret Agent," *Proceedings of the Northumblerland County Historical Society* 30 (Dec. 1990): 107–15; Samuel Wallis to Samuel Meredith, Oct. 11, 1792, *SCP* 10:161.

steads. These migrants were part of a much larger wave of pioneers who occupied and improved more frontier land in the thirty years between 1790 and 1820 than in the previous two centuries of European colonization. Entrepreneurs, sensing that there was money to be made from selling land to these immigrants, redoubled their efforts to purchase and develop property along the Pennsylvania frontier. This lively market in frontier lands, combined with heavy migration into the region, reinvigorated Yankee resistance.[2]

Wild Yankees renewed their fight against Pennsylvania by harnessing their insurgency to the commercial and social energies bound up in frontier expansion. In the last decade of the eighteenth century, the Connecticut claim attracted speculators who wanted to take advantage of America's robust land market and thus gained advocates who had the means to fill northern Pennsylvania with Yankee immigrants. Reinforced by this growing body of recruits, Wild Yankees overwhelmed isolated Pennsylvania claimants and dominated local governmental and judicial institutions. Instead of resisting the imposition of Pennsylvania's political institutions as they had done in the past, Yankee rebels now used them to serve their own ends.

More than ever, Yankee resistance depended on the combined efforts of settlers and speculators. Yankee settlers and Susquehannah Company speculators, though they possessed different aims and aspirations, continued to find a common ground in their mutual opposition to Pennsylvania.[3] In the closing years of the eighteenth century, this coalition of frontier yeomen and eastern entrepreneurs intensified the challenge to Pennsylvania's authority and dramatically expanded the geographical scope of Yankee resistance.

"A Matter of Great Speculation"

Pennsylvania contributed to the revival of Wild Yankee resistance when it repealed the Confirming Act in 1790. The act, which had promised to legitimate

---

2. Much has been written about America's post-Revolutionary land boom. Works pertinent to this study include Norman B. Wilkinson, *Land Policy and Speculation in Pennsylvania, 1779–1800: A Test of the New Democracy* (Ph.D. diss., University of Pennsylvania, 1958); Wilkinson, "The 'Philadelphia Fever' in Northern Pennsylvania," *Pennsylvania History* 20 (Jan. 1953): 41–56; and William Wyckoff, *The Developer's Frontier: The Making of the Western New York Landscape* (New Haven, CT, 1988). For insights into the link between frontier speculation and agrarian unrest, see Alan Taylor, "Agrarian Independence: Northern Land Rioters after the Revolution," in *Beyond the American Revolution: Explorations in the History of American Radicalism*, ed. Alfred F. Young (DeKalb, IL, 1993), 232–33.

3. Alan Taylor, "'To Man Their Rights': The Frontier Revolution," in *The Transforming Hand of Revolution: Reconsidering the American Revolution as a Social Movement*, ed. Ronald Hoffman and Peter J. Albert (Charlottesville, VA, 1995), 233–36, 244–46.

Connecticut deeds that predated the Trenton Decree, had never actually gone into operation but instead remained in a sort of legislative limbo. Ultimately, the state assembly struck down the law in the face of mounting pressure from Pennsylvania landholders.[4] After the law's repeal, these same Pennsylvania claimants brought a flurry of ejectment suits against Yankee settlers. Even Timothy Pickering, who held land in the town of Wilkes-Barre under the Connecticut claim, became a target of prosecution.[5] This legal battle came to a head in 1795 when Pennsylvania claimant Robert Fenn brought ejectment suits against John Dorrance, William Slocum, Samuel Allen, and Pickering. The suit between Fenn and Dorrance, which became a test case for all other ejectment proceedings, was decided in a federal court in favor of Fenn.[6] This victory for Pennsylvania's land claimants, though significant, proved to be extremely limited. Yankee settlers largely ignored the legal ramifications of the verdict and continued to hold their land through force.

With this legislative turnaround, Pennsylvania accomplished what John Franklin and his associates had failed to do: bring together half-share men and old settlers in the common defense of their property. Soon after the repeal of the Confirming Act, Connecticut claimants entered into an agreement in which they promised to stand together against ejectment suits and to establish a fund to help defray legal expenses. Yankee hard-liners James Finn, Justus Gaylord, and Chester Bingham joined with Zebulon Marcy, Abraham Westbrook, Obadiah Gore, and other moderates in signing the compact. Later, Yankee settlers formed a committee that included representatives from both moderate settlements in the Wyoming Valley and enclaves of Yankee hardliners farther up the Susquehanna. This body organized the legal response to ejectment suits and administered the funds collected to defray settlers' court costs.[7]

The repeal of the Confirming Act helped to reinvigorate Yankee resistance, but America's lively land market converted opposition to Pennsylvania into a concrete plan of action. In March 1797, Justice Asahel Gregory highlighted the link between the land market and agrarian unrest in a report he sent to Governor Thomas Mifflin. Detailing the deterioration of state rule in northeastern Pennsylvania, Gregory explained that the Susquehannah Company had illegally sold large tracts of land, making the Connecticut claim "a matter of Great

4. *SCP* 10:xiv–xiv–xx; Repeal of the Confirming Act, April 1, 1790, *SCP* 10:112–13.
5. Timothy Pickering to William Lewis, Feb. 3, 1791, and Timothy Pickering to Jesse Root, April 25, 1792, *SCP* 10:138, 159.
6. *SCP* 10:xxi–xxxii; Evidence Presented in *VanHorne's Lessee v. Dorrance* and William Paterson's Charge to the Jury in *VanHorne's Lessee v. Dorrance*, April 1795, *SCP* 10:232–307, 308–27.
7. Agreement by the Connecticut Claimants, 1790, and Minutes of a Meeting of Representatives of the Connecticut Claimants, March 4, 1793, *SCP* 10:130–31, 165.

Speculation" among unprincipled men in New York and New England. In turn, he continued, these predatory land speculators promoted settler resistance in order to secure their investments.[8] The timing of the company's move was critical to its success, for it came just when settlers and speculators were focusing their attention on Northeast Pennsylvania.

After the Revolution, land speculation, rather than commerce or manufacturing, became the principal venture of America's economic elite. Cut off from Britain's trade networks, powerful merchants cast their eyes toward America's vast, unexploited hinterlands.[9] Northern Pennsylvania, like the Ohio country, upstate New York, and Kentucky, became the focus of speculating schemes and land development projects. Pennsylvania's determination to exploit its land reserves, combined with the insecurity of the United States' western territories, made Northeast Pennsylvania a popular destination among settlers and a choice investment among speculators. Before the United States defeated the Ohio Indians' Western Confederacy at the Battle of Fallen Timbers in 1795, many pioneers were unwilling to journey into the Trans-Appalachian West while land could be found in more sheltered backcountry regions like the upper Susquehanna Valley.[10]

More than any other factor, the availability of large quantities of land at low prices sparked the speculating frenzy that swept over northern Pennsylvania. In 1784 Pennsylvania sold its northern lands for about eighty cents an acre. Five years later, the state lowered its price to fifty-three cents. Finally, in the spring of 1792, Pennsylvania started selling undeveloped frontier land at the rock-bottom rate of twenty cents an acre. For back lands in the rough hill country east of the Susquehanna, prices went even lower. In northern Luzerne County, land could be had for about seven cents an acre while along the upper reaches of the Delaware River prices dropped to six cents an acre. Such low prices, combined with the federal government's decision to fix its price for land in the Northwest Territory at two dollars an acre, caused land sales to soar. Between 1792 and 1794, Pennsylvania's land office received applications for nearly 10 million acres spread throughout the northern and western portions of the state.[11]

8. Asahel Gregory to Thomas Mifflin, March 14, 1797, *SCP* 10:431–32.
9. Wilkinson, *Land Policy and Speculation in Pennsylvania*, 64; Thomas M. Doerflinger, *A Vigorous Spirit of Enterprise: Merchants and Economic Development in Revolutionary Philadelphia* (New York, 1987), 314–16.
10. Norman B. Wilkinson, "The 'Philadelphia Fever,' " 41–44; Wilkinson, *Land Policy and Speculation*, 26–27.
11. Wilkinson, *Land Policy and Speculation*, 38, 48, 129–31, 209–10; David Craft, *History of Bradford County, Pennsylvania* (Philadelphia, 1878), 41; Phineas G. Goodrich, *History of Wayne County* (Honesdale, PA, 1880), 100.

The opportunities for profit offered by land speculation in Northeast Pennsylvania drew the attention of prominent men throughout America and Europe. Samuel Wallis obtained possession of more than forty thousand acres in Luzerne and Northampton counties. He developed some of this land himself and sold off the balance to Timothy Pickering, Tench Coxe, Samuel Hodgdon, and other gentlemen. Henry Drinker and John Nicholson also accrued extensive claims in northern Pennsylvania. Drinker purchased more than fifty thousand acres in a region between the Delaware and Susquehanna rivers known as the Beech Lands; Nicholson gained title to twelve thousand acres along Tunkhannock Creek as well as sizeable tracts of land elsewhere in Northeast Pennsylvania. William Bingham, who acquired large amounts of land in Maine and New York, also laid claim to about a million acres across northern Pennsylvania.[12]

There were significant differences between speculators who obtained land under Pennsylvania deeds and speculators who operated under the auspices of the Susquehannah Company. Henry Drinker, Tench Coxe, William Bingham, and other powerful Pennsylvania landholders were more familiar with the drawing rooms and counting houses of Philadelphia and New York than backcountry settlements and thus were more inclined to view their frontier holdings as commodities to be bought and sold for a profit. In contrast, Joseph Hamilton, Caleb Benton, Zerah Beach, and other Yankee speculators who at first glance appear to be newcomers to Northeast Pennsylvania, possessed longstanding ties to the region. Hamilton, though he resided in New York after the Revolution, was born in Connecticut, purchased a right in the Susquehannah Company in 1773, and briefly resided in the Wyoming Valley before fleeing the war-torn frontier in 1778. He returned to Connecticut and then moved to Hudson, New York, in 1785. From his new home, Hamilton pushed for the Susquehannah Company to reassert its claim and renewed his ties with Wyoming's settlers.[13] Zerah Beach possessed a similar background. He joined the Susquehannah Company and was a prominent inhabitant of the Wyoming Valley before the Revolutionary War. Even after he left the valley, Beach remained involved in the company and affairs in Northeast Pennsylvania.[14]

12. Wilkinson, *Land Policy and Speculation*, 75; Stewart Pearce, *Annals of Luzerne County* (Philadelphia, 1866), 192–93; John Lincklaen, *Travels in the Years 1791 and 1792 in Pennsylvania, New York, and Vermont: Journals of John Lincklaen Agent of the Holland Land Company* (New York, 1897), 41–45; Margaret L. Brown, "William Bingham, Eighteenth-Century Magnate," *PMHB* 61 (Oct. 1937): 412–13; Doerflinger, *Vigorous Spirit of Enterprise*, 319–22.
13. Oscar Jewell Harvey and Ernst G. Smith, *History of Wilkes-Barre, Luzerne County, Pennsylvania*, 6 vols. (Wilkes-Barre, PA, 1927–30), 3:1569–70.
14. John Franklin's Diary, July 3 to Dec. 7, 1784, and John Franklin's Diary, July 1 to Nov. 15, 1785, *SCP* 8:158, 276–78.

Like Hamilton and Beach, Susquehannah Company proprietor Solomon Strong demonstrates that it is misleading to categorize people as speculators or settlers, insiders or outsiders. On the surface, Solomon Strong seemed to be the sort of frontier opportunist Pennsylvania accused of fomenting rebellion along its frontier. Strong's name repeatedly turned up in the 1780s in reports describing Yankee plots to form new states out of portions of Pennsylvania and New York. Strong fled from Claverack, New York, in 1786 and sought refuge among Pennsylvania's Yankee settlers after New York authorities sought his arrest for "counterfeiting Dollars."[15] Strong's fugitive status and his association with separatist schemes, though they highlight some aspects of his character, do little to explain his relationship to Pennsylvania's Yankee inhabitants. No stranger to the Wyoming dispute, Solomon Strong had settled along the Susquehanna in 1773 and represented Westmoreland County in Connecticut's legislature in 1776. During the Revolution he led Westmoreland's inhabitants as a captain in the Connecticut Line. After the Battle of Wyoming, Strong returned to his home state of Connecticut and then took up residence in Berkshire County, Massachusetts. In 1782 he moved to Claverack, New York, where he reacquainted himself with an old friend and business associate from the Wyoming Valley, Jeremiah Hogeboom.[16]

Northern Pennsylvania's booming land market not only brought Yankee speculators like Solomon Strong and Joseph Hamilton into conflict with powerful Pennsylvania land developers, but also furnished them with the means to wage this struggle. The relationship between land speculation, frontier settlement, and resistance evolved piecemeal in the decade after the Trenton Decree. In 1786 the Susquehannah Company began to authorize new towns north of the Wyoming Valley in order to provide lands for its half-share men.[17] For instance, the company laid out the town of Athens at the juncture of the Susquehanna and Chemung rivers just south of the New York State line. From the start, this town acted as a magnet for radical Connecticut claimants.[18] John Jenkins, Elisha Mathewson, Zerah Beach, William Slocum, Waterman Baldwin, Elisha Satterlee, and John Swift all held proprietors rights in the new settlement. John Franklin, another Athens proprietor, moved there after his release from prison in September 1789. Christopher Hurlbut, William Miller,

15. Solomon Strong to Zebulon Butler, Apr. 22, 1786, and George Clinton to Benjamin Franklin, Dec. 13, 1786, SCP 8:316, 423.
16. Pearce, *Annals of Luzerne County*, 78; Harvey and Smith, *History of Wilkes-Barre*, 3:1498.
17. Joseph Hamilton to John Franklin, March 24, 1786, SCP 8:311; Grants for the Towns of Whitehaven, Athens, and Claverack, May 17, May, 22, and Aug. 31, 1786, SCA Liber C:97, 98, 100; Samuel Gordon to Obadiah Gore, Oct. 15, 1787, SCP 9:240.
18. Louise Welles Murray, *A History of Old Tioga and Early Athens* (Wilkes-Barre, PA, 1907), 269; Certificate and Survey for the Town of Athens, May 22, 1786, SCA Liber C:98.

Daniel Moore, Mason Cary, and Eldad Kellogg became Athens's first settlers and served as a vanguard for other half-share men.[19]

Athens was only one of a number of new towns established by the Susquehannah Company. By the summer of 1786, company agents had laid out the town of Allensburgh on Wyalusing Creek, regranted the town of Claverack (which had been located at the confluence of Sugar Creek and the Susquehanna River before the Revolutionary War but never settled) to a new group of proprietors, and established the town of Ulster along the Susquehanna River just south of Athens.[20] In the fall the company laid out Hamilton, Goresburgh, Bentonsburgh, and Johnson along the south branch of the Tioga River. Caleb Benton, Joseph Hamilton, Ethan Allen, and John McKinestry received the rights to these towns, garnering more than sixty thousand acres.[21]

The creation of new company towns furnished both commercial opportunities for speculators and homesteads for settlers. In December 1785, Solomon Strong and Jeremiah Hogeboom obtained possession of the entire town of Claverack with the stipulation that the partners seat twenty settlers in the town by May.[22] Hoping to attract inhabitants, Strong and Hogeboom offered one hundred acres free of charge to any settler who would occupy the town. Arnold Franklin, a half-share man, was among the first to locate his family in "Strong and Hogeboom's town." Drawing on their Hudson Valley connections, the two proprietors also attracted Ezra Rutty and his oldest son, Ezra Jr., from Dutchess County, New York. Jonas Smith and his son, Nathan; Daniel Guthry; and Isaac, Rufus, and Abial Foster soon followed.[23]

As was the case with Strong and Hogeboom's efforts to secure possession of Claverack, concerted efforts to recruit settlers and develop backcountry communities accompanied speculation in the Connecticut claim. Caleb Benton worked hard to attract inhabitants for the towns he obtained from the company and, by the summer of 1787, he had drawn at least twenty families to his lands.[24] Likewise, Zerah Beach and Joseph Hamilton served their interests, the Connecticut

19. Craft, *History of Bradford County*, 270–74; Murray, *History of Old Tioga*, 252–53, 304; Harvey and Smith, *History of Wilkes-Barre*, 3:1647; Half-shares entered into Athens, May 8–June 1, 1786, SCA Liber I:60–66.

20. Certificate and Survey for Claverack, Aug. 31, 1786, and Certificate and Survey for Whitehaven, May 17, 1786, SCA Liber C:100, 97; Certificate and Survey for Ulster, July 21, 1786, SCA Liber I:25.

21. Caleb Benton to John Franklin, Aug. 9, 1787, *SCP* 9:157–58; Certificates and Surveys for Hamilton, Goresburgh, Johnson, and Bentonsburgh, Nov. 26, 1786, SCA Liber I:18–25; Harvey and Smith, *History of Wilkes-Barre*, 3:1537.

22. Harvey and Smith, *History of Wilkes-Barre*, 3:1498; Craft, *History of Bradford County*, 85.

23. Craft, *History of Bradford County*, 324, 362–63.

24. Town grants of Hamilton, Goresburgh, Johnson, and Bentonsburg, Nov. 24, 1786, and Pitches laid out for Caleb Benton, Nov. 24, 1786, SCA Liber I:18–24, 26–27; John Franklin to Joseph Hamilton, Nov. 25, 1786, *SCP* 8:421; Murray, *History of Old Tioga*, 311–12; Obadiah

claim, and the needs of Yankee settlers by converting their company shares into settlements.[25] John Jay AcModer followed a similar path: he purchased thirty-two whole share rights from Joseph Hamilton, promoted settlement along the Pennsylvania–New York border, and acted as an agent in Benton's, Hamilton's, and Beach's efforts to people their lands.[26] Unlike many Pennsylvania landholders, Yankee speculators offered generous terms to secure prospective inhabitants. Ezekiel Hyde, a leading proprietor of the Delaware Company, sold his lands at one dollar an acre while Pennsylvania claimants demanded two to three times as much for land of similar quality. Likewise, Nathan Morgan drew David Watkins, Oliver Canfield, Joseph Batterson, and other Yankee migrants to his lands by granting fifty acres free of charge to each prospective settler. Yankee speculators Gordon Fowler and Reed Brockway also offered their settlers a fifty-acre land bounty. In the long run, Fowler's and Brockway's strategy worked to their advantage as their rapidly growing settlement attracted immigrants who could pay for their freeholds. One newcomer, Timothy Alden, purchased eight hundred acres from Brockway and paid for it in hard cash.[27]

Yankee speculators came to realize that by tapping into the energies of frontier settlement they could forward their economic interests while striking a blow against Pennsylvania. The profitability of any speculating scheme depended on attracting settlers. In paying for their farms, settlers transformed land developers' holdings into cash. In addition, by improving their freeholds they increased the value of (and the prices that speculators could charge for) the surrounding land. In turn, settlers looked to frontier speculators for credit, legitimate titles, and even the construction of roads, mills, and other improvements. Pennsylvania's Wild Yankees transformed this reciprocal relationship into a successful strategy of resistance. Newly arriving settlers provided the manpower needed to oppose state authorities and intimidate Pennsylvania claimants. In exchange, speculators contributed their wealth and leadership to the Connecticut cause.[28]

Gore and Mathias Hollenback to Timothy Pickering, July 3, 1787; Timothy Pickering to Samuel Hodgdon, Aug. 9, 1787; and Zerah Beach to John Franklin. Sept. 14, 1787, *SCP* 9:149–50, 154, 192–93.

25. For details on Beach and Hamilton's land dealings see "600 Whole Share Proprietors," SCA, Liber A; Zerah Beach to Zebulon Butler, Sept. 21, 1785, *SCP* 8:262; Zerah Beach to John Franklin, Sept. 14, 1787 and John Franklin to Caleb Benton, June 26, 1787, *SCP* 9:192–93, 147.

26. Timothy Pickering to Samuel Hodgdon, Aug. 9, 1787; Obadiah Gore and Mathias Hollenback to Timothy Pickering, July 3, 1787; and Deposition of John Jay AcModer, Dec. 22, 1788, *SCP* 9:154, 149–50, 524–25.

27. Tench Coxe to Thomas McKean, Aug. 12, 1800, *SCP* 11:529; Town of Granby Granted to Nathan Morgan, Mar. 1, 1795, SCA Liber E:164; Craft, *History of Bradford County*, 302–3, 320–22.

28. Alan Taylor, *William Cooper's Town: Power and Persuasion on the Frontier of the Early American Republic* (New York, 1995), 98; Charles E. Brooks, *Frontier Settlement and Market Revolution: The Holland Land Purchase* (Ithaca, NY, 1996), 23.

Though the Susquehannah Company first linked speculation and settlement to insurgency in the late 1780s, it greatly expanded the scale of this process in the mid 1790s. Whereas the company only created a handful of new towns between 1786 and 1793, it established 16 new towns in 1794 and an astonishing 218 new towns in 1795.[29] This drastic increase in town grants marked the beginning of a new phase in the struggle for Northeast Pennsylvania. On February 18, 1795, company shareholders gathered in Athens, Pennsylvania, at a tavern owned by Yankee land speculator James Irwin. During this meeting, the company forged policies through which it channeled the energies of frontier expansion into agrarian insurgency.[30] To encourage speculation in the Connecticut claim, the shareholders increased the amount of acreage contained in a company share from six hundred to two thousand acres. They also reduced the number of proprietors needed to establish a new town from twenty to eight. In addition to creating a climate ripe for land speculation, the company, realizing that peopling the land with settlers loyal to the Connecticut claim would be the surest way to secure control over Northeast Pennsylvania, stipulated that each right issued by the company would be revoked if it was not located and occupied within two years.[31]

News of the "Franklemites" meeting soon reached the ears of Pennsylvania authorities, and it did not take them long to discern that land offered under such generous terms would attract troublemakers. To head off the arrival of more Yankee insurgents, the state passed the Intrusion Act. This piece of legislation made it a crime to sell, buy, and settle lands under Connecticut titles issued after the Trenton Decree. Settlers who illegally occupied lands faced a two-hundred-dollar fine and a year-long prison term. Speculators (or their emissaries) who conspired to survey and sell lands under the Connecticut claim were subject to a fine between five hundred and one thousand dollars and up to eighteen months in prison at hard labor. The punishment for resisting arrest was even more severe: the law stipulated fines between five hundred and five thousand dollars and three to seven years imprisonment at hard labor. Finally, the law provided for calling out the militia to combat intruders.[32]

Because the enforcement of the Intrusion Act was dependant on local justices and juries who were partial to the Connecticut claim, the law failed to deter Yankee settlers or diminish the activities of Yankee speculators. The Susquehannah Company's liberal policies made the Connecticut claim an at-

29. *SCP* 10:xxxiii; The Susquehannah Company Commissioners Authorize a New Township, Nov. 6, 1793; The Susquehannah Company Authorize Two New Townships, Jan. 20, 1794; and Grants of Townships in the Susquehannah Company Purchase, *SCP* 10:191, 193, 566–77.
30. Craft, *History of Bradford County*, 41; Murray, *A History of Old Tioga*, 334–36.
31. Minutes of a Meeting of the Susquehannah Company, Feb. 18, 1795, *SCP* 10:215–18.
32. Extract of Letter from Jesse Fell, Feb. 26, 1795, and The Intrusion Act, Apr. 11, 1795, *SCP* 10:219–20, 227–29.

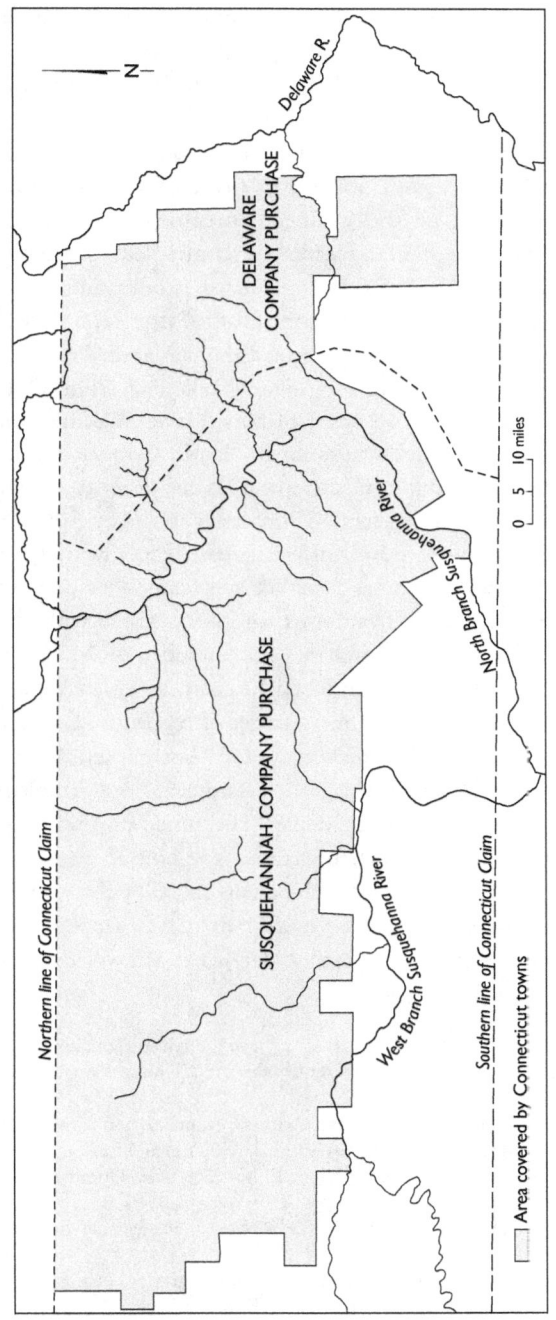

Map 3. The Expansion of Connecticut Towns, 1785–1800

tractive investment and company shares a sought-after commodity. Putnam Catlin, a New Englander who worked as a land agent for Pennsylvania landholders, described the process by which Connecticut deeds had been "bought up by companies of wealthy men at the Eastward." Likewise, Yankee speculator Clement Paine (a brother of David Paine, the Susquehannah Company's assistant clerk) asserted that "a great number of persons of respectability, property, and influence" had taken up the Connecticut cause, "not thro' inadvertance, but from a full knowledge of all the leading circumstances" surrounding the dispute with Pennsylvania. One of these speculator associations came together in February 1795 when William Wynkoop, Elisha Satterlee, Labius Hammond, John Spalding, Durance Irwin, and Chester Bingham agreed to jointly purchase and develop Susquehannah Company towns.[33] Likewise, Elihu C. Goodrich of Claverack, New York, and Seth Turner of New Haven, Connecticut, formed a partnership and dealt extensively in company lands. Goodrich and Turner became the proprietors of Nankin, Canton, and several other towns after scouring Connecticut and New York in search of unseated company rights.[34]

Silas Pepoon was another powerful gentleman who invested heavily in the Connecticut claim. His activities as a Yankee speculator shed additional light on how the commercial aspects of frontier expansion coexisted with agrarian insurgency. Pepoon, an innkeeper, merchant, and member of Massachusetts's rural gentry, acquired lands under the Connecticut claim in 1795. Although his conservative political stance had made him a target of regulator mobs during Shays's Rebellion, Pepoon did not allow his distaste for Massachusetts's agrarian radicals to dissuade him from taking advantage of commercial opportunities that grew out of backcountry unrest in Pennsylvania.[35] He gained possession of more than sixty thousand acres in the Connecticut claim. As was the case across northeastern Pennsylvania, these grants conflicted with patents issued by the state of Pennsylvania. One of Pepoon's holdings, the town of Franklin, overlapped a ten-thousand-acre tract claimed by Pennsylvania landholder James Strawbridge.[36] In a unique

---

33. Putnam Catlin to John Nicholson, Dec. 12, 1798, Asylum Company Papers, HSP; Articles of Agreement by William Wynkoop and Others and Clement Paine to Seth Paine, Sept. 20, 1796, *SCP* 10:212–13, 386.

34. Town Grants of Nankin, Canton, and Calcutta, March 2, 1795 and Conveyances from Charles Foot, John Wells, Aaron Dewey, David H. Jewitt, Eneas Munson, Bishop Dodd, and Margaret Cook, SCA Liber C:251–56, 290–99; Elihu Chauncey Goodrich to John Jenkins, Nov. 18, 1794, *SCP* 10:209.

35. David P. Szatmary, *Shays' Rebellion: The Making of an Agrarian Insurrection* (Amherst, MA, 1980), 109–10.

36. Grant of Lancaster, Mar. 10, 1795, and Grant of Braintree, Feb. 27, 1795, SCA Liber D:112, 110; Conveyance from David Paine to Silas Pepoon, Sept. 7, 1795, SCA Liber C:134; Grant of the town of Franklin, SCA Liber E:190.

episode, Pepoon wrote Strawbridge and suggested that they make a deal, noting that disputes between Connecticut and Pennsylvania claimants had produced a situation in which "neither party can avail himself with any where near the [lands] real worth." He asked Strawbridge to transfer to him the Pennsylvania deeds covering the town of Franklin and, in return for this favor, promised to find settlers to fill the town. Pepoon assured Strawbridge that whatever loss he suffered from losing this property would be more than compensated by the value his settlers' labor would add to Strawbridge's remaining lands.[37] Pepoon's offer did contain a subtle threat. If Strawbridge refused to cooperate, the same Yankee settlers who could increase the value of his lands might just as easily take them by force.

Settlers were the key to gaining possession of the land. Connecticut's land companies were in a far better position to win this war of settlement than Pennsylvania. Yankee proprietors offered land for less money and with fewer restrictions than the state and its landholders. Moreover, they drew on a larger pool of potential recruits. New England's rapidly growing population, combined with its shrinking pool of arable land, produced a wave of migrants who turned to the backcountry to seek their fortune. Many of these land-hungry Yankees would end up settling the hardscrabble hills of Northeast Pennsylvania.

Easternites

Like the speculators who fueled the fires of Northeast Pennsylvania's land market, the thousands of ordinary people who migrated to the region in the 1790s and early 1800s took a hand in transforming Yankee resistance. The most critical link between migration and insurgency in Northeast Pennsylvania was the simple fact that most of the people who settled the region at the turn of the century hailed from New England or Yankee communities in eastern New York. William Cooper, the renowned land developer and founder of Cooperstown, New York, touched on why Northeast Pennsylvania became a home to New Englanders rather than Pennsylvanians when he observed that heavily forested hill country "would frighten a Pennsylvania farmer" but prove the "support of an Easternite." He explained that Pennsylvanians who were familiar with the rich soils and gently rolling countryside of southeast Pennsylvania avoided the rough terrain and dense stands of timber that covered much of the Northeast frontier, while New Englanders, who were familiar with the difficulties of farming such marginal lands, pushed into the region to take advantage of low land

---

37. James Strawbridge to William Maclay, Dec. 30, 1796, and Silas Pepoon to James Strawbridge, Feb. 10, 1796, *SCP* 10:390, 330–31.

prices. Putnam Catlin echoed Cooper's sentiments in a report to Pennsylvania landholder John Nicholson. He explained that the "soil and situation" of Nicholson's lands would not "invite the Penna farmers to settle." "On the other hand," he warned, "the quality, soil, and situation of this land is precisely such as to attract the New England farmer." To drive home his point, Catlin compared Yankees, who were so eager to settle in northern Pennsylvania "that Sanguinary laws can hardly check them from it," with Pennsylvanians who could "scarcely be hired at any rate to undertake the cultivation of such land."[38]

Yankee migration to the Northeast frontier was part of a larger postwar folk movement that saw thousands of families leave New England and set out for central and western New York, northern Pennsylvania, and the Ohio country. Out-migration from New England, which started as a trickle in the 1750s and 1760s, became a steady stream in the 1780s and a flood by the turn of the century. During one three-day period in February 1795, more than twelve hundred sleighs carrying Yankee migrants and their possessions passed through Albany on their way to the frontier. In 1797, New Englander Samuel Law asserted that the flow of Yankee immigrants into "the Northern & Western parts of N. York, the upper parts of Penna" and the Ohio Country had become "more formidable than ever," adding that Connecticut and Massachusetts were "alive" with plans for settling in Pennsylvania under the Connecticut claim. All together, between 1790 and 1820, more than 800,000 people left New England in search of land and opportunity.[39]

Economic and social conditions in New England contributed to this folk movement. The debt litigation and social unrest that plagued the region in the 1780s forced many farmers to try their luck elsewhere. Revolutionary war veteran William Hencher was one of thousands of people who became caught up in Shays's Rebellion. Fearing government prosecution for the role he played in the insurrection, Hencher left his Brookfield, Massachusetts, home and made his way to Newtown, New York. Once there, his family joined him and, soon after, they made another move to the nearby settlement of Big Flat. Amos Stone was another Shaysite driven to the frontier by economic hardship and the threat of prosecution. He ended up taking up land along the south branch of the Tioga River under a Connecticut deed. In addition to short-term social

38. William Cooper to Henry Drinker, Nov. 3, 1791, quoted from Taylor, *William Cooper's Town*, 94–95; Putnam Catlin to John Nicholson, Dec. 12, 1798, Asylum Company Papers, HSP.
39. David Maldwyn Ellis, "Rise of the Empire State, 1790–1820," *New York History* 56 (Jan. 1975): 5–28; David Maldwyn Ellis, "The Yankee Invasion of New York, 1783–1850," *New York History* 32 (Jan. 1951): 4–8; Taylor, *William Cooper's Town*, 89–91; Samuel A. Law to Tench Coxe, Feb. 14, 1797, SCP 10:411.

and political turmoil, long-term ecological and demographic factors such as soil exhaustion and population growth contributed to out-migration from New England.[40]

Not all Yankee migrants were pushed by adversity; many were pulled to the frontier by hopes of cheap land and prosperity. A growing European market for American produce, a declining Indian threat, and land developers' willingness to offer land at low prices and on credit made frontier settlement an increasingly attractive option. Thomas Rice was one of many New Englanders drawn to the backcountry. In September 1791, John Lincklaen, a land agent for a group of European speculators known as the Holland Company, visited Rice at his home in Clarendon, Vermont. Lincklaen had first met the Vermonter earlier that year in New York's Genesee Country where Rice intended to take up residence on a newly purchased four-hundred-acre tract. After laying eyes on Rice's well-tilled Vermont farm, Lincklaen expressed his astonishment at seeing "a man 50 years old who has spent the best part of his life in clearing his land & enhancing its value, leaving it all just as he begins to enjoy the fruits of his labor, in order to bury himself anew in the forest, & expose himself to all the difficulties of forming a new settlement!"[41] No matter what Lincklaen thought of the wisdom of Rice's decision to head west, the Vermont farmer's determination to trade a well-developed farm for unimproved frontier land testifies to the powerful pull that the prospect of obtaining large frontier freeholds at low prices exerted on Yankee yeomen.

Whether they were pushed out of New England by hardship or drawn to the frontier by the promise of prosperity, the course of Yankee migration brought increasing numbers of New Englanders into northern Pennsylvania. Resolved Sessions was one Yankee who made his way to Pennsylvania's Susquehanna Valley. Sessions's starting point remains obscure, but it is clear that he moved from Vermont to New York before settling along Towanda Creek in 1794.[42] For many Yankee pioneers, Northeast Pennsylvania was not a destination but a way station in a longer chain of migration that took them into central and western New York. The Duc de la Rochefoucault-Liancourt, one of the many French noblemen who took refuge in the American republic during the French Revolution, witnessed this movement. In 1795, he found Athens's only inn "crowded with travellers from the Jerseys, Pennsylvania, and New York, who intended to

---

40. Szatmary, *Shays' Rebellion*, 32–33, 107–8; Orsamus Turner, *History of the Pioneer Settlement of Phelps and Gorham's Purchase, and Morris' Reserve* (Rochester, NY, 1852), 410; Edwin A. Glover, *James Strawbridge, Esquire* (Elkland, PA, 1954), 4; Kenneth Lockridge, "Land, Population, and the Evolution of New England Society, 1630–1790," *Past and Present* 39 (Apr. 1968): 62–80.
41. Lincklaen, *Travels in the Years 1791 and 1792*, 83–84.
42. Deposition of Resolved Sessions, July 31, 1797, *SCP* 10:442–43.

settle on the lakes" of central New York. Roswell and Jehiel Franklin joined the force of northbound migrants described by Rochefoucault. Jehiel abandoned his half-share right in the Susquehannah Company and kept moving north till he eventually ended up in Canada. Roswell Franklin, a Yankee moderate who took a leading role in rounding up Timothy Pickering's kidnappers, became a squatter in central New York and eventually committed suicide after facing repeated setbacks in his attempt to secure a homestead.[43] Likewise, Solomon Teasy, who came to Pennsylvania from New York in 1790 and managed to clear thirty acres of a five-hundred acre tract by mid-decade, set his sights on western New York's Genesee Valley.[44]

No matter if they stayed only briefly or put down permanent roots, the steady flow of Yankee migrants meant that New Englanders greatly outnumbered Pennsylvanians in the region. Yankee settlers were not only numerous but united by family ties and common places of origin. For instance, New Englanders monopolized settlement along Wyalusing Creek. James Rockwell came to Wyalusing from East Windsor, Connecticut, in 1790. Seth Rockwell, a kinsman and fellow East Windsor native, joined James a year later. Two sets of brothers, Darius and Elijah Coleman and Dimon and Benajah Bostwick, arrived from Connecticut the following year. In 1793, half a dozen more Yankee families arrived. Most of the settlers along Wyalusing Creek hailed from a handful of Connecticut towns and were bound by ties of kinship. In addition to the Bostwick and Coleman brothers, the creek sported three other sets of pioneering brothers. By migrating as groups of townsmen and kinsmen, Yankees eased the pains of frontier settlement and presented competing Pennsylvania claimants with a united front of resistance.[45]

In the same way that prominent speculators could promote community building and agrarian unrest in their pursuit of profit and power, frontier yeomen engaged in commercial ventures and embraced land speculation as a way to secure property and independence.[46] Martin Dudley's experiences as a settler along the New York frontier illustrate the permeability of the lines that separated yeomen from gentlemen and agrarian insurgents from frontier entrepreneurs. A Yankee

---

43. James W. Darlington, "Peopling the Post-Revolutionary New York Frontier," *New York History* 74 (Oct. 1993): 341–81; Duc de la Rochefoucault-Liancourt, *Travels through the United States of North America, The Country of the Iroquois, and Upper Canada in the Years 1795, 1796, and 1797*, 2 vols. (London, 1799), 1:100; Craft, *History of Bradford County*, 455.

44. Rochefoucault-Liancourt, *Travels through the United States*, 1:97–98. For examples of Connecticut claimants who ended up in the Genesee country, see Turner, *Pioneer History of Phelps' and Gorham's Purchase*, 223, 252–53, 552–53.

45. Craft, *History of Bradford County*, 337–40.

46. Stephen Aron, "Pioneer and Profiteers: Land Speculation and the Homestead Ethic in Frontier Kentucky," *Western Historical Quarterly* 23 (May 1992): 182; Paul W. Gates, "The Role of the Land Speculator in Western Development" *PMHB* 66 (July 1942): 315–16; James A. Henretta, "Families and Farms: *Mentalité* in Pre-Industrial America" *WMQ* 35 (Jan. 1978): 27.

farmer who also plied his trade as a carpenter, Dudley removed to Kanadesaga after his run-in with Pennsylvania authorities in 1788. Though he was an ordinary settler and backcountry rebel in Pennsylvania, he took on a very different persona in New York. At first, Dudley continued to work as a farmer and carpenter; however, he seems to have made a change in his status by 1789. In that year he agreed to build a barn on William Walker's house lot in Canandaigua, New York. A contract drawn up to finalize the deal referred to Dudley as a "Gentleman." If he fit this title, then he did not build Walker's barn with his own hands but probably supervised workmen under his employ. This document furnishes the first glimpse of Dudley's improving fortunes in New York and serves as a reminder that backcountry migrants not only traversed geographical space but, at times, crossed lines of class and social status.[47]

In addition to transforming himself from an ordinary farmer into a rough-hewn gentleman of the New York frontier, Martin Dudley was one of many Wild Yankees who engaged in modest speculating ventures. Once in New York, Dudley set himself up as a middleman between Connecticut claimants who had left Pennsylvania for the Finger Lakes region and speculators who maintained their interest in the Susquehannah Company. In December 1794, Martin Dudley, who had now gained the title of "Merchant," purchased company shares from his son Gideon Dudley and other half-share men. Weeks later, Dudley transferred these rights to Elisha Satterlee and John Hutchinson "in consideration of a valuable sum." In a separate deal, Dudley sold a six-hundred-acre tract along the Lackawanna River to Satterlee and Hutchinson for a hundred pounds.[48]

Peter Bortle, a small-time speculator from the Hudson Valley, was another Wild Yankee who turned agrarian insurgency into an instrument of commercial gain. Bortle briefly took up residence in Northeast Pennsylvania as a Connecticut claimant in 1786 before leaving the state for Ontario County, New York. Once there, he began buying up the Connecticut rights of other Yankee migrants and selling them for a profit. In March 1794, Bortle purchased a number of half-share rights and handed them over to Guy Maxwell, a merchant from Athens. Maxwell, in turn, agreed to sell them and share the profit with Bortle. Maxwell lived up to his promise and completed Bortle's speculative venture when he sold the half-share rights to another Athens resident, David Paine.[49] A number of other Wild Yankees, instead of trading Connecticut rights,

47. Agreement between Martin Dudley and William Walker, Aug. 25, 1789, William Walker Papers, New York Historical Society.
48. Conveyances between Martin Dudley and Gideon Dudley, Dec. 29, 1794; Conveyance from Aaron Kilborn to Martin Dudley, Dec. 29, 1794; and Conveyances from Martin Dudley to Elisha Satterlee and John Hutchinson, Jan. 7, 1795, SCA Liber C:311, 304, 301–3.
49. Conveyances from Enos Tubbs, David Woodward, and Jeptha Earl to Peter Bortle, Mar. 1794; Agreement between Peter Bortle and Guy Maxwell, Dec. 14, 1794; and Conveyance from Guy Maxwell to David Paine, Dec. 20, 1794, SCA Liber C:315, 316, 317–18.

became small-scale land developers. John Swift and John Jenkins became the proprietors of a twenty-one-thousand-acre township in New York which later became the bustling frontier settlement of Palmyra. In a similar fashion, Uriah Stevens, Joel Thomas, and several other Yankee insurgents joined together to purchase and develop lands around Newtown, New York.[50]

The pursuit of agrarian independence and the maintenance of kin networks shaped the contours of frontier migration just as much as land prices, soil quality, and transportation networks. John Lincklaen's account of Thomas Rice's move to western New York sheds light on the social context of frontier expansion. Lincklaen may have doubted the wisdom of Rice's decision to go west but he understood the reasons that lay behind it, noting that it was common for Americans to spend years developing a farm and then sell it for a profit in order to purchase a larger tract along the frontier. In doing so, Lincklaen concluded, yeomen hoped to secure enough property "to maintain & establish around them a dozen children." Thus, frontier migration served to sustain two processes central to the survival of a freehold society: the creation of close-knit social networks and the passage of landed property from one generation to the next.[51]

Rather than breaking families apart, frontier expansion often served to keep them together. For eastern households facing declining crop yields and land shortages, remaining in place often meant splitting up to find work in neighboring communities or distant towns. More important, a shortage of arable land worked to undermine farmers' efforts to maintain cohesive kin networks as sons and daughters had to move farther and farther away from their parents in order to set up a homestead. The frontier offered farmers the land they needed to maintain close-knit families.[52] While traveling in central New York, the Duc Rochefoucault-Liancourt met several groups of immigrants on their way to the Genesee Country. He commented that the migrants' "friendly connections also are mostly confined to their own families, which move about with them," illustrating that settlers did not abandon familiar social networks or sever emotional ties when they entered the backcountry.[53]

---

50. Murray, *History of Old Tioga*, 305, 306 n. 5; "Sketch of the Life of Lt. Col. John Jenkins," *Proceedings and Collections of the Wyoming Historical and Geological Society* 18 (1922): 249–51.

51. Lincklaen, *Travels in the Years 1791 and 1792*, 83–84; William Herbert Siles, "A Vision of Wealth: Speculators and Settlers in the Genesee Country of New York" (Ph.D., diss., University of Massachusetts, 1978), 125.

52. Thomas Bender, *Community and Social Change in America* (New Brunswick, NJ, 1978), 71–72; Wyckoff, *The Developer's Frontier*, 108.

53. Rochefoucault-Liancourt, *Travels through the United States*, 107; Lucy Jayne Botscharow-Kamau, "Neighbors: Harmony and Conflict on the Indiana Frontier," *Journal of the Early Republic* 11 (winter 1991): 521; Taylor, *William Cooper's Town*, 97.

That migrants traveled in the company of kin, friends, and neighbors means that frontier settlements, instead of lacking meaningful social ties, often supported extensive neighborhood and family networks. The settlement of Sugar Creek illustrates that kin and neighbors quickly became one and the same in backcountry communities. In 1790 Amos Bennett came to Sugar Creek; Joseph Baily arrived two years later. As was commonly the case, family ties and regional background shaped Baily's and Bennett's decision to settle near one another. Both men hailed from Orange County, New York. In addition, Joseph Baily was Amos Bennett's brother-in-law, having married Bennett's sister, Susan. Martin Stratton, a millwright and carpenter from Hartford, came to Sugar Creek in 1794 and further reinforced the creek's growing kinship network when he married Rebecca Rutty, the daughter of another Sugar Creek pioneer, Ezra Rutty. A couple of years later, Martin Stratton's brother, Surager, joined the settlement.[54]

In many cases, kinship and neighborhood networks were not so much rebuilt as relocated. Captain Jonathan Terry, who took up land along the west bank of the Susquehanna River in 1787, was soon joined by an uncle, his father, and six of his siblings. Not surprisingly, the settlement they formed became known as Terrytown. Another group of Connecticut claimants joined by ties of kinship settled just west of Lake Wallenpaupack. Here Silas Purdy and his sons Jacob, Amos, and Isaac started a new community in 1787. In the years that followed several other Purdys joined the settlement, including Reverend William Purdy who was accompanied by his six sons and two daughters.[55] The common origin of migrants was another important source of cohesion for frontier communities. Standing Stone, a Yankee enclave just north of Terrytown, drew a large proportion of its early inhabitants from two towns in eastern New York. Benjamin Ackla, Richard Benjamin, and Amos Bennett all hailed from Florida, New York, while Anthony Vander Pool, Isaac Wheeler, and Wheeler's brother-in-law, Nicholas Johnson, all resided in Kinderhook before coming to the settlement.[56]

Next to the desire to maintain familiar social relationships, access to markets and the quality of the land shaped where migrants chose to settle.[57] Rather than

---

54. Clement F. Heverly, *History of the Towandas, 1776–1886* (Towanda, PA, 1886), 66–77.

55. Ellen Eslinger, "Migration and Kinship on the Trans-Appalachian Frontier: Strode's Station, Kentucky," *Filson Club Historical Quarterly* 62 (Jan. 1988): 52–66; Botscharow-Kamau, "Neighbors," 521; Craft, *History of Bradford County*, 267–68; Goodrich, *History of Wayne County*, 165–67.

56. Craft, *History of Bradford County*, 383. A similar process of kinship migration is described in David J. Goodall, "New Light on the Border: New England Squatter Settlements in New York during the American Revolution" (Ph.D. diss., State University of New York at Albany, 1984), 104–6.

57. Brooks, *Frontier Settlement*, 2–4; Darlington, "Peopling the Post-Revolutionary Frontier," 346–47.

representing an escape route from market relationships, frontier migration placed yeomen at the center of the early republic's greatest commercial enterprise: the development and exploitation of land. Some pioneers transformed the very process of settlement into a speculative venture by sinking their labor into the land and selling their improvements to those who followed them. Settlers' involvement in commercial relationships did not emerge slowly but started as soon as they began to clear the land. Cutting down trees provided pioneers with lumber, potash, and pearl ash—valuable commodities that settlers marketed in order to defray the costs of farm building. Another commercial opportunity avidly exploited by backcountry farmers was selling provisions to frontier-bound migrants who passed through their communities.[58]

At the grassroots level, frontier expansion rested on a set of intertwined social and economic aspirations. Yeomen went to the frontier to maintain relationships rooted in household, kin, and neighborhood networks as well as to provide themselves with a level of material security and economic opportunity absent in older eastern communities. Whatever their motives, as the number of Yankee settlers in Northeast Pennsylvania increased so did tensions. Pennsylvania landholders, instead of realizing profit from their investments, found themselves playing host to cantankerous Yankees who held very little respect for their property rights. During the last decade of the eighteenth century, Wild Yankees found themselves in a position to take the offensive against Pennsylvania. Frontier migration had strengthened their hand, giving them the numbers needed to dominate local government and crowd Pennsylvanians off the land.

"Yankee-play"

The arrival of large numbers of New Englanders in Northeast Pennsylvania caused a considerable amount of apprehension among state land claimants. Samuel Preston, a Quaker and land agent for fellow Quaker Henry Drinker, witnessed the growth of Yankee settlements along the upper reaches of the Delaware River. Writing from his home in Harmony, Pennsylvania, Preston informed Drinker that his lands were being occupied by settlers but warned that "too many of the emigrants are from the eastward, and more disposed to purloining of timber than of cultivating of farms." He claimed that New Englanders were "universally given to thieving" and "abundantly more impudent and debauched than any other clan." Preston's prejudice against Yankees ran so

---

58. Taylor, "William Cooper's Town," 100–103; Ellis, "Rise of the Empire State," 13–14; Siles, "A Vision of Wealth," 123.

deep that he wished they would simply stop coming—in this respect, as in most others, the New Englanders disappointed him.[59]

Arthur Erwin was another Pennsylvania claimant who felt threatened by the flood of Yankee immigrants. In the spring of 1791, he wrote to Governor Mifflin begging protection from Wild Yankees. Erwin explained that he had purchased five thousand acres along the Tioga River from the state in 1785 and, since that time, had "patented, settled, cleared, and improved" his property. A lone Pennsylvania claimant in a sea of New Englanders, he found himself a target of "Insult and abuse" by neighbors who disputed his soil rights. On one occasion, Wild Yankees attacked Erwin and broke one of his arms with the handle of a pitchfork. He took his assailants to court and, though "every necessary proof" was made of their guilt, they went unpunished. Erwin's adversaries consolidated their victory in court by stealing his crops and abusing his farmhands.[60] Outnumbered and without effective support, Erwin became another victim of agrarian violence. One evening, while on a visit to his tenant Daniel McDuffee, Erwin was shot and killed by an unknown gunman. Joel Thomas, a resident of Athens, was brought to trial for the murder but escaped punishment after being acquitted by a Luzerne County jury.[61]

As Erwin's ordeal attests, Wild Yankees were able to take the offensive against Pennsylvania and its land claimants in the last decade of the eighteenth century. They were also to do so because they effectively linked agrarian insurgency to the demographic forces of frontier expansion. The migration of Connecticut claimants into Pennsylvania made it possible for Wild Yankees to muster more settlers than Pennsylvania and its landholders could contend with. William Judd had this situation in mind when he happily observed that New Englanders were "flocking" to the Northeast frontier "and daily strengthening the Claim." Judge Jacob Rush, the president of Pennsylvania's Fifth Court of Common Pleas, echoed Judd's words when he warned Governor Mifflin of the difficulties the state would bring on itself if it allowed large numbers of Yankee settlers to gain a foothold. He concluded that every "Encrease of Inhabitants" under the Connecticut claim equalled "an Accession to *their* Strength."[62]

---

59. Samuel Preston to Henry Drinker, May 1, 1791; Samuel Preston to Henry Drinker, Nov. 19, 1792; and Samuel Preston to Henry Drinker, June 26, 1793, HDP, Journal and Land Records, 1789–1809.

60. Arthur Erwin to Thomas Mifflin, April 5, 1791, SCP 10:143–45; Murray, *History of Old Tioga*, 313–14.

61. Proclamation of Governor Mifflin, June 20, 1791, PA9 1:135–36. Murray, *History of Old Tioga*, 315–18.

62. William Judd to Timothy Pickering, Mar. 24, 1794, and Jacob Rush to Thomas Mifflin, July 1, 1797, SCP 10:195, 440.

Besides restive Yankee settlers, Pennsylvania had to contend with parties of Yankee surveyors who spread across northeastern Pennsylvania to lay out new towns and fresh lines of resistance. State officials began to receive reports describing this campaign of insurgent surveys late in 1794. Soon after, Governor Thomas Mifflin issued a proclamation against the "ill-disposed persons" who "unlawfully intruded upon and surveyed" lands in Pennsylvania under the Connecticut claim. The state quickly followed up this warning with the passage of the Intrusion Act.[63] However, warnings and legislative initiatives did little to dampen the tide of illegal surveys. Well-armed, well-equipped surveying parties traversed the whole of Northeast Pennsylvania, spreading insurgency in their wake. In 1797 a state commission formed to investigate the growing crisis concluded that "the country west of the Susquehannah, nearly to the Allegheny River, along the northern boundary" had been mapped out under the Connecticut claim by as many as fifteen different groups of surveyors.[64] State officials were able to discover the names of several of the surveyors but, lacking the support of local inhabitants, failed to find or apprehend them. Pennsylvania surveyor John Adlum testified that Connecticut claimants treated government authority with "ridicule and contempt" and refused to inform on Yankee surveyors. Likewise, Judge Rush complained that backcountry inhabitants either supported the intruders or feared to speak out against them, shrouding the illegal survey and sale of lands in "the thickest Veil of Darkness." Court records support the judge's statement: by the summer of 1797 not a single person had been successfully prosecuted under the Intrusion Act.[65]

Pennsylvania speculators who laid claim to lands in Northeast Pennsylvania found securing their possessions a difficult and laborious task. James Strawbridge experienced all the difficulties faced by state landholders. In December 1796, Strawbridge wrote a letter to fellow Pennsylvania claimant William Maclay narrating the troubles he had with Yankees seated on his property. In 1790 Strawbridge found five families squatting on his lands but decided to take no action against them after they promised not to oppose his property rights. Two years later, the squatter population on Strawbridge's tract had grown to twenty families. Confident that their numbers would enable them to fend off any threat, the settlers "openly declared their rights from the Susquehannah Company." Tensions rose between Strawbridge and the New Englanders. On

---

63. Deposition of Alexander Brown, Dec. 16, 1794; Proclamation by Thomas Mifflin, Jan. 26, 1795; and The Intrusion Act, Apr. 11, 1795, *SCP* 10:210, 211, 227–29.
64. Report of the Committee on the Wyoming Controversy, Jan. 16, 1797, *SCP* 10:396–97.
65. William Carter to Thomas Mifflin, June 28, 1796; Deposition of John Adlum, Dec. 31, 1796; and Jacob Rush to Thomas Mifflin, July 1, 1796, *SCP* 10:352, 392–93, 441.

"ALL THE DIFFICULTIES OF FORMING A NEW SETTLEMENT"   115

one occasion, the Yankees even opened fire on Strawbridge and a group of surveyors under his employ.⁶⁶ Strawbridge eventually initiated ejectment suits against the intruders, but for every Yankee family he got rid of, two came to take their place. Ultimately, it was the Wild Yankees who forced Strawbridge to abandon his lands.⁶⁷

Though the problems faced by Pennsylvania speculators were considerable, they paled in comparison to the troubles faced by ordinary Pennsylvania claimants who attempted to settle their lands in the teeth of Yankee resistance. Casper Singer, who occupied a 120-acre farm near the mouth of Towanda Creek, gained firsthand knowledge of the intimidation and violence Pennsylvanians suffered at the hands of Wild Yankees. Singer's troubles began in the fall of 1795 when Orr Scovill challenged his claim and proceeded, along with half a dozen other Yankee settlers, to survey Singer's "improved fenced fields" and divide them into lots. When Singer demanded by what authority Scovill and his accomplices usurped his lands, they replied that Connecticut deeds in their possession justified their "Yankee-play." Soon after, Connecticut claimants pulled down Singer's home and forced him off the land.⁶⁸ Likewise, in the summer of 1796, Pennsylvania claimants in Northampton County became "seriously alarmed" when Wild Yankees threatened them with violence and ejectment. Samuel Preston believed that these settlers, many of whom were New Englanders, would have willingly joined the Wild Yankees if they had not already made payments toward Pennsylvania titles.⁶⁹

The same commitment to community that led to the creation of close-knit frontier neighborhoods shaped these episodes of violence and dispossession. In a land torn by disputes over land and authority, supportive neighbors could quickly turn into menacing adversaries. Resolved Sessions discovered this when he renounced the Connecticut claim and repurchased his land along Towanda Creek under a Pennsylvania deed. Casper Singer, who sold the land to Sessions, wisely told him to hide the fact from his neighbors (all of who were Connecticut claimants). For as long as Sessions's secret remained hidden, he enjoyed good relations with his fellow settlers. But in the fall of 1796 his infidelity to the Connecticut claim became known. Soon after, Sessions's neighbors plundered his

---

66. James Strawbridge to William Maclay, Dec. 30, 1796, *SCP* 10:390. Glover, *James Strawbridge, Esquire*, 1–6. For a discussion of the settlement of the south branch of the Tioga River see John Franklin Meginness, *History of Tioga County Pennsylvania* (Chicago, 1897), 56–58, 526–27.

67. James Strawbridge to William Maclay, Dec. 30, 1796, *SCP* 10:391–92.

68. Heverly, *History of the Towandas*, 49–50; Deposition of Casper Singer, Nov. 11, 1796, *SCP* 10:388–90.

69. Deposition of Casper Singer, Jan. 26, 1797, *SCP* 10:399–401; Samuel Preston to Henry Drinker, Aug. 9, 1796, HDP, Journal and Land Records, 1789–1809.

property and installed a newly arrived Yankee migrant, Aaron Gillet, in his home. To replace his losses, Sessions leased land and a house from Casper Singer and restarted the process of farm-building. Sessions's troubles followed him to his new homestead. One day, while Sessions and his son were at work on their new farm, Jacob Bowman, Aaron Gillet, and a third Yankee strode up and warned them "not to plough another Inch," saying that the land belonged to Bowman.[70]

These tales of violence and dispossession provide only a partial picture of the difficulties faced by Pennsylvania claimants, for individuals who accepted Pennsylvania titles also experienced a sustained campaign of legal harassment. While rank-and-file Wild Yankees carried out acts of physical violence, their leading men commandeered local government and turned it against those settlers who aligned themselves with the state. Samuel Preston recognized that the New Englanders' "uncommon propensity to do something at politicks" posed a grave threat to state authority. He prayed that no more Yankees would come to Northeast Pennsylvania, noting that if they became a majority, "all goes to ruin." But the creation of a politically potent Yankee majority is just what the insurgents had in mind. During the last decade of the eighteenth century, Wild Yankees shifted their emphasis from toppling Pennsylvania's political apparatus to using it to serve their own ends.[71]

This Yankee tactic was not entirely new. The New Englanders had been using legal and political means to vex their opponents since the 1780s. In one of the first episodes in which the insurgents used state institutions to undermine state authority, Connecticut claimants chose five well-known Wild Yankees to serve as militia officers in Luzerne County's upper battalion. County courts became another target of Yankee usurpation. Control of the county-level legal apparatus not only helped to shield Connecticut claimants from the power of the state, but also served as a useful weapon against Pennsylvania claimants. In 1789 Pennsylvanian William Miller accused Elisha Mathewson, Elisha Satterlee, and others of forcible entry but lost his suit and his lands after a jury drawn from the region's Yankee inhabitants decided in the defendants' favor. The following year, a Yankee-dominated jury found two Pennsylvania settlers, Daniel McDuffee and John Doran, guilty of forcible entry and detainer after they attempted to recover lands occupied by Yankee intruders.[72]

---

70. Deposition of Resolved Sessions, July 31, 1797, *SCP* 10:442–48.
71. Samuel Preston to Henry Drinker, May 20, 1794; Samuel Preston to Henry Drinker, May 28, 1794; and Samuel Preston to Henry Drinker, May 22, 1799, HDP, Journal and Land Records, 1789–1809.
72. Zebulon Butler to Benjamin Franklin, Aug. 26, 1788, *SCP* 8:479; Murray, *History of Old Tioga*, 313, 326–27. For another example of Yankee bias in Luzerne County courts, see the Petition of Thomas Martin to the Pennsylvania Council, Mar. 7, 1790, *SCP* 10:66.

The arrival of large numbers of New Englanders in the 1790s made it possible for Wild Yankees to expand and strengthen their hold on Pennsylvania's political and judicial institutions. After 1795 even an outsider like the Duc de la Rochefoucault-Liancourt could discern that Wild Yankees "acted on the principle, that an increase of the number of colonists would increase the force of resistance against the sentence of judicial dispossession." In a letter to Tench Coxe, Ephraim Kirby described the dismal prospects faced by Pennsylvania claimants who sought justice from Yankee-controlled courts. Kirby declared that "the shameful neglect of the magistrates in the County of Luzerne has been a subject of boast among the Connecticut claimants and a great encouragement to lawless adventure." He believed, and rightly so, that the insurgents would "multiply in numbers and grow strong in confidence" as long as local courts failed to check their illegal actions. Luzerne County was not the only district in which Yankee settlers bent state institutions to their will. To the west, Pennsylvania officials in Lycoming County had to contend with Yankee settlers who dominated its northern townships. Wayne County's Yankee majority also used the law as a weapon against Pennsylvania claimants.[73]

Pennsylvania, armed with the Intrusion Act, struggled to regain control of the Northeast frontier, but as long as local justices and juries remained under the thumb of Yankee insurgents, there was little the state could do to punish lawbreakers or protect Pennsylvania claimants. In July 1797, Judge Rush ordered the sheriff of Luzerne County to arrest Elisha Satterlee and a dozen other Connecticut claimants for illegally surveying and settling lands. But this effort, like those that proceeded it, foundered in Luzerne County courts. Likewise, Tench Coxe registered his disapproval when a Luzerne County jury failed to find John Jenkins guilty of resisting the progress of a Pennsylvania surveying party, "tho the proof of the interruption . . . was clear and positive."[74] Without the cooperation of juries and witnesses, the Intrusion Act, no matter how potent it seemed on paper, proved ineffective.

Wild Yankees also discovered the numbers on the ground translated into victories at the ballot box. Joseph Kinney became a judge of Luzerne County's court of common pleas in 1789. A year later, three other Yankee agitators joined Kinney as justices of the peace and judges for the court of common pleas.[75] Likewise, John Franklin became a local political figure. Franklin, who had only

---

73. Rochefoucault-Liancourt, *Travels through the United States*, 1:85–86; Ephraim Kirby to Tench Coxe, Feb. 6, 1797, SCP 10:404; Goodrich, *History of Wayne County*, 133–34.
74. Jacob Rush to Thomas Mifflin, July 1, 1797, and Jacob Rush to the sheriff of Luzerne County, July 17, 1797, SCP 10:440–42; Tench Coxe to Presley C. Lane, Jan. 3, 1801, SCP 11:4.
75. Murray, *History of Old Tioga*, 334; Timothy Pickering to Thomas Mifflin, Aug. 16, 1791, SCP 10:147–48; Pearce, *Annals of Luzerne County*, 242–43.

recently been pardoned of his crimes against the state, became sheriff of Luzerne County in 1792, a post he held for four years. With Franklin in charge of this key position, it is little wonder that Pennsylvania found it difficult to enforce the Intrusion Act. Franklin's rise to sheriff marked only the beginning of his political career. In 1793 he became the lieutenant colonel of Luzerne County's upper militia battalion; later, Franklin served as a representative in the Pennsylvania legislature in 1795, 1796, 1799, and from 1800 to 1803.[76]

Casper Singer and Resolved Sessions experienced all the difficulties Pennsylvania claimants faced at the hands of Yankee officials. When insurgents trespassed on his land, Singer made a complaint to three Yankee justices who, instead of offering any aid, "laughed at him for pretending to hold any lands under Pennsylvania." Later, Singer lost thirty-one dollars in court fees after a grand jury failed to support his charges of intrusion against neighboring Connecticut claimants.[77] In a similar fashion, Sessions became subject to verbal abuse and threats from Yankee leading men. On one occasion, Joseph Kinney reproached Sessions for purchasing a Pennsylvania title and told him that he would never hold land under the state "as long as water runs in the susquehanna."[78]

The threats and abuse of Yankee settlers, combined with the power of Yankee officeholders, eventually squeezed many Pennsylvania claimants off the land. The end came for Resolved Sessions when local "poormasters" and Yankee stalwarts Job Irish and Jehiel Franklin came to Sessions's home accompanied by another Connecticut claimant, Justice Moses Coolbaugh. The three men accused Sessions's recently deceased landlord, Casper Singer, of having "unlawfully" fathered two children by Elizabeth Freeton. Irish and Franklin then inventoried Singer's property—including the home Sessions occupied, the crops he stored, and the tools he used—and confiscated them under the pretense that the proceeds would go toward the support of Freeton's children. To add insult to injury, they also forced Sessions's son to pay twenty dollars for the use he had gotten of the property since Singer's death. Hiding behind a facade of due process, Connecticut claimants robbed Sessions and his son of their property and drove them from their home.[79]

Frontier expansion played an important role in shaping agrarian unrest in Northeast Pennsylvania. Unbridled speculation and high levels of migration

76. Pearce, *Annals of Luzerne*, 524; James Edward Brady, "Wyoming: A Study of John Franklin and the Connecticut Settlement into Pennsylvania" (Ph.D. diss., Syracuse University, 1973), 275–76, 288, 301.

77. Depositions of Casper Singer, Nov. 11, 1796, and Jan. 26, 1797, *SCP* 10:389, 400–401.

78. Deposition of Resolved Sessions, July 31, 1797, and George Head and Others to Thomas Mifflin, June 19, 1797, *SCP* 10:444, 438–39.

79. Deposition of Resolved Sessions, July 31, 1797, *SCP* 10:446–47.

"ALL THE DIFFICULTIES OF FORMING A NEW SETTLEMENT" 119

generated new interest in the Connecticut claim. Furthermore, the surge in frontier settlement that followed the Revolutionary War brought large numbers of Yankee insurgents to the region. Speculators and settlers, the pursuit of profit and personal independence, came together and, for a time, worked together to undermine state rule.

As quickly as it had arisen, however, Pennsylvania's speculation boom came to an end. Once federal land west of the Ohio River became more accessible to settlers, demand for land in northern Pennsylvania declined. More important, the land fever of the 1790s had been built on irresponsible investments and shady land-grabbing schemes. It was only a matter of time before the land market suffered from its own excesses.[80] Early in 1797 Tench Coxe received word from an associate in New York City that land speculation had reached a low ebb and that "a man would be pitied or laughed at who should let it be known he had a wish to effect sales." The rapid decline of the land market caused financial ruin for many prominent speculators. Connecticut claimant Clement Paine wrote that "many persons of the first respectibility in business" were hardly able to "keep their heads above water." The great land magnates Robert Morris, James Wilson, and John Nicholson ended up bankrupt or in debtors' prison as a result of unwise investments and their fate reflected that of scores of frontier speculators.[81]

Changes in Pennsylvania's land market continued to shape Yankee insurgency. The declining value of the state's frontier lands did not stop the flow of migrants, but tough financial conditions drove away many speculators and caused those who remained to take a much less indulgent attitude toward settlers. As the profit-making potential of the Pennsylvania backcountry declined, speculators found that it was increasingly important to squeeze more money out of settlers who occupied their lands. In short, land developers who faced financial difficulties passed on the pressure to frontier inhabitants. One result of this was the decline of settler-speculator relations. Many Susquehannah Company proprietors pulled out of the Connecticut claim, leaving Yankee settlers to fend for themselves. Meanwhile, Pennsylvania landholders, determined to fight for every acre of their property, banded together to promote a fresh wave of anti-Yankee initiatives.

---

80. Wyckoff, *The Developer's Frontier*, 10–11; Wilkinson, *Land Policy and Speculation*, 184; Doerflinger, *Vigorous Spirit of Enterprise*, 323–26.
81. Samuel A. Law to Tench Coxe, Feb. 14, 1797, and Clement Paine to Seth Paine, May 10, 1799, SCP 10:411, 474; Peter C. Mancall, *Valley of Opportunity: Economic Culture along the Upper Susquehanna, 1700–1800* (Ithaca, NY, 1991), 170; Wilkinson, *Land Policy and Speculation*, 236–54.

CHAPTER 5

"A Perfect Union with the People"

Cultures of Resistance along the Revolutionary Frontier

By the summer of 1804, Yankee settlers along Sugar Creek found themselves struggling to shield their community from intruding sheriff's deputies, surveyors, and land agents. In the spring, they got word that a group of Pennsylvania surveyors were at work near their settlements. Three parties of settlers scoured the woods for the Pennsylvanians but failed to intercept them. A short time later, word spread that Lycoming County magistrate Henry Donnell was in the neighborhood cajoling Connecticut claimants into purchasing Pennsylvania titles and bringing ejectment suits against those who refused. Responding to this threat, Sugar Creek's Wild Yankees rallied and, after "a good deal of hard work," captured Donnell and submitted him to a gauntlet of verbal and physical abuse before releasing him. Though under increasing pressure, Connecticut claimants along Sugar Creek asserted that there was "a perfect union with the people" and that they were "determined to share an equal fate" in defense of their families and farms.[1]

After 1800 Yankee resistance changed from a regional movement that enjoyed the support of well-connected, nonresident speculators into a fragmented, highly localized insurgency manned and managed by backcountry settlers. Two developments undermined the settler-speculator alliance that had buoyed Yankee resistance since the 1780s. First, with the collapse of the speculating boom that had swept over northern Pennsylvania in the 1790s, profit-minded land

---

1. Nathaniel Allen to John Jenkins, June 25, 1804, in Louise Wells Murray, *A History of Old Tioga Point and Early Athens* (Wilkes-Barre, PA, 1907), 420–21.

developers fell back from the commitment to the Connecticut claim. Second, the state and its most powerful land speculators moved to impose their authority and soil rights over Northeast Pennsylvania. Through the deft combination of compromise and punitive legislation, Pennsylvania undercut support for the Connecticut claim among Yankee settlers and further discouraged nonresident speculators from sponsoring settler resistance. Eventually, local leading men who were more concerned with protecting themselves and their neighbors from ejectment than defending the integrity of the Connecticut claim filled the leadership vacuum created by the decline of the Susquehannah and Delaware companies.

Exploring Yankee insurgency during this period reveals how ordinary settlers battled to defend their farms, neighborhoods, and independence and provides insight into the behaviors and beliefs that constituted rural cultures of resistance. Incidents of unrest highlight that the insurgents waged both an "external" campaign of resistance aimed at protecting their communities from invading state officials and an "internal" campaign of purges and intimidation aimed at Yankee turncoats. They also demonstrate that Wild Yankees drew on venerable traditions of popular protest, the memory and experience of the American Revolution, and the experience of frontier life in mounting these parallel efforts. Most important, the desperate battle Wild Yankees fought after the turn of the century illustrates that ordinary settlers' efforts to achieve and secure independence continued to propel agrarian unrest in Northeast Pennsylvania.[2]

"a Determination to Survey Disposes Sel & turn the world upsidedown"

That Wild Yankee resistance became more localized and fragmented after 1800 was a result of Pennsylvania's renewed efforts to win control over the Wyoming region. Pennsylvania offered secure titles to compromise-minded Yankees while meting out harsh punishments to those who continued to support the Connecticut claim. This strategy broke the settler-speculator alliance that had bolstered Yankee resistance. Moreover, the new legislation opened a fissure between settlers who lived in the Wyoming Valley and those who occupied raw backcountry settlements to the north.

---

2. Alan Taylor has uncovered similar patterns and similar ideological components in his examination of agrarian resistance in Maine: see *Liberty Men and Great Proprietors: The Revolutionary Settlement on the Maine Frontier, 1760–1820* (Chapel Hill, NC, 1990), 118–21, and " 'Stopping the Progress of Rogues and Deceivers': A White Indian Recruiting Notice of 1808," *WMQ* 41 (Jan. 1985): 90–103.

In the spring of 1799, Pennsylvania made the first in a series of moves that would ultimately resolve land disputes in and around the Wyoming Valley. On April 4, the state assembly passed the Compromise Act, which allowed settlers who held Connecticut deeds that predated the Trenton Decree to obtain Pennsylvania titles to their lands. The legislation established a three-man commission empowered to assess the legitimacy of settlers' claims, survey their tracts, and ascertain their value. Settlers who had their Connecticut deeds confirmed by the commissioners had to pay, depending on the value of their farms, between eight cents to two dollars per acre in eight annual installments. The proceeds from these sales went toward defraying the cost of compensating Pennsylvania claimants who lost property to Connecticut settlers.[3]

As with the Confirming Act of 1787, the new law encouraged Connecticut claimants holding deeds issued before 1783 to move toward reconciliation with the state and to turn their backs on settlers who held titles issued after the Trenton Decree. After some initial hesitation, the lure of secure titles at low prices assured the act's acceptance among Yankee settlers in the fifteen Susquehannah Company towns established before the Trenton Decree. These settlements covered the Wyoming Valley and adjacent lands extending up the Susquehanna River as far as the town of Claverack at the mouth of Sugar Creek.

More than any other person, Thomas Cooper can be credited with the success of the Compromise Act. Appointed to serve on the commission created under the law, he quickly established himself as its leading member. Cooper was able to break that deadlock that had foiled negotiations between Pennsylvania and its Yankee inhabitants in the past because he treated Connecticut claimants with fairness, understanding, and compassion. His background gives some hints as to why he was able to empathize with rebellious backcountry farmers. An Englishman by birth, a scientist and freethinker by nature, a religious dissenter by conscience, and a lawyer by profession, Cooper and his family came to the United States in 1794 after his support of the French Revolution and denunciations of England's aristocracy had earned him the enmity of the British government. Cooper settled along the west branch of the Susquehanna in Northumberland, Pennsylvania, where he continued his activities as a political dissident. His writings in favor of freedom of the press and in opposition to Federalist policies made him an asset to Pennsylvania's Democratic-Republican gubernatorial candidate Thomas McKean in the election of 1799. They also resulted in his prosecution and imprisonment under the Sedition Act. After Cooper's release, Governor

---

3. The Compromise Act of 1799, Apr. 4, 1799, *SCP* 10:468–74.

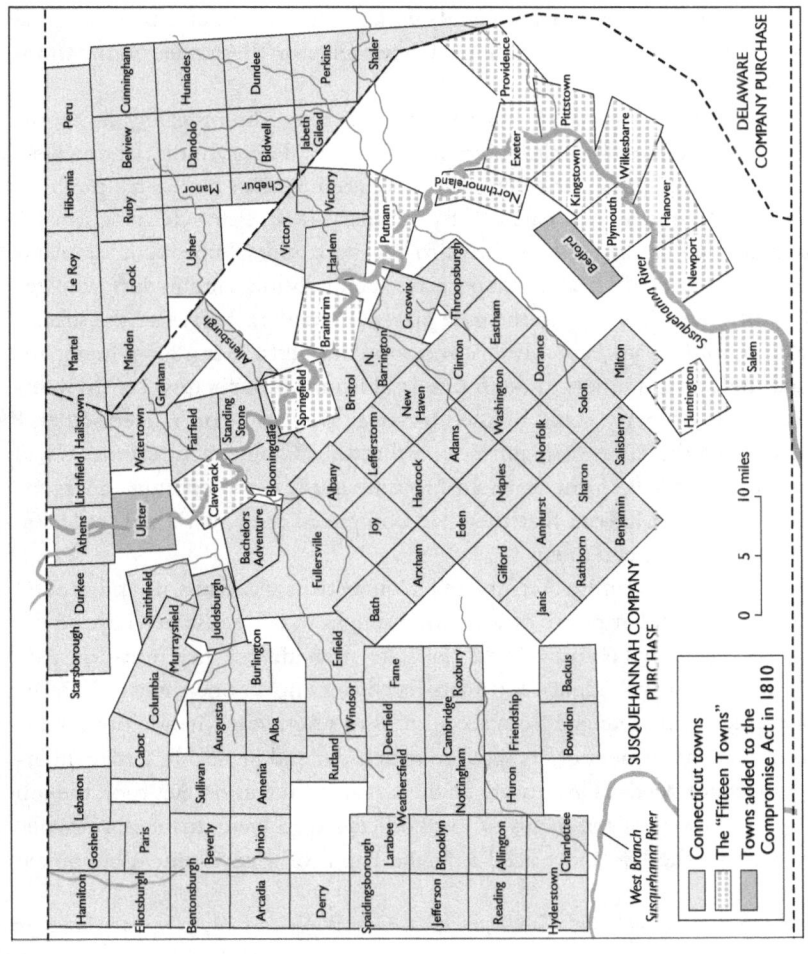

Map 4. Pennsylvania's Upper Susquehanna Valley, 1790–1810

McKean rewarded him with an appointment to the Compromise Act commission.[4] Cooper represented a new breed of Jeffersonian Republican officeholder. Though not leveling radicals by any stretch of the imagination, Republicans like Cooper brought a democratic ethos to government that their more elitist Federalist predecessors lacked. In Pennsylvania, Maine, and elsewhere, such Jeffersonian Republicans were more accommodating to the demands of backcountry farmers and worked hard to quiet rebellious rural folk without undermining private property rights or the landed foundations of elite power.[5]

Thomas Cooper took a no-nonsense approach to administering the Compromise Act and brooked little interference from Pennsylvania landowners, Connecticut claimants, or state officials who attempted to hinder his progress. Cooper's single-mindedness paid off. By February 1800, Pennsylvania claimants had relinquished almost 100,000 acres to the state and Connecticut claimants had applied for title to nearly 50,000 acres. Pennsylvania landholders who refused to turn over their land to the state presented the final barrier to the success of the compromise law. Pennsylvania overcame this obstacle in 1802 when it authorized the commissioners to confiscate land from uncooperative Pennsylvanians so that the property could be used to satisfy the claims of Yankee settlers.[6] By October of the same year, almost one thousand Connecticut claimants had submitted their deeds to the state. In November 1803, the commissioners informed Governor McKean that they had completed their work and settled all land claims in the fifteen towns.[7]

While the Compromise Act quieted Connecticut claimants in and around the fifteen towns, other pieces of legislation sought to end resistance beyond the Wyoming Valley. In February 1801, the state strengthened the Intrusion Act. Under the revised law, Yankee intruders faced fines up to one thousand dollars and prison terms that ranged from six months to seven years. In addition, it authorized the appointment of an agent to search out and prosecute settlers holding Connecticut deeds. This feature of the amended Intrusion Act took the job of enforcement out of the hands of local officials who were unable, or unwilling, to enforce the law and placed it in the hands of a government appointee

---

4. John A. Garraty and Mark C. Carnes, eds., *American National Biography*, 24 vols. (New York, 1999), 5:462.

5. Taylor, *Liberty Men*, 209–32; Alan Taylor, "Agrarian Independence: Northern Land Rioters after the Revolution," in *Beyond the American Revolution: Explorations in the History of American Radicalism*, Alfred F. Young, ed. (DeKalb, IL, 1993), 235–37.

6. Tench Coxe to the House of Representatives, Feb. 13, 1800, and Amendments to the Compromise Act, April 26, 1802, *SCP* 10:494–95, 311–15.

7. Thomas Cooper to Thomas McKean, Oct. 20, 1802, and Thomas Cooper and John M. Taylor to Thomas McKean, Nov. 18, 1803, *SCP* 11:336, 431.

Figure 3. Thomas Cooper. Portrait by Charles Willson Peale. Courtesy, The College of Physicians of Philadelphia

who reported directly to the governor and the assembly.[8] Lawmakers also made it more dangerous for speculators to dabble in the Connecticut claim and freed the courts of Northeast Pennsylvania from Yankee influence. In the spring of 1802, the state passed the Territorial Act. This law struck at the Susquehannah

8. Amendment to the Intrusion Act, Feb. 16, 1801, *SCP* 11:27–31.

and Delaware companies by making it illegal to purchase, sell, or transfer Connecticut deeds issued after the Trenton Decree. Those found guilty of doing so faced heavy fines and imprisonment. Equally important, the act worked to undo Yankee dominance over Northeast Pennsylvania's county courts by barring individuals holding Connecticut titles from serving as judges or jurors in cases concerning the Connecticut claim.[9]

The state of Pennsylvania was not the only power working to undermine the Connecticut claim and uproot Yankee resistance. In 1801 powerful speculators created the Pennsylvania Landholders' Association. The syndicate met at Dunwoody's Tavern in Philadelphia and from this headquarters coordinated their efforts to subdue Yankee resistance. The Landholders' Association brought together men of considerable wealth and social standing. Among the association's members were Henry Drinker, William Bingham, Samuel Meredith, Samuel Hodgdon, Edward Tilghman, Timothy Pickering, James Strawbridge, and other prominent land developers who had battled Wild Yankees through the 1780s and 1790s. Drinker, Strawbridge, and Tilghman served on the association's executive committee while Hodgdon held the position of association president.[10]

Samuel Meredith, who held more than eighty thousand acres in Northeast Pennsylvania, epitomized the power of the association's members. Meredith was a successful Philadelphia merchant and one of the twelve original directors of the Bank of North America. He complemented his extensive commercial and landed interests with a wealth of political connections. In the late 1770s and the 1780s, Meredith served a number of terms in the Pennsylvania Assembly and the Confederation Congress. Between 1789 and 1801, he served as the first Treasurer of the United States.[11] Like many of his associates, Meredith was well placed to forward the Landholders' interests at both the state and national levels.

With the creation of the Landholders' Association, Pennsylvania speculators finally found themselves in a position to exploit their superior wealth and political power. Fully aware of the clout wielded by the association, many state officials sought their patronage and became willing instruments of their designs. Abraham Horn, who was appointed in 1801 as the agent to enforce the intrusion law, read-

---

9. Proposed Act to Maintain the Territorial Rights of Pennsylvania, Feb. 6, 1801, *SCP* 11:34–36.

10. Meeting of the Pennsylvania Claimants, 1801, *PA2* 18:757–58; William Tilghman to Tench Coxe, Jan. 13, 1801, and Organization of the Pennsylvania Landholders Association, Apr. 9, 1801, *SCP* 11:14, 40–43.

11. Phineas G. Goodrich, *History of Wayne County* (Honesdale, PA, 1880), 199–200; *Dictionary of American Biography*, 15:335–36.

ily cooperated with the association and, in return for a salary from the landholders, submitted reports to them detailing the location and disposition of Yankee settlers. Tench Coxe also cooperated with the association while he served as secretary of the Pennsylvania land office between 1800 and 1801. He did so, not for a salary, but to help himself secure his own claims in Northeast Pennsylvania.[12]

As Pennsylvania and the Landholders' Association moved forward, the Delaware and Susquehannah companies lost momentum. Intimidated by Pennsylvania's aggressive stance, the nonresident speculators who had proved so crucial to development of Yankee resistance in the past ncw abandoned the Connecticut claim. In September 1801, John Franklin noted that Silas Pepoon and other prominent Yankee speculators had largely cut their ties with the Susquehannah Company. Even Joseph Hamilton, a firebrand of Yankee resistance during the 1780s and 1790s, neglected to answer Franklin's calls for aid. In the following year, Franklin openly criticized the company's nonresident proprietors, complaining that Yankee settlers bore the brunt of persecution while speculators failed to pay company dues or attend its meetings.[13] Without the assistance of nonresident speculators such as Caleb Benton and Joseph Hamilton support for the Connecticut claim in New England and New York withered, further isolating Pennsylvania's Wild Yankees. Edward Tilghman traveled through Connecticut in the summer of 1802 and happily reported that he found no one in the state who would admit to membership in the Susquehannah and Delaware companies. By 1803 the Susquehannah Company—whose sphere of influence was now restricted to the area around Athens, Pennsylvania—found itself bereft of outside support and badly in need of money.[14]

Deserted by nonresident proprietors, disavowed by the state of Connecticut, and faced with growing dissention among their settlers, the Susquehannah and Delaware companies distanced themselves from agrarian violence and became advocates of accommodation. In the summer of 1801, the guiding light of the Susquehannah Company, John Franklin, wrote to a Pennsylvania landholder expressing his willingness to compromise and settle the dispute before a federal court. In October 1802, company proprietors appointed John Franklin and Samuel Avery to open talks with the Landholders' Association.[15] But the Pennsylvanians refused to recognize the right of Connecticut claimants to bargain

---

12. *SCP* 11:xiv, xviii, xx.
13. John Franklin to John Jenkins, Sept. 16, 1801; John Franklin to Ira Allen, June 27, 1802; and Joseph Kingsberry to Ezekiel Hyde, Aug. 4, 1803, *SCP* 11:195, 331–32, 403–4.
14. Edward Tilghman to Jason Torrey, Sept. 1802, JTP.
15. Letter of May 22, 1801, CCP 1:62; John Franklin to John Jenkins, Apr. 22, 1801; John Franklin to John Field, July 21, 1801; and John Franklin and Samuel Avery to Samuel Hodgdon and Edward Tilghman, Dec. 6, 1802, *SCP* 11:45, 141–42, 344–45; Murray, *A History of Old Tioga*, 409

collectively or appoint representatives for what they preferred to see as a series of individual disputes between legitimate landholders and illegal squatters. The association also refused the company's requests to settle their differences before a federal court or extend the terms of the Compromise Act to lands beyond the fifteen towns. Seeing no other option for salvaging their claims, the Connecticut land companies remained committed to negotiations in spite of the Landholders' Association's uncompromising stance. Talks sputtered on into 1805 without any result.[16]

Not everything went Pennsylvania's way after the passage of the Compromise Act. State efforts to settle property disputes in the Wyoming Valley suffered from incompetence and infighting. The same aggressive attitude that enabled Thomas Cooper to forge ahead with the Compromise Act also brought him into conflict with more conservative officials in the Pennsylvania land office. Cooper alluded to this friction when he wrote to the head of the land office, Tench Coxe, admitting that his "liberal construction" of the act clashed with Coxe's "notions of Prudence and legal precision." Cooper and Coxe's different approaches became glaringly apparent when Yankee settlers continued to hand in Connecticut deeds after the deadline for submitting them had passed. Cooper and the commissioners welcomed these latecomers while Coxe considered the Yankees' tardiness grounds for dismissing their claims. Cooper and Coxe's like-minded successor, Andrew Ellicott, also clashed over the administration of the Compromise Act. On several occasions, Cooper complained of Ellicott's failure to issue state deeds to Connecticut settlers whose claims had been confirmed by the Compromise Act commission. Such foot-dragging, Cooper asserted, only served to spread "far and wide distrust of the State proceedings."[17]

The Pennsylvania Landholders' Association also experienced difficulties in their efforts to break Yankee resistance beyond the fifteen towns. One of the problems the association faced was finding competent agents to promote their interests. James Ralston, who took over the enforcement of the Intrusion Act in 1803, believed that settler resistance would only lessen once the association

---

16. Memorial of the Susquehannah Company to the Pennsylvania Legislature and Connecticut Claimants to the Pennsylvania Landholders' Association, Feb. 23, 1803, SCP 11:360, 373–74; Samuel Hodgdon and Edward Tilghman to Samuel Avery, Joseph Kingsberry, and John Spalding, Mar. 16, 1803, RPLA. Correspondence between John Franklin and the Pennsylvania Landholders' Association is printed in *The Luzerne County Federalist*, Apr. 6 and Apr. 13, 1805, WHGS.

17. For evidence of Cooper's cantankerous relations with Pennsylvania's land office see Thomas Cooper to Tench Coxe, Aug. 1801; Thomas Cooper to Andrew Ellicott, July 8, 1802; Thomas Cooper to Andrew Ellicott, Jan. 14, 1804; and Thomas Cooper to Thomas McKean, Aug. 1, 1804, SCP 11:185–86, 333–34, 496–71, 495–96.

hired men able enough "conduct the business with fairness, temper & decision" and scrupulous enough to forebear from taking "those petty advantages of the Settlers, which Appears to be the Order of the day among those already appointed."[18] Abraham Horn was guilty of the abuses decried by Ralston. Horn became the Landholders' Association's chief agent in 1801—a post he held simultaneously with his appointment by the state as enforcement officer under the Intrusion Act.[19] While serving in these capacities he mixed public duties with private interest. The Intrusion Act specified that any person who provided information that led to a prosecution under the law would receive half of any fine levied.[20] Horn took advantage of this provision. He brought prosecutions against settlers in behalf of the Landholders' Association, used his position as agent of the Intrusion Act to push these indictments through the courts, and then pocketed his share of the fines. Instead of opening good-faith negotiations with settlers, he attempted to entrap them. Both Cooper and Ralston censured this practice, arguing that it only deepened Yankees enmity and did "incalculable" damage to the process of reconciliation.[21]

The indiscretion of association agents was often compounded by their ineffectiveness. After the Landholders' Association replaced Abraham Horn in 1803, they discovered that more than three-fourths of the submissions he had collected during his tenure were not from Connecticut claimants, but from squatters who held neither Pennsylvania nor Connecticut deeds. This practice not only failed to uproot Yankee resistance but created a false impression of progress. State officials also exhibited incompetence. James Ralston, for all his criticisms of Abraham Horn, was equally unwilling to confront Wild Yankees. One Pennsylvania claimant complained that Ralston had failed to familiarize himself with Yankee settlers and remained "ignorant" of their location and strength. After traveling deep into territory controlled by Wild Yankees, association agent Robert Rose bitterly remarked, "Mr. Ralston has not been here, and where he slumbers I do not know."[22]

Another obstacle in the way of the state and the Landholders' Association was their failure to successfully prosecute Yankee settlers under the Intrusion

---

18. James Ralston to the Landholders' Committee, May 17, 1803, RPLA.
19. SCP 11:xix–xx; Samuel Hodgdon to Timothy Pickering, March 21, 1801; Abraham Horn to the Committee of the Pennsylvania Landholders, Sept. 14, 1801; James Strawbridge to Edward Tilghman, July 13, 1801; and Abraham Horn to the Connecticut Intruders, June 24, 1801, SCP 11:38, 95, 126–27, 85.
20. Amendment to the Intrusion Act, Apr. 11, 1795, SCP 11:28.
21. Thomas Cooper to Tench Coxe, Aug. 1801, SCP 11:186–87; James Ralston to the Landholders' Committee, May 17, 1803, RPLA.
22. Robert Rose to Samuel Hodgdon, Aug. 4, 1803, SCP 11:406; John Kidd to Edward Tilghman, Feb. 18, 1803, and Robert Rose to Samuel Hodgdon, Nov. 2, 1803, CCP 2:10, 60.

Act. Although Connecticut claimants were barred from serving as jurors or justices in cases involving land disputes, Yankees found other ways to hobble the legal process. For instance, county commissioners partial to the Connecticut claim refused to pay witnesses involved in the prosecution of Yankee settlers any compensation for the time they spent at court. Without compensation, witnesses balked at the prospect of participating in lengthy court proceedings and, without witnesses to testify against them, those indicted under the Intrusion Act went free.[23] Even after the passage of the Territorial Act in March 1802, Yankees continued to escape prosecution by questioning the legality of the intrusion law.[24] In the summer of 1801, a Luzerne court indicted John Franklin, John Jenkins, Elisha Satterlee, and Joseph Biles for illegally conspiring to sell state lands. Their trial became a test case for the legitimacy of the Intrusion Act when a jury found Franklin and Jenkins guilty but made their verdict contingent on the law being found constitutional. Pennsylvania's Supreme Court decided this question in the state's favor in December 1802. Thus only in 1803 did the Intrusion Act rise above its legal challenges and begin to take effect.[25]

The final stumbling block facing the Landholders' Association was the attitudes and actions of its members. Many of these speculators were unfamiliar with their lands and clung to exaggerated notions of their value. This led many of them to set their prices far beyond what Yankee settlers were willing or able to pay. Robert Rose explained that Connecticut claimants who lived on land not worth more than half-dollar an acre stared "with astonishment" when he told them they would have to pay five times that amount to purchase a Pennsylvania deed. Settlers who could not afford to pay exorbitant prices continued to resist. Land disputes between association members presented another obstacle to quieting Yankee dissidents. James Ralston reported that opposition to state rule had reemerged along Towanda Creek after a Pennsylvania claimant brought ejectment proceedings against settlers who had recently purchased state titles from another Pennsylvania landholder.[26] Finally, landholders held up the process of reconciliation through their own neglect. On more than one occasion, Rose had to inform the association's executive committee that his

23. Report of Abraham Horn to the Landholders' Committee, Feb. 18, 1802, CCP 1:117.
24. Summary of Court Proceedings in Luzerne and Wayne Counties, Dec. 17, 1801, SCP 11:250–51; Robert Rose to Samuel Hodgdon, Nov. 26, 1803, CCP 2:68; Documents no. 1 and no. 2 attached to Samuel Hodgdon and James Strawbridge to Landholders' Committee, Nov. 26, 1801, MPLA.
25. Jury Verdict in the Trial of John Franklin and Others, May 6, 1802, and Ebenezer Bowman to Samuel Hodgdon, May 10, 1802, SCP 11:318–19, 322–23; SCP 11:xxiii; Murray, *History of Old Tioga*, 415.
26. Robert Rose to Henry Drinker, Oct. 10, 1803, and James Ralston to the Committee of the Pennsylvania Landholders, Dec. 10, 1803, SCP 11:420, 442.

negotiations with Connecticut claimants had been foiled by the failure of Pennsylvania landholders to transfer power of attorney to him.[27]

In spite of these setbacks, Pennsylvania and the Landholders' Association managed to mount an effective offensive against the Connecticut claim. As one Connecticut claimant put it, the state and its landholders flooded Northeast Pennsylvania with men who came "with a Determination to Survey Disposes Sel & turn the world upsidedown."[28] Standing alone against Pennsylvania and its most powerful land speculators, Wild Yankees retreated into isolated backwoods settlements from whence they waged a fierce, last-ditch struggle.

"though Yankees are wilde they will not thus be taimed"

Faced with the combined weight of the state of Pennsylvania and the Pennsylvania Landholders' Association, Yankee resistance became more atomized, defensive, and inward looking. The insurgents turned their attention from maintaining the integrity of the Connecticut claim to protecting their farms, their communities, and their status as independent yeomen. Instead of mounting an offensive against state authority as they had done in the 1790s, Wild Yankees only roused themselves on occasions when it was necessary to shield their communities from intruding land agents and surveyors or to punish Connecticut claimants who defected to Pennsylvania. Gone were the days when Yankee rebels plotted to kidnap leading state officials or contemplated independent statehood. However, just because opposition became more guarded and conservative does not mean that it became less determined or violent.

The targets chosen by Wild Yankees reflect the increasingly parochial nature of their resistance. The insurgents focused their attacks on the sheriffs' deputies, land agents, and surveyors who invaded their settlements. Resistance remained particularly strong in a rectangular region that spanned from the headwaters of Wyalusing Creek to the south branch of the Tioga River and from the New York State line to Sugar Creek. On one occasion, the inhabitants of the town of Ulster gathered together and drove off association surveyor William Ellis when he attempted to run lines near their settlement. In a similar episode, people from the town of Smithfield beat the woods for Richard Caton, a land agent and surveyor for Pennsylvania landholder Charles Carroll, when they got

---

27. Robert Rose to Samuel Hodgdon, July 28, 1803; Robert Rose to Samuel Hodgdon, Aug. 11, 1803; Robert Rose to Henry Drinker, Sept. 1, 1803; Robert Rose to Samuel Hodgdon, Sept. 10, 1803; and Robert Rose to Samuel Hodgdon, Sept. 17, 1803, CCP 2:40, 43, 59, 57, 58.

28. Nathaniel Allen to John Jenkins, June 25, 1804, in Murray, *History of Old Tioga*, 420–21.

wind of the fact that he was at work nearby. John Cummings, the association's deputy agent for Lycoming County, managed to escape rough handling at the hands of a settler mob when he narrowly evaded a band of Wild Yankees equipped with all the fixings necessary to administer a coat of tar and feathers.[29] The hostility Ellis, Caton, and Cummings faced was fed by suspicions that were deeply ingrained in struggling farmers across the revolutionary frontier. Settlers who held contested or extralegal claims to the land saw such men as the vanguard of a phalanx of land speculators, lawyers, and government officials who would cheat them out of their lands or, at the very least, make them pay exorbitant prices to maintain possession of their farms. Pennsylvania surveyor John Adlum alluded to this animus when he noted that he and his compatriots were "generally looked upon as a tricky kind of people" by frontier inhabitants and claimed that settlers greeted the news of a surveyor's arrival "with as much satisfaction of a visit from his Satanic Majesty."[30]

In at least one instance, Yankee efforts to defend their communities turned deadly. In the summer of 1803, Henry Donnell, a justice of the peace and association agent for Lycoming County, made repeated attempts to initiate ejectment proceedings against Connecticut claimants along Sugar Creek. In response to Donnell's challenge, the settlers vowed to take action that would "witness to him that though Yankees are wilde they will not thus be taimed." They soon lived up to their promise. On July 27, Edward Gobin, a surveyor working for the Landholders' Association, was shot "through the body with a rifle bullet" and "grievously wounded" while standing near the door of Henry Donnell's home along the south branch of the Tioga River. The leading suspects in Gobin's shooting were "eighteen persons, dressed as Indians, and said to be employed by persons residing on Sugar Creek."[31]

Besides fending off the threat posed by invading surveyors and land agents, Wild Yankees strove to maintain a local base of support for their resistance by threatening (or worse) any Connecticut claimant who cooperated with the state or its landholders. Thomas Smiley became one victim of the insurgents' internal campaign of violence and intimidation. A Baptist preacher and a self-proclaimed "born citizen of Pennsylvania," Smiley came from Hanover, Pennsylvania, and

29. Thomas Cooper to Thomas McKean, Nov. 15, 1802, and Thomas Cooper to Robert Rose, July 2, 1803, *SCP* 11:339, 393; Tench Coxe to the Commissioners, July 29, 1801, Letters from the Secretary of the Land Office to the Commissioners, 1801–04, PHMC.

30. Quote from Adlum in Norman Wilkinson, "The 'Philadelphia Fever' in Northern Pennsylvania," *Pennsylvania History* 20 (Jan. 1953): 47.

31. Nathaniel Allen to John Jenkins, June 25, 1804, in Murray, *History of Old Tioga*, 420–21; Proclamation of Reward for the Perpetrator of the Murder of Edward Gobin, Aug. 11, 1804, *PA4* 4:535–36; Tench Coxe to the Commissioners, July 29, 1801, Letters from the Secretary of the Land Office to the Commissioners, 1801–04, PHMC.

settled along Wyalusing Creek in 1795. Five years later he moved his homestead to Towanda Creek. Like many backcountry inhabitants, Smiley squatted on his land instead of purchasing it. On May 18, 1801, Smiley wrote to Abraham Horn on behalf of neighboring settlers who, like himself, desired to obtain Pennsylvania titles to their lands. Horn not only accepted Smiley's application but also appointed him the associations' deputy agent for Luzerne County. In accepting this post, Smiley claimed that he was a "sincere philanthropist" who only wished to bring peace and prosperity to his community. Wild Yankees saw him in a far less generous light.[32]

Thomas Smiley became a target of Yankee insurgents because of his ties to Pennsylvania claimants and because he threatened local solidarity. Acting on behalf of the association, Smiley collected more than forty signed relinquishments from people who wished to turn in their Connecticut deeds and repurchase their farms from Pennsylvania landholders. His actions soon provoked a response from Wild Yankees. In the predawn hours of July 8, a band of armed men, their faces obscured with blacking, entered a house where Smiley lodged and roused him from his sleep. The insurgents placed a pistol to his chest and forced him to give up relinquishments he had collected. The rioters examined the papers (taking note of who signed them) and then ordered Smiley to burn them. Next, the insurgents marched their captive into the woods. There, in the seclusion of the forest, they covered Smiley's head with tar and feathers and, before letting him go, threatened to do worse if he continued his work for the Landholders' Association.[33]

Bartlett Hinds was another settler who threatened to compromise Yankee resistance and, in doing so, fell victim to violence. In 1801 Hinds broke ranks with his neighbors by turning in his Connecticut deeds and replacing them with Pennsylvania titles. He later compounded this offense when he committed the unpardonable sin of providing state officials with information that led to the prosecution of several Connecticut claimants under the Intrusion Act.[34] On a December night in 1802, Wild Yankees took their revenge when they caught Hinds in a settlement along Wyalusing Creek known as Usher. They forced their way into a home where Hinds was lodging and dragged him outside.

---

32. Clement F. Heverly, *Patriot and Pioneer Families of Bradford County, Pennsylvania*, 2 vols. (Towanda, PA, 1915), 1:250; Thomas Smiley to Abraham Horn, May 18, 1801 and July 16, 1801 and Abraham Horn to the Intruders in Luzerne and Lycoming Counties, June 24, 1801, in David Craft, *History of Bradford County, Pennsylvania* (Philadelphia, 1878), 45–46.

33. Deposition of Thomas Smiley, July 15, 1801, in Craft, *History of Bradford County*, 45–46; Document no. 1 attached to a letter from Samuel Hodgdon and James Stewart to Pennsylvania Landholders Committee, Nov. 26, 1801, RPLA.

34. Abraham Horn to Tench Coxe, Sept. 18, 1801, CCP 1:87.

The rioters then tied Hinds to a horse's tail and, prodding the animal to a gallop, dragged him through Wyalusing Creek. Next, the mob pulled their victim from the water, tore off his clothes, and drew him around (and sometimes through) a bonfire topped with his own flaming effigy. The rioters then released their burnt and beaten victim, warning Hinds that if he did not leave the country in three months they would put him to death. Thomas Cooper later assured Governor McKean that the riot arose "from [a] *private* revenge against Hinds" and that it owed "more to the fumes of liquor more than to any permanent, or systematic opposition." Cooper's assessment of the disturbance rested on a false distinction: the assault on Bartlett Hinds was as much a feature of the Northeast Pennsylvania's contest over property and power as a local quarrel between settlers.[35]

The attacks on Smiley and Hinds were but two episodes in a growing struggle between Wild Yankees and their more compromise-minded neighbors. The insurgents increasingly had to shift their attention from threats that emanated from beyond the borders of their settlements to challenges that emerged from within. This deepening internal conflict was reflected in the bitter comments of an anonymous "Yankee Farmer" that appeared in the *Luzerne County Federalist* in the fall of 1801: "Let those dastardly souls who are intimidated by the Intrusion law . . . creep and cringe to the agents of Pennsylvania land jobbers—abandon their lands, and apply for counterfeit grace where nothing just and equitable is to be granted—such men are not worthy to be called Yankees." Ulster's Wild Yankees echoed these sentiments when they announced that those who relinquished their Connecticut deeds were "traitors unworthy to live among full blooded Yankees" and vowed to punish anyone who cooperated with the state by refusing to "oblige them with the least thing to support life." Thomas Smiley testified to the effectiveness of these tactics when he informed Samuel Hodgdon that several of his neighbors wanted to purchase Pennsylvania titles but "dare not for the mob."[36]

Neighborhood-level conflicts that pitted Yankees against Yankees increasingly set the tone of Northeast Pennsylvania's agrarian disturbances. On one occasion, George Welles, a native of Glastonbury, Connecticut, "was obliged [to] make his escape" from his Athens home when his work for the powerful Pennsylvania claimant Charles Carroll brought him into open conflict with his

---

35. Samuel Hodgdon to Timothy Pickering, Jan. 13, 1803, *SCP* 11:368; Emily C. Blackman, *History of Susquehanna County, Pennsylvania* (Philadelphia, 1873), 21–22; Thomas Cooper to Thomas McKean, Jan. 18, 1803, *SCP* 11:369. For a list of Hinds's assailants see Craft, *History of Bradford County*, 46–47, and *The Luzerne County Federalist*, Apr. 25, 1803, WHGS.

36. *The Luzerne County Federalist*, Oct. 10, 1801; Joseph Kingsbury to John Jenkins, June 28, 1801; and Thomas Smiley to Samuel Hodgdon, July 16, 1801, *SCP* 11:212–13, 96, 130.

neighbors. Zephon Flower, another Athens resident, became a target of Wild Yankees when he abandoned his Connecticut rights and began working for the Landholders' Association as a surveyor. Settlers cut off the mane and tail of Flower's horse, threatened him with violence, and shot at him from ambush. Likewise, along Wyalusing Creek, an inhabitant who had offered to work for Pennsylvania surveyor Jason Torrey had a change of heart after several of his neighbors threatened to kill him.[37]

As resistance retreated into backwoods communities so did conflict. Busy defending their hold on local allegiance, Wild Yankees relinquished the initiative to the state and its landholders and soon surveyors and land agents crisscrossed Northeast Pennsylvania looking for opportunities to undermine settler insurgency. The localization of Yankee resistance placed a greater burden on settler solidarity, for it enabled Pennsylvania and its land claimants to focus more and more pressure on holdouts. As a result, struggles over individual loyalty and community allegiance only intensified.

"the eternal rules of right"

Wild Yankees forged a culture of resistance that both informed and grew out of their decades-long fight for land and autonomy. This process was not unique to Northeast Pennsylvania but occurred whenever disputes over land, debt, and taxes threatened the independence of farm families. On one level, Yankee resistance culture was nothing more than a collection of tactics, rituals, and motifs the insurgents borrowed from Old World traditions of popular protest, the memory of the American Revolution, and the experience of frontier life. On another, more meaningful level, Yankee resistance culture was a product of the ideas and aspirations that motivated their insurgency. Specifically, it was a visible, often violent expression of their pursuit of landed independence.

Reconstructing the constellation of ideas, values, and beliefs that constituted agrarian insurgents' mental world is no easy task. In a time when few people penned written accounts of their lives and when only a fraction of these actively reflected on themselves and their society, it is not surprising that hardworking farmers have left behind precious little in the way of documents that describe their attitudes and beliefs. Although it is difficult to come to grips with the mental outlook of agrarian insurgents, it is possible to examine behaviors that express and reflect it.

37. Extract of a Letter from Wayne County, CCP 1:76; Heverly, *Pioneer and Patriot Families*, 2:22; Murray, *History of Old Tioga*, 419; Jason Torrey to Edward Tilghman, Apr. 20, 1803, JTP.

The ways in which the insurgents punished their victims reveals that Yankee resistance drew on trans-Atlantic traditions of popular protest. A European practice variously known as "rough music," "skimmington," or in France, *charivari* contributed to the texture of agrarian violence in Northeast Pennsylvania and across the revolutionary frontier. No matter what it was called or where it was found, the practice was largely the same. Rough music was a form of popular, extralegal justice aimed at those—usually wife beaters, adulterers, and prostitutes—who challenged community-sanctioned moral and social norms. People commonly turned to rough music in cases where courts, due to a lack of jurisdiction or inclination, would not intercede. A typical episode of rough music began with a riotous procession of people, often disguised, who marched to the dwelling of an offender accompanied by the "rough music" of banging pots and pans, shouting, and discordant instruments. The mob might satisfy itself with "serenading" its target or perhaps burning them in effigy. On other occasions, however, rough music would culminate in a brutal physical attack.[38] This European practice made its way to America. In Elizabeth, New Jersey, a band of about a dozen disguised men stripped and flogged several known wife beaters in the early 1750s. Likewise, in Rye, New York, a man who had abandoned his wife and children also became the victim of a violent skimmington in 1768.[39]

The rituals of rough music framed Wild Yankee attacks. In 1799, Yankee rioters along the upper Delaware mobbed Long Island immigrant Judge Post and burned him in effigy for his support for the authority and soil rights of Pennsylvania. The 1802 assault upon Bartlett Hinds also contained several

38. On European traditions of rough music, see Violet Alford, "Rough Music or Charivari," *Folklore* 70 (Dec. 1959): 505–18; Martin Ingram, "Ridings, Rough Music, and Mocking Rhymes in Early Modern England," in *Popular Culture in Seventeenth-Century England*, ed. Barry Reay (London, 1985), 166–97; Natalie Zemon Davis, "The Reasons of Misrule: Youth Groups and Charivaris in Sixteenth-Century France," *Past and Present* 50 (Feb. 1971): 41–75; and David Underdown, "The Taming of the Scold," in *Order and Disorder in Early Modern England*, ed. Anthony Fletcher and John Stevenson (New York, 1985), 116–36.

39. For a discussion of the transmission of European traditions of rough music to the New World and how they shaped popular unrest in Anglo-America, see Alfred F. Young, "English Plebeian Culture and Eighteenth-Century American Radicalism," in *The Origins of Anglo-American Radicalism*, ed. Margaret and James Jacob (London, 1984), 184–212, and Steven J. Stewart, "Skimmington in the Middle and New England Colonies," in *Riot and Revelry in Early America*, ed. William Pencak, Matthew Denis, and Simon P. Newman (University Park, 2002), 41–86. For a fuller description of the skimmingtons in Elizabeth, New Jersey, and Rye, New York, see Brendan McConville, "The Rise of Rough Music: Reflections on an Ancient New Custom in Eighteenth-Century New York," and Thomas J. Humphrey, "Crowd and Court: Rough Music and Popular Justice in Colonial New York," in *Riot and Revelry*, 87, 107.

elements common to European and American rough music including the stripping and parading of Hinds by a riotous procession and the burning of his effigy.[40] In a similar fashion, Wild Yankees drew on traditions of popular protest when they cut off the mane and tail of Zephon Flower's horse. Shaving, cutting, or burning the hair of their victims was a common punishment meted out by rough music mobs. In 1735, a group of women near Philadelphia cut off half the hair and beard of a man who beat his wife. Fifty years later, Pennsylvania farmers, outraged at the federal government's whiskey excise, assaulted tax collector William Graham and, in a grotesquely comic skimmington, "cut off one half of his hair, cued the other half on the side of his head, cut off the Cock of his Hat, and made him wear it in a form to render his Cue the most Conspicuous." Perhaps the Wild Yankees, unable to lay their hands on Flower, contented themselves by applying the rites of rough music to his horse.[41]

The violent rituals employed by Yankee rioters also reflect the degree to which the memory and experience of the American Revolution colored their struggle against Pennsylvania. The settlers who attacked Thomas Smiley in 1801 acted in ways that would have been familiar to the patriot mobs of the 1760s and 1770s. In an act that mimicked the numerous instances where crowds forced imperial officials to renounce their loyalty to Britain by compelling them to destroy official documents, Smiley's assailants had him turn over papers related to his work as agent for the Landholders' Association and made him burn them. Moreover, Smiley's attackers evoked the unruly spirit of America's independence movement by subjecting him to a punishment that had become synonymous with revolutionary-era crowd actions: a coat, or in Smiley's case, a cap, of tar and feathers.[42]

A second practice that bears scrutiny is agrarian insurgents' habit of donning disguises when carrying out acts of resistance. Timothy Pickering's kidnappers, Thomas Smiley's assailants, and the Wild Yankees who shot Edward Gobin all disguised themselves by blacking their faces and donning "Indian" garb that

40. Goodrich, *History of Wayne County*, 28; Samuel Hodgdon to Timothy Pickering, Jan. 13, 1803, and Thomas Cooper to Thomas McKean, Jan. 18, 1803, *SCP* 11:368–69; Blackman, *History of Susquehanna County*, 21–22.

41. Murray, *History of Old Tioga*, 419; Steven J. Stewart, "Skimmington in the Middle and New England Colonies," in *Riot and Revelry*, 46; Dorsey Pentacost to Council, Apr. 16, 1786, *PA1* 10:757.

42. A description of the assault on Smiley can be found in Craft, *History of Bradford County*, 46. For a discussion of mob behavior during the Revolution see Dirk Hoerder, "Boston Leaders and Boston Crowds, 1765–1776," in *The American Revolution: Explorations in the History of American Radicalism*, ed. Alfred F. Young (DeKalb, IL, 1976), 233–71; and Young, "English Plebeian Culture," 194.

usually included a handkerchief wrapped around the head and a blanket draped over the body.[43] Such behavior was not limited to Northeast Pennsylvania. Vermont's Green Mountain Boys disguised themselves as Indians in order to intimidate settlers, speculators, and officials from New York. Likewise, Maine's Liberty Men wore blankets and other elements of an Indian disguise when they assaulted sheriffs' deputies and proprietary agents. Their native persona was so elaborate that they later became known as "White Indians." The land riots that periodically erupted in New York's Hudson Valley between the mid eighteenth and mid nineteenth centuries also featured rural insurgents dressed as Indians. As in Maine, the disguise developed by New York's antirent Indians became quite elaborate, which points to the fact that such garb was not just a disguise meant to hide one's identity but also a visual symbol meant to convey messages.[44]

This use of disguise again calls attention to the ways in which Old World traditions of popular protest contributed to agrarian resistance. The European folk custom of mummery—a form of mocking, rowdy street theater performed by costumed or otherwise disguised players—provided rural insurgents with a set of protest motifs.[45] Mumming was but one aspect of a much larger tradition of festive misrule that undergirded popular protest. With their identities hidden from view, mummers could abrogate social norms and criticize their social betters without fear of reprisals.[46] The traditions of festive misrule survived in American celebrations like Boston's "Pope's Day." Pope's Day was a New England rendition of Britain's Guy Fawkes's Day, which every November 5 commemorated the failure of a 1605 plot by Fawkes and several other English Catholics to blow up Parliament. This holiday saw rowdy processions of revelers with blacked faces and outlandish costumes fill Boston's streets and culminated in a brawl between gangs drawn from the city's plebeian North and

---

43. Charles W. Upham, *The Life of Timothy Pickering*, 4 vols. (Boston, 1873), 2:381–82; Proclamation of Reward for the Perpetrator of the Murder of Edward Gobin, Aug. 11, 1804, *PA4* 4:535–36.

44. Michael Bellesiles, *Revolutionary Outlaws: Ethan Allen and the Struggle for Independence on the Early American Frontier* (Charlottesville, VA, 1993), 91; Taylor, *Liberty Men*, 89, 184–90; Reeve Huston, *Land and Freedom: Rural Society, Popular Protest, and Party Politics in Antebellum New York* (New York, 2000), 116–24. Taylor and Huston's works include good discussions of the symbolic and psychological dimensions of Indian disguise.

45. For a discussion of European traditions of mumming, see Herbert Halpert, "A Typology of Mumming," in *Christmas Mumming in Newfoundland*, ed. Herbert Halpert and G.M. Story (Toronto, 1969), 35–61.

46. Peter Burke, *Popular Culture in Early Modern Europe* (New York, 1978), 178–204, esp. 185–91, 199–204; Simon P. Newman, *Parades and the Politics of the Street: Festive Culture in the Early American Republic* (Philadelphia, 1997), 11, 19–20, 24; Young, "English Plebeian Culture," 184–212.

South Ends—the victor of which won the privilege of burning an effigy of the Pope on Boston Common. Besides asserting their Protestant identity, the revelers readily pounced on any gentleman or officer of the law who foolishly tried to interfere with their violent celebrations. Thus Pope's Day was an occasion for the city's lower classes to subvert, if but in a temporary and limited way, order and social restraint.[47]

Like their European counterparts, early America's rural inhabitants blacked their faces and donned disguises to hide their identities from authorities and—in the role-shifting tradition of European mummery—to transform themselves from farmers into agrarian rebels. However, unlike mummers and rioters in Europe, who dressed as devils, wild men, or women, America's agrarian insurgents invariably disguised themselves as Indians. That rural rebels habitually took on an Indian persona points to the ways in which the American Revolution and the experience of frontier life framed agrarian resistance. In the wake of the Boston Tea Party and numerous other episodes of anti-imperial protest, the Indian became an image associated with the patriot movement, America, and the Revolution. Thus, in dressing like Indians, agrarian insurgents associated themselves with the memory of, and drew legitimacy from, America's independence movement.[48] The use of Indian disguise was also a product of intercultural contact along the frontier. In a curious cross-cultural coincidence, blacking one's face was a custom both among European rioters and Indian men who set out on the warpath.[49] Frontier settlers who had once lived under the threat of Indian war parties usurped the image of the bloodthirsty Indian and turned it into an effective terror tactic.[50] Land agents and surveyors who ventured into the backcountry feared that people who looked like Indians might be as savage as Indians. As it turned out, their fears were not groundless. In Pennsylvania, Wild Yankees disguised as Indians shot and dangerously wounded Pennsylvania surveyor Edward Gobin. In New

---

47. Gary Nash, *The Urban Crucible* (Cambridge, MA, 1979), 260–61; Hoerder, "Boston Leaders and Boston Crowds," 242; Newman, *Parades and the Politics*, 20–22.

48. America was consistently represented as an Indian in the prolific and lively political cartoons of the revolutionary era. Examples of this can be found in Peter D. G. Thomas, *The American Revolution*, The English Satirical Print Series (Cambridge, 1986), 48–49, 60–61, 70–71, 84–85; H. T. Dickinson, *Caricatures and the Constitution, 1760–1832*, The English Satirical Print Series (Cambridge, 1986), 58–59, 74–75, 84–85; and John D. Dolmetsh, *Eighteenth-Century Prints in Colonial America* (Williamsburg, VA, 1979), 184–85, 192–95.

49. Paul A. W. Wallace, *Indians of Pennsylvania*, 2d ed., revised by William A. Hunter (Harrisburg, PA, 1981), 24; Reuben Gold Thwaites, ed., *The Jesuit Relations and Allied Documents: Travels and Explorations of the Jesuit Missionaries in New France, 1610–1791* (Cleveland, OH, 1899), 38:249–53, 49:231.

50. Taylor, *Liberty Men*, 190–94, 197–99.

York's Hudson Valley and Maine, agrarian insurgents dressed in "Native" garb gunned down several men.[51]

The language insurgents deployed to portray their cause provides another window into Yankee resistance culture. It is important not to equate words with belief. On one level, such polemics are simply propaganda and, as such, are rife with interpretive pitfalls. However, insight can be gained by focusing, not so much on what agrarian insurgents said, but how they said it. Approached in this way, Yankee rhetoric again reveals the Revolution's influence on Yankee resistance. In a petition sent to the Pennsylvania legislature, Connecticut claimants complained about the agents employed by the Landholders' Association, referring to them as "Pimps, Spies, tidewaiters, and Informers." This language was steeped in the memory of America's battle against Britain's revenue-gathering policies during the 1760s and 1770s. That Wild Yankees described association agents as "tidewaiters" shows that they drew a parallel between them and the imperial officials who had sought to enforce unpopular economic regulations. When Connecticut claimants referred to their opponents at "court sycophants," they were drawing on the country versus court imagery that framed patriot diatribes against Britain. Yankee settlers clearly had the Revolution on their minds when they declared that "an equal distribution of property, and not engrossing large domains, is the basis of a free and equal government, founded on republican principles."[52]

Wild Yankees, Massachusetts's Shaysites, western Pennsylvania's whiskey rebels, and Maine's Liberty Men all summoned popular understandings of the Revolution to inspire and legitimize their uprisings.[53] The ideas of English philosopher John Locke gained currency during the Revolution and provided agrarian insurgents with concepts that justified their actions. Locke's contention that only labor could transform land in a state of nature into property legitimized squatters' extralegal possession of their farms and undermined speculators' "paper" claims to undeveloped frontier land.[54] While it was unlikely that backcountry farmers had direct access to Locke's writings, a handful of

---

51. Proclamation of Reward for the Perpetrator of the Murder of Edward Gobin, Aug. 11, 1804, *PA4* 4:535–36; Taylor, "Agrarian Independence": 222–23; Taylor, *Liberty Men*, 199–205; Huston, *Land and Freedom*, 147.

52. Memorial of the Susquehannah Company to the Pennsylvania Legislature, *SCP* 11:365; Minutes of a Meeting Held in Wyoming, July 20, 1786, *SCP* 8:371–72.

53. David P. Szatmary, *Shays' Rebellion: The Making of an Agrarian Insurrection* (Amherst, MA, 1980), 92–97; Leonard Richards, *Shays's Rebellion: The American Revolution's Final Battle* (Philadelphia, 2002), 67–68; Taylor, *Liberty Men*, 5–6, 14–17, 112–14; Thomas Slaughter, *The Whiskey Rebellion: Frontier Epilogue to the American Revolution* (New York, 1986), 29–36, 127–33; Bellesiles, *Revolutionary Outlaws*, 105–7.

54. Bernard Bailyn, *The Ideological Origins of the American Revolution* (Cambridge, MA, 1967), 27–30; John Locke, *Second Treatise of Government*, Richard Cox, ed. (Arlington Heights, IL, 1982), 17–31, 58–78, 130–48.

agrarian pamphleteers such as Massachusetts's James Shurtleff exposed rural people to his ideas. Pennsylvania's Wild Yankees expressed themselves in ways that were consistent with Locke's thinking. In July 1786, a gathering of Connecticut claimants proclaimed "that the labours bestowed in subduing a rugged wilderness were our own, and can never be wrested from us without infringing the eternal rules of right."[55]

In addition to salting their writings with references to the Revolution, Wild Yankees frequently turned to religious themes. In 1793 Samuel Baker wrote a scathing letter to James Strawbridge in which he observed that Strawbridge might "excape punishment by the Law of men" but would be surely brought to justice by "the Law of God" for his crimes against Connecticut claimants. On another occasion, an anonymous Yankee author who styled himself the "Luzerne Lay Preacher" asserted that the only way to account for the behavior of the Landholders' Association was to blame it on the influence of the "arch deceiver," Satan. Sugar Creek's settlers also couched their support of the Connecticut claim in religious terms. They declared that the titles to their lands were "derived and can be regularly traced from the Great Proprietor and Master of the Universe" and that Pennsylvania had no better claim to the land than "Satan had to the kingdom of the Earth." Here and elsewhere, Wild Yankees portrayed their struggle as a cosmic battle between the forces of good and evil. This language was not limited to the insurgents' rank and file. The leading Connecticut claimant John Jenkins wrote that, if worse came to worst, God would vindicate their soil rights through a "Supernatural Interference."[56]

That Wild Yankees employed such religious rhetoric is consistent with the relationship between religion and agrarian unrest elsewhere along the revolutionary frontier. A series of religious revivals swept through the United States in the decades surrounding independence. This religious upheaval saw evangelical Protestant denominations—Baptists, Free Will Baptists, Universalists, Methodists—grow in power and numbers at the expense of older, more traditional denominations such as the Congregational, Episcopalian, and Presbyterian churches. For example, the Methodist Episcopal Church experienced an unprecedented surge of growth, expanding from about a thousand members in 1770 to over a quarter of a million just fifty years later. In keeping with the Revolution's republican ethos, these denominations forwarded a more popular,

---

55. Taylor, *Liberty Men*, 101–5; Minutes of a Meeting Held in Wyoming, July 20, 1786, *SCP* 8:371.
56. Samuel Baker to James Strawbridge, 1793, James Strawbridge Papers, HSP; The "Luzerne Lay Preacher" No. 2, Mar. 23, 1805, and Proceedings of a settlers meeting held at Sugar Creek on Aug. 10, 1803, *The Luzerne County Federalist*, WHGS; John Jenkins to Noah Murray, March 21, 1802, *SCP* 11:304–5.

democratic brand of Christianity in which lay people played a dominant role in shaping religious life and institutions.[57]

The Baptists, Methodists, Universalists, and other evangelical denominations that grew out of America's revolutionary-era revivals did make deep inroads into religious life in Northeast Pennsylvania. The Baptists, who had been active in the Wyoming Valley before the Revolutionary War, established several congregations in roughhewn Yankee settlements along the Pennsylvania–New York border during the 1790s. The Universalists joined the Baptists in Northeast Pennsylvania and, under the tutelage of one-time Baptist mister, Noah Murray, soon developed a strong following in Athens and the surrounding area.[58] In keeping with national patterns, the Methodists also gained a substantial number of adherents. In 1788, blacksmith and lay preacher Anning Owen formed a Methodist "class" at Ross Hill in the Wyoming Valley. In the 1790s a number of Methodist congregations sprang up along the Pennsylvania–New York state line and, ultimately, came to constitute a series of stops for itinerant Methodist clergy known as the Tioga Circuit.[59]

These same evangelical denominations promoted a set of beliefs that supported backcountry farmers in their clashes with powerful speculators and government officials. Religious dissenters in North Carolina played a prominent role in the colony's regulator movement in the 1760s and 1770s. Likewise, people associated with a number of evangelical sects in Maine promoted the region's agrarian insurgency; indeed, many leading religious seekers were also prominent White Indians. Drawing on Martin Luther's concept of the "priesthood of all believers"—that all devout Christians could commune directly with God without the aid of religious authorities—evangelical Christianity imbued its adherents with a sense of spiritual equality and self-worth. In turn, this spiritual leveling furnished backcountry inhabitants with a religiously inspired critique of wealth and authority. Agrarian insurgents justified their rebellion against traditional sources of authority by claiming that they obeyed a higher, spiritual law. In addition, they challenged the very sources of

---

57. Nathan O. Hatch, *The Democratization of American Christianity* (New Haven, CT, 1989); Jon Butler, *Awash in a Sea of Faith: Christianizing the American People* (Cambridge, MA, 1990), 220–22; John Wigger, *Taking Heaven by Storm: Methodism and the Rise of Popular Christianity in America* (New York, 1998), 3–6; Alan Taylor, *Liberty Men*, 131–42.

58. Craft, *History of Bradford County*, 127–32, 168–69, 363; Murray, *History of Old Tioga*, 324–25, 556–57.

59. Craft, *History of Bradford County*, 148–58; Amasa F. Chaffee, *History of the Wyoming Conference of the Methodist Episcopal Church* (New York, 1904), 3–4, 12–14, 36–37; *Minutes of the Annual Conferences of the Methodist Episcopal Church for the Years 1773–1828* (New York, 1840), 46–47, 92–94, 183–88.

elite power—money, the law, and political office—by claiming that such things had little merit in God's eyes.[60]

European traditions of popular protest, the American Revolution, and evangelical Christianity constitute important dimensions of Yankee resistance culture but they do not fully encompass it. These cultural and historical antecedents provided rural insurgents with a ready-made set of tactics, rituals, and rhetorical devices. Nonetheless, these instruments of agrarian resistance should not be confused with the larger goal and motivating force behind it. Rural unrest was fueled by the pursuit of independence and anchored in ordinary farmers' efforts to secure land and the economic, political, and social benefits its possession conveyed.

Wild Yankee polemics were laden with religious references, but Yankee resistance was not predicated on any specific religious outlook. Faith in the concept of landed independence transcended differences in religious outlook and crossed denominational lines. In particular, evangelical Christians numbered both among Wild Yankees and their opponents. Unlike Maine or North Carolina, where backcountry insurgents faced off against elites who were almost invariably members of the state-supported Congregationalist and Anglican churches, Pennsylvania's history of religious pluralism helped to keep denominational membership from becoming enmeshed in the revolutionary frontier's struggle over property and power.[61] A number of deeply committed Wild Yankees were prominent figures in the region's evangelical churches. One active proponent of Yankee resistance in the 1780s was the minister of Pittston's Baptist congregation, James Finn. Another was Stephen Ballard, a prominent Methodist layman whose home along Sugar Creek became the site of the Tioga Circuit's quarterly meetings. But there were also evangelicals who actively promoted accommodation to the state. The Baptist minister Thomas Smiley was one of these; Bartlett Hinds, a leading Baptist along Wyalusing Creek, was another.[62]

---

60. Marjoline Kars, *Breaking Loose Together: The Regulator Rebellion in Pre-Revolutionary North Carolina* (Chapel Hill, NC, 2002), 83, 86–87, 98–100; Taylor, *Liberty Men*, 134–36, 141–47; Alan Taylor, "Nathan Barlow's Journey: Mysticism and Popular Protest on the Northeastern Frontier" in *Maine in the Early Republic*, ed. Charles E. Clark James S. Leamon, and Karen Bowden (Hanover, NH, 1988), 100–117.
61. Kars, *Breaking Loose Together*, 107–10, 180–81, 184; Taylor, *Liberty Men*, 131–42.
62. Stewart Pearce, *Annals of Luzerne County* (Philadelphia, 1866), 300–301; Craft, *History of Bradford County*, 148–49; Blackman, *History of Susquehanna County*, 302. Historians who have explored the relationship between religion and backcountry unrest in Massachusetts have noted a similar lack of correlation between an evangelical outlook and agrarian activism: William G. McLoughlin, *New England Dissent, 1630–1881*, vol. 2, *The Baptists and the Separation of Church and State* (Cambridge, MA, 1971), 752–53, 777–80; John L. Brooke, "A Deacon's Orthodoxy: Religion, Class, and the Moral Economy of Shays's Rebellion," in *In Debt to Shays*, ed. Robert A. Gross (Charlottesville, VA, 1993), 206–8, 210, 221.

A close inspection of Yankee rhetoric also demonstrates that settlers drew inspiration more from the ideal of agrarian independence than from the ideology of the American Revolution. Pioneers who labored to clear forests and build farms did not have to read Locke to understand how labor transformed land into valuable property. Likewise, the idea that those who occupied and worked a piece of land had more of a right to it than those who held legal title was not something a backcountry farmer needed to learn from the Founding Fathers. Such an argument would have been second nature to people who battled land speculators for possession of their farms and who were familiar with the common law principle that "possession is nine parts of the law."[63] Yankee settlers bolstered their resolve, not by referencing America's recent struggle against Britain, but by remembering their struggles against Pennsylvania, Pennsylvania landholders, Indians, and Tories. In a petition to Congress, Yankee settlers spoke of converting a "howling wilderness into cultivated fields" that had been "repeatedly fertilized with their blood" and the "bones and ashes of their brethren." Similar addresses told Yankees that they were fighting against Pennsylvania's "Popish Inquisitors" for land "still reaking with the mangled carcases and blood of your dearest friends, whose scattered bones are still whitening in the sun." In sum, Connecticut claimants believed that they and their forbearers had paid for their lands in ways that could never be compensated with anything short of full possession of their farms.[64]

The parallels that have been drawn between the behavior of America's rural rebels and European mobs also need to be carefully considered in light of what they can reveal about agrarian insurgents' attitudes, values, and motives. Some scholars have argued that these similar behaviors reflect a deeper ideological continuity; namely, a popular, class-conscious mentality rooted in a "moral economy" of long-standing notions of economic and social justice.[65] Wild Yankees and European rioters may have used similar methods and motifs, but they did not share a similar outlook. They were different people with different aspirations who lived in very different worlds. The premise that agrarian insurgents who acted like European rioters possessed the mental outlook of Europe's underclass is no more likely than the assertion that frontier rebels who dressed like Indians thought like Indians.

---

63. Patricia Seed, "Taking Possession and Reading Texts: Establishing the Authority of Overseas Empires," *WMQ* 49 (Apr. 1992): 190.

64. Petition to Congress from Connecticut Claimants, Nov. 1801, *SCP* 11:234; William Judd's Address to the Settlers at Wyoming, Apr. 13, 1787, *SCP* 9:98. Other examples of such talk can be found in Petition of John Franklin and Others to the Connecticut General Assembly, Oct. 20, 1784, and Minutes of a Meeting Held in Wyoming, July 20, 1786, *SCP* 8:123–26, 370.

65. Kars, *Breaking Loose Together*, 120–21, 215; Ruth Bogin, "Petitioning and the New Moral Economy of Post-Revolutionary America," *WMQ* 45 (July 1988): 397–402; Barbara Clark Smith, "Food Rioters and the American Revolution," *WMQ* 51 (Jan. 1994): 4–5, 8–15.

Similarities in behavior between European and American, rural and urban rioters do not necessarily equate into similar beliefs because the meaning of any activity greatly depends on the context in which it takes place. What made mummery and festive misrule such an effective method of social protest in Europe was that they were aimed at an elite audience. Old World protesters dressed and behaved as they did because they were trying to communicate messages to their social betters. This also appears to be the case with festive misrule in early American cities. A description of Boston's eighteenth-century Christmas celebrations provided by Samuel Beck, a gentleman of that city, illustrates how mumming functioned in America, as it did in Europe, as a form of role-reversal and incipient social protest. Beck told of "a set of the lowest blackguards" called "Anticks" who, "with masked faces" and "great insolence," went from house to house invading "rooms that were occupied by parties of ladies and gentlemen" and did not leave until their "hosts" rewarded them with money, food, or drink. Besides the prospect of gaining some cash or a good meal, Boston's mummers entered the homes of the well-to-do to temporarily assert themselves over their social betters, remind the rich of their obligations to the poor, and at least on a symbolic level, coerce a redistribution of wealth.[66] The American backcountry did not possess the same social landscape as Europe or America's cities. In the case of Northeast Pennsylvania, there was often no elite audience to observe the rituals of agrarian protest, for the wealthy Pennsylvanian landholders who opposed Yankee soil rights lived far away from the contested region. Wild Yankees directed their actions, not against their social betters, but against people much like themselves. They may have borrowed the outward forms of European unrest, but these elements did not operate in a similar context or convey the same class-infused meanings.

Rather than being propelled by a common, trans-Atlantic "moral economy," agrarian resistance in early America was driven by a distinct set of moral imperatives that revolved around the ideal of personal independence. The moral economy of Europe's lower orders rested on issues like the fair pricing for basic necessities such as food, the protection of time-honored rights, and the enforcement of long-standing customs of noblesse oblige. Riots and protest erupted when people transgressed this moral economy by engaging in price gouging, by threatening people's traditional rights, or by refusing to fulfill their obligations to others.[67] For Wild Yankees and other agrarian insurgents, the struggle to obtain social justice did not revolve around the price of bread but

66. For a discussion of European traditions of mumming, see Herbert Halpert, "A Typology of Mumming," 35–61 (quote from Samuel Beck on 52).

67. E. P. Thompson, "The Moral Economy of the English Crowd in the Eighteenth Century," *Past and Present* 50 (1971): 76–131.

the price of land. More to the point, it hinged on the deeper issues of land ownership and independence. The moral economy of early America's land rioters was a vision of a society in which the economic, political, and social benefits conveyed to white men through land ownership would trump all other claims to property—be they from wealthy gentlemen, government officials, or Indians.[68]

The independence-oriented moral economy of early America's rural folk comes through in the words Wild Yankees used to portray their struggle. In an address to Wyoming's settlers, Yankee stalwart William Judd described the Connecticut claim as the "fair inheritance of your fathers, purchased, settled, and defended by your prowess" and reminded them that their freehold farms were "unclogged by the shackles of rents or tyths or any other engine of despotism." Having painted this picture of propertied independence, Judd went on to warn of Pennsylvania's "avowed design to impoverish and thereby disable" Connecticut claimants "from holding and enjoying the fruits of your purchase and labour." In a similar fashion, the anonymous "Yankee Farmer" explained that the farm "I now possess and occupy is considered a valuable one" but warned his readers that, on submission to state and its landholders, they "must either become tenants to the Pennsylvania land jobbers or abandon their land forever and seek a precarious subsistence elsewhere." Once again, independence and competency was juxtaposed with dependency and want to spur resistance. On another occasion, Connecticut claimants declared their determination to have their "liberty, reputation, and property . . . duly secured; beyond the reach of the covetous, over-bearing, licentious, and designing" minions of Pennsylvania.[69]

Besides their words, the deeds of Yankee insurgents demonstrate that the concept of independence lay at the center of their resistance culture. A brief reconsideration of the types of people the insurgents targeted in their attacks confirms the essential link between rural discord and the pursuit of property. Wild Yankees perpetrated violence against Pennsylvania claimants whose claims to or presence on the land threatened their hold on property and, thus, their independence. Likewise, Yankee rioters focused their ire on the agents of the Pennsylvania Landholders' Association, surveyors, sheriff's deputies, and

---

68. Bogin, "Petitioning and the New Moral Economy," 392–95, 402–7; Edward Countryman, " 'Out of the Bounds of the Law': Northern Land Rioters in the Eighteenth Century," in *The American Revolution*, 40–43; Taylor, *Liberty Men*, 6–9, 112–14; Allan Kulikoff, "The Revolution and the Making of the American Yeoman Classes," in Kulikoff, *The Agrarian Origins of American Capitalism* (Charlottesville, VA, 1992), 139–41.

69. William Judd's Address to the Settlers at Wyoming, Apr. 13, 1787, *SCP* 9:98, 100; "Yankee Farmer," *Luzerne County Federalist*, Oct. 10, 1801, WHGS; Minutes of a Meeting Held in Wyoming, July 20, 1786, *SCP* 8:370.

other emissaries of the state because they represented an immediate threat to their soil rights and independence. Finally, Wild Yankees waged their campaign of terror and harassment against Connecticut claimants who sought to come to terms with the state and the Landholders' Association because, in doing so, they challenged the local consensus on which resistance depended. More important, by undermining resistance, they threatened the soil rights and independence of Yankee settlers.

Though they found a powerful motive in their struggle for independence, Wild Yankees found it increasingly difficult to maintain their resistance after the turn of the century. The tide began to turn against them in 1799 with the passage of the Compromise Act. This legislation eventually quelled dissent in older Yankee settlements in the Wyoming Valley. Meanwhile, armed with a series of punitive laws, the Pennsylvania Landholders' Association and state officials exerted pressure on Wild Yankee strongholds that lay beyond it. For example, eighteen of the Wild Yankees who attacked Bartlett Hinds in December 1802 found themselves before a Luzerne County magistrate the following spring. Freed from Yankee influence by the Territorial Act, the court found fourteen of the settlers guilty of riot and assault and punished them with jail terms and fifteen hundred dollars in fines.[70] Ultimately, Pennsylvania's offensive cut off Yankee insurgents from the support of nonresident speculators and destroyed any hopes of maintaining the Connecticut claim.

The demise of the Connecticut claim did not spell the end of agrarian unrest in Northeast Pennsylvania. Yankee settlers cast aside hopes that the legal merits of the Connecticut claim would vindicate their soil rights, but they did not give up on keeping possession of their farms. Though settlers remained committed to holding their land, this common aspiration did not translate into a united front. While some hard-pressed Yankees maintained violent opposition to the state, others turned to negotiation in order to save their freeholds.

---

70. Thomas Cooper to Thomas McKean, Jan. 18, 1803, *SCP* 11:369; Craft, *History of Bradford County*, 46–47; *The Luzerne County Federalist*, Apr. 25, 1803, WHGS.

CHAPTER 6

"POOR AND IGNORANT BUT INDUSTRIOUS SETTLERS"

Frontier Development and the Path to Accommodation

The chief agent of the Pennsylvania Landholders' Association, Robert Rose, made his way to Sugar Creek in July 1803 with the aim of subduing its Wild Yankees. Knowing that the only way to conquer resistance was to break it down one person at a time, he hoped to meet individually with each householder along the creek. The settlers upset this plan when they intercepted Rose and brought him before a gathering of the area's inhabitants. Luckily for him, the Yankees were more interested in talk than tar and feathers. Rose explained that the Landholders' Association was willing to let them purchase their lands at a "very moderate price" but warned that, if they ignored this offer, they "would be ruined by expensive law-suits, that would drive them from their farms." After the meeting ended, Rose mingled with the local inhabitants and "laughed & talked to them in their own style." He even jested about the Wild Yankees' blood-thirsty reputation, saying that the Pennsylvania landholders hired him as their agent because he was "something of an Indian" himself and would not "be alarmed if he found them [the settlers] dressed in leggins & breechcloths." That evening, Rose lodged with Sugar Creek settler Ezra Goddard and entered into a conversation with his host about the merits of the Connecticut claim. Eventually, he convinced Goddard to purchase a Pennsylvania title for his lands. Later that same night, Rose made his pitch to Ezra's brother, Luther, and Stephen Ballard, a staunch Wild Yankee who once claimed he would "lose the last drop of his blood in the Connecticut cause." Before long, Rose had also persuaded them to accept the landholders' offer. The divisive impact of Rose's efforts was clear even before he left Sugar Creek the following day. When he caught wind of his neighbors' capitulation, Moses Calkins confronted Stephen Ballard and told him that "he was worse than [Benedict] Arnold & deserved to be tarred & feathered a thousand times more than Smiley."[1]

Rose's work along Sugar Creek soon bore additional fruit: shortly after his visit, thirty of the creek's settlers forwarded a petition to the Landholders' Association in which they offered to relinquish their Connecticut deeds. In a report to the association's executive committee, Rose proudly stated that his plan to create discord among Sugar Creek's settlers had met with success and that Connecticut claimants who had once prided themselves on their solidarity now viewed each other with suspicion. He observed that each settler was "averse to an action being brought against himself" by the landholders but had "no objection to its being brought against his neighbors." This statement cut to the heart of the collapse of agrarian resistance in Northeast Pennsylvania. Whenever and wherever Yankees turned their backs on their neighbors, opposition to the state declined. Without trust there was no unity. Without unity there could be no effective resistance.[2]

This story demonstrates how the pursuit of independence and agrarian resistance parted company after the turn of the century. During both his public meeting and private conversations with Sugar Creek's settlers, Rose portrayed submission to the Pennsylvania landholders as the surest path toward securing possession of their lands. In this way he turned the desire for personal independence against continued opposition to the state. Of course, this appeal toward self-interest did not work with all settlers and, for some, independence remained inseparable from resistance. Where settlers and their communities stood in the process of frontier development shaped whether they continued their opposition or embraced accommodation. Those who had invested time and labor in developing productive farms and possessed access to markets held the motive and means to repurchase their farms from Pennsylvania. Meanwhile, settlers who occupied isolated or undeveloped freeholds that provided only a bare subsistence continued to view insurgency as the best way of avoiding, or at least putting off, the financial burdens of accommodation. No matter which course settlers took, the aim remained the same: securing property and independence. Nevertheless, that Yankees took different paths to reach this goal spelled the end of settler insurgency in Northeast Pennsylvania. Settlers who believed that they could achieve their goals within the bounds of the law broke ranks with neighbors who

---

1. Robert Rose to Samuel Hodgdon, July 21, 1803, CCP 2:38–40.
2. Robert Rose to Samuel Hodgdon, July 28, 1803, and Rose to Hodgdon, Aug. 4, 1804, CCP 2:40, 97.

continued to rely on violence to hold their lands and undermined the consensus that was essential to the survival and success of agrarian resistance.

Resistance and Reconciliation

After 1800 a growing number of Yankees pursued a course of accommodation. In May 1801, more than forty settlers along Towanda Creek agreed to relinquish their Connecticut claims.[3] The following month, twenty-seven inhabitants of the Nine-Partners settlement in Wayne County submitted to the Pennsylvania Landholders.[4] At the same time, dozens of Yankee settlers along Tunkhannock Creek accepted an offer from the Landholders' Association to sell them Pennsylvania deeds. By August more than a hundred settlers outside the fifteen towns had agreed to relinquish their Connecticut deeds.[5] By 1803 this stream of relinquishments had grown into a flood. In January, Connecticut claimants along the upper reaches of Wyalusing and Wysox creeks agreed to open negotiations with the Pennsylvania Landholders. Robert Rose found the majority of these settlers "well disposed, or capable of being made so with a little trouble."[6] In May, James Ralston informed the Landholders' Association that "all kind[s] of opposition" in Wayne County had "completely ceased" and presented them with an offer to buy state titles signed by more than one hundred Towanda Creek settlers. In October, Pennsylvania land agent Samuel Baird obtained relinquishments from forty-three out of forty-eight Yankees seated on lands south of Towanda Creek. A month later, settlers from Smithfield and Murraysfield north of Sugar Creek forwarded a written declaration expressing their willingness to abandon the Connecticut claim and repurchase their lands from Pennsylvania.[7]

But this progress sometimes proved more illusory than real. For every report detailing the success of negotiations between Connecticut claimants and

---

3. Joseph Van Sick to Tench Coxe, May 19, 1801, and List of Connecticut Relinquishments, June–Aug. 1801, SCP 11:61, 193; Abraham Horn to the Landholders' Committee, June 9, 1801, MPLA.

4. Enclosure accompanying letter from Henry Drinker to Tench Coxe, Aug. 8, 1801, CCP 1:83; John Thacher to Henry Drinker and Samuel Hodgdon, Aug. 26, 1801, SCP 11:184; Committee of the Pennsylvania Landholders to Thomas McKean, Feb. 1804, CCP 2:83.

5. List of Connecticut Relinquishments, June–Aug., 1801, SCP 11:191–94.

6. Dimon Bostwick to Ebenezer Bowman, Jan. 30, 1803; Robert Rose to Samuel Hodgdon, Aug. 4, 1803; and Robert Rose to Samuel Hodgdon, Aug. 21, 1803, CCP 2:8, 42, 49.

7. James Ralston to the Landholders' Committee, May 17, 1803, RPLA; Samuel Baird to Thomas Cooper, Oct. 7, 1803, Letters from the Pennsylvania Claimants to the Commissioners, PHMC; George Welles to Governor McKean, Nov. 7, 1803, in Louise Welles Murray, *A History of Old Tioga Point and Early Athens* (Wilkes-Barre, PA, 1907), 368.

Pennsylvania landholders, there was another claiming that resistance was still alive—even among inhabitants who had pledged to relinquish their Connecticut deeds and accept state authority. In 1806, three years after its settlers had agreed to purchase state titles, Wyalusing Creek remained, according to Pennsylvania land agent John Wallace, "a hot-bed of opposition to the Pennsylvania Land holders."[8] Ebenezer Bowman, who served as an agent for several Pennsylvania landholders, also encountered contradictory testimony concerning Yankee settlers. In May 1803, Bowman received word that Connecticut claimants along Wyalusing and Towanda creeks were "disposed to purchase" their lands from the Landholders' Association. But only a few weeks earlier Bowman's sources had informed him that settlers "from the forks of the Wyalusing to Tioga point on both sides of the [Susquehanna] river" were "determined not to purchase the Pennsyla title" and ready to "stand and fall by the Connecticut title." Likewise, in the spring of 1803, Wayne County officials reported an end to settler opposition, yet surveyors working for state landholders still encountered hostility in parts of that county the following fall.[9]

Even as Pennsylvania landholders received petitions expressing settlers' willingness to purchase state titles, some of their agents and surveyors continued to be harassed, beaten, and even shot. More often than not, efforts to subjugate Yankee resistance only served to split backwoods communities into factions of accommodationists and hard-liners. While dividing settlers was productive in the long run, it did not necessarily make things easier for state officials and association agents in the short run. Insurgents who felt power slipping from their grasp became even more violent and unpredictable. It was only after Robert Rose visited Sugar Creek and set many of its inhabitants on the path toward accommodation that unreconciled militants took to the woods and shot Pennsylvania surveyor Edward Gobin. In November 1803, Samuel Hodgdon forwarded a brace of pistols to Robert Rose. Rose later explained that, while he did not think he would have "any occasion for them," he thought it wise "to be provided against things that may occur." Clearly, he felt that Yankee insurgents still posed a threat. With the shooting of Gobin foremost in his mind, Rose asserted that any Pennsylvania surveyor working near settlements dominated by Wild

---

8. Connecticut claimants to the Pennsylvania Landholders' Association, Feb. 23, 1803, *SCP* 11:373; John B. Wallace to Samuel Meredith, Dec. 1, 1806, Samuel Meredith Papers, WHGS.

9. Ebenezer Bowman to Edward Tilghman, May 14, 1803, and Ebenezer Bowman to Edward Tilghman, Apr. 8, 1803, *SCP* 11:387, 384–85; James Ralston to the Landholders' Committee, May 17, 1803, RPLA; Jason Torrey to Edward Tilghman, Oct. 10, 1804, JTP; Samuel Preston to Samuel Meredith, Sept. 26, 1804, *SCP* 11:506–7.

Yankees would be violently resisted, even killed, "by persons disguised so as not to be known."[10] This prediction was born out by future events. On several occasions Yankee insurgents fired on state and association surveyors. In one incident a bullet narrowly missed a man employed by Rose.[11]

The move toward reconciliation in Northeast Pennsylvania was halting and uneven for a number of reasons. After 1800, the Susquehannah and Delaware companies no longer orchestrated Yankee resistance, but neither did they coordinate a coherent move toward accommodation. Instead, individual Yankee settlements were left to pursue independent courses of action. Oscillation between resistance and accommodation was also a product of the divisions existing within Yankee settlements. Until settlers were of one mind they found it difficult to speak with one voice. Finally, opposition and negotiation, instead of being mutually exclusive, became intertwined. Pennsylvania discovered that settlers could sign a pledge of loyalty with one hand and maintain resistance with the other. Rather than renouncing violence once they opened talks with the state and the Landholders' Association, Connecticut claimants continued to use it as leverage in their negotiations. In some instances negotiation became just another instrument of resistance. Settlers who had no real desire to purchase state titles opened talks with Pennsylvania and its landholders merely to forestall ejectment suits. In other cases insurgents fought a sort of delaying action and stalled for time in order to improve their bargaining position.

Even in the face of this complex welter of motives and actions, it is possible to discern patterns of opposition and reconciliation across Northeast Pennsylvania. The move toward accommodation was contingent, in part, on whether or not there existed an effective legal process for both the resolution of land disputes and the punishment of those who continued to challenge government authority. Settlers quickly came to terms when such a framework existed, but when it was absent, accommodation made little headway. The passage of the Compromise Act in 1799, an amended version of the Intrusion Act in 1801, and the Territorial Act in 1802 transformed the legal context of the Wyoming controversy. Taken together, they both opened the door to a negotiated settlement between Pennsylvania and its Yankee inhabitants and heightened the risks of continued resistance.

Depending on where they lived, settlers experienced these legislative initiatives in very different ways, which goes a long way toward explaining the region's

---

10. Robert Rose to Samuel Hodgdon, Nov. 17, 1803 and Robert Rose to Samuel Hodgdon, Aug. 11, 1804, CCP 2:66, 98; Emily C. Blackman, *History of Susquehanna County, Pennsylvania* (Philadelphia, 1873), 23; David Craft, *History of Bradford County, Pennsylvania* (Philadelphia, 1878), 369.

11. Blackman, *History of Susquehanna County*, 23; Robert Rose to Samuel Hodgdon, Sept. 17, 1803, CCP 2:58; H. C. Bradsby, *History of Bradford County, Pennsylvania* (Chicago, 1891), 448.

landscape of resistance and accommodation. Connecticut claimants in Susquehannah Company towns that were laid out before the Trenton Decree of 1782 came into contact with the more benevolent (and ultimately more successful) side of the state's efforts to end the Wyoming dispute. The Compromise Act provided these settlers with a procedure through which a peaceful settlement could be reached. Out of the fifteen towns included under the terms of the act, eleven of them were in or adjacent to the Wyoming Valley. The other four were strung along the Susquehanna River between Tunkhannock Creek and Sugar Creek. These were the same areas that moved most rapidly toward accommodation after the turn of the century. The compromise law allowed these towns' inhabitants to purchase Pennsylvania deeds at rates below market value. Under the law's provisions, Connecticut claimants only had to pay two dollars an acre for land of the highest quality—land for which the state was paying up to five dollars an acre in order to compensate dispossessed Pennsylvania claimants.[12] The inhabitants of the fifteen towns embraced accommodation because the Compromise Act provided them with a means to secure their lands on reasonable terms. By contrast, Yankees who occupied claims laid out after the Trenton Decree experienced the more punitive side of Pennsylvania's legal offensive. For these settlers there was no clear path to a negotiated settlement but only the threat of legal prosecution under the Intrusion and Territorial acts. Resistance endured outside of the fifteen towns because the state did not present settlers with a real alternative. The Landholders' Association also failed to come up with a comprehensive plan for compromise. Faced with legal sanctions and aggressive Pennsylvania landholders who threatened their farms and independence, Yankees in backwoods communities fought on.

Changes in the legal context surrounding land disputes outside of the fifteen towns contributed to the decline of Yankee resistance after 1803. For many years state officials and association agents labored under serious disadvantages. On the one hand, the aggressive stance of Pennsylvania and its landholders served only to alienate Yankee settlers. On the other, the state and the Landholders' Association did not possess effective instruments to coerce Yankees into giving up their Connecticut deeds. The Intrusion and Territorial acts remained largely toothless where local juries failed to enforce them and while state courts debated the laws' constitutionality. The tide began to turn in the final weeks of 1802 when the Pennsylvania Supreme Court upheld both acts. Besides gaining better means to punish recalcitrant settlers, the Landholders' Association stopped asking exorbitant prices for marginal frontier lands and set forth terms for payment that most Yankee settlers were willing and able to

---

12. The Compromise Act, May 23, 1799, *SCP* 10:470–71.

meet. Starting in 1803, the Landholders' Association ended opposition along Towanda Creek, Sugar Creek, and elsewhere by asking settlers to pay not what their lands were worth at current market value, but "in a state of nature." These developments led many backwoods Yankees to turn away from violence and toward a negotiated settlement.

By the early nineteenth century, the struggle over property in Northeast Pennsylvania was largely a battle over price. Connecticut claimants, even those who remained committed to resistance, were not agrarian extremists contending over what constituted legitimate ownership of the land but aspiring yeomen whose only capital was the time and labor they devoted to the creation of productive farms. Thomas Cooper echoed this characterization when he described Yankees as "poor and Ignorant but industrious settlers thinly Scattered over a wild country." Likewise, Robert Rose found that most settlers "expressed their wishes to purchase the Pennsylvania title, if it could be got on reasonable terms." In sum, Yankee insurgents were not opposed to the concept of property as a legal right or even to accepting the state's definition of what constituted legitimate possession of the land. They only struggled over the process by which state titles could be obtained and the price it would cost them.[13] Whether or not Yankee settlers could afford to purchase state deeds was determined by their economic standing which was, in turn, framed by the larger process of frontier development.

Communities

The collective enterprise whereby settlers knit themselves together into social and economic networks was a critical component of frontier development. How settlers went about this endeavor and what the communities they created looked like speak volumes about their outlook and aspirations. In the case of Northeast Pennsylvania's Yankee migrants, the communities they created provide some clues to the premium they placed on independence and shed light on patterns of resistance and reconciliation.

Kinship networks were foundational to community building in the backcountry. It has already been established that Yankee migrants preferred to confront the struggles of settlement, not alone, but alongside family and neighbors. However, to these preexisting social ties they soon added new ones forged along the frontier. Such connections enabled pioneers to marshal the labor

---

13. Thomas Cooper to Thomas McKean, Nov. 15, 1802, SCP 11:339; Robert Rose to Samuel Hodgdon, July 10, 1803, CCP 2:36.

"POOR AND IGNORANT BUT INDUSTRIOUS SETTLERS" 155

necessary to transform forests into farms. Tree-cutting bees and cabin raisings furnished occasions for backcountry inhabitants to form and reinforce ties between kin and neighbors. These face-to-face ties provided an important safety net against hunger, illness, and misfortune that often spelled the difference between success and failure for pioneer families.

The Yankee enclave of Juddsburgh along Sugar Creek provides a good example of the dense thicket of kinship that characterized backwoods neighborhoods. The settlement, which was first pioneered in the early 1790s, contained forty-eight adult men according to a list drawn up by Robert Rose in 1803. These forty-eight individuals shared thirty-eight surnames: a sign that many of them belonged to larger family networks. The Ballards formed one such extended frontier family. Stephen Ballard came from Framingham, Massachusetts, to Sugar Creek in 1792. His twin cousins, John and Nathan Ballard, and their father, Joseph, arrived a year later. Other Ballards soon followed. The pervasive kin ties that bound together Juddsburgh's inhabitants only come into full view when ties of marriage are taken into account. All told, well over half (thirty out of forty-eight) of the settlement's households were connected by blood or marriage. In some cases these ties could be quite extensive and complex. Within a decade of their arrival, the Ballards were linked by marriage to several other Sugar Creek families. John and Nathan Ballard married Mary and Susannah Dobbins, the daughters of William Dobbins. Stephen Ballard's daughter, Elizabeth, married Sugar Creek settler John Gamage. Finally, Joseph Ballard's daughter, Mehitabel, married David Miller, the son of another Juddsburgh householder, Derrick Miller. Through the Dobbins family, the Ballards were linked with the Kendalls and McKeans. William Dobbins's daughter, Jane, married Ebenezer Kendall while his son, John, married Rebecca McKean, daughter of Juddsburgh pioneer James McKean.[14]

The kinship networks that were so important to the process of community-building also influenced settlers' choices concerning opposition and accommodation. It is hard not to notice the clusters of surnames that appear on petitions Yankees forwarded to Pennsylvania landholders signaling their willingness to relinquish their Connecticut deeds. In one sent by Wyalusing settlers appear the names of Ezra and Walter Lathrop; Samuel and Elisha Lewis; Jesse, Daniel, and Joseph Ross; Peter and Aden Stevens; and other sets of fathers, sons, and brothers who chose to embark on the process of accommodation—as they did with all the challenges of frontier life—together. Meanwhile, other family networks stood together in their commitment to the Connecticut claim. All of the

---

14. Robert Rose to Samuel Hodgdon, Aug. 11, 1803, CCP 2:43. The genealogical information in this paragraph was drawn from Clement F. Heverly, *Pioneer and Patriot Families of Bradford County, Pennsylvania, 1770–1800*, 2 vols. (Towanda, PA, 1913). The page references are too numerous to list, but the people I discuss can be easily looked up in Heverly's index.

household heads in the Bostwick and Bosworth clans (several of who were involved in the 1802 mobbing of Bartlett Hinds) are conspicuously absent from the petition drawn up by Wyalusing Creek's compromise-minded inhabitants. If the settlement of Juddsburgh is any guide, the lines separating hard-liners from accommodationists followed ties of marriage as well as consanguinity.[15]

But ties of blood and marriage were by no means sacrosanct, and when individual settlers had to finally choose between accommodation and opposition they pursued the course that best served their interests. Robert Rose divided his list of Juddsburgh men into two categories: those who recently signed a proresistance declaration and those who did not. Rose happily noted that only twenty-four of the settlement's forty-eight householders signed the petition, seeing it as a sign of the collapse of Juddsburgh's collective commitment to resistance. What is even more telling is that the petition divided the community's kin networks. Joseph Ballard refused to sign the petition while his twin sons, John and Nathan, put their names to the document. John and Nathan were married to Mary and Susannah Dobbins whose father, William, also failed to sign the petition. William Dobbins may not have signed but his son, John, did. In doing so, John Dobbins went against his father and his brothers-in-law, John McKean and James McKean, Jr. Luther Goddard, who signed the petition, also split from his brother, Ezra Jr., who did not.[16]

How frontier inhabitants divided up the land is another aspect of community building that speaks directly to how the pursuit of independence intersected with resistance and accommodation. Patterns of landholding illuminate how rural folk envisioned community. They shed light on the relationship between communities and the individual households that constituted them. To fully understand the significance of landholding practices among Northeast Pennsylvania's Yankee settlers it is first necessary to put them into context with over a century's worth of New England land policies.

Though methods of land distribution varied from town to town and colony to colony in seventeenth-century New England, some general procedures did emerge. First, the region's land policies were predicated on the idea of communal settlement. The New England colonies did not issue land grants to individuals but to *groups* of like-minded proprietors who petitioned for allotments of land. Once a group of settlers had obtained a grant, or "town," they set about dividing it up among themselves. This process was shaped by a combination of the law, local custom, and personal preference. The result was a patchwork of

---

15. Robert Rose to Samuel Hodgdon (with enclosures), Aug. 21, 1803, CCP 2: 49–54; Craft, *History of Bradford County*, 46–47.
16. Robert Rose to Samuel Hodgdon, Aug. 11, 1803, CCP 2:43.

land use and distribution policies. Some towns continued the age-old tradition of consolidating individual farmers' lands into "common fields" and organizing field labor along collective lines. Others eschewed such practices, and allowed their inhabitants to work their individual holdings much as they pleased.[17] Regardless of these differences, there were some widely practiced methods of land distribution. Town proprietors commonly organized their lands into two sorts of "divisions." They designated certain portions of the town's lands as "house lots," "meadow lots," and "wood lots," reflecting each division's intended use. In addition, proprietors did not distribute all of the town's lands at once but over the course of several decades. "First division" lands were distributed at the time of settlement, and land in "second," "third," and "fourth" divisions as they were needed. Between the 1640s and 1660s, for example, the inhabitants of Andover issued four divisions of land. The upshot of all this is that individual land holdings, instead of being consolidated in a single farmstead, were often spread across towns. This scattering was not accidental, but integral to New England's land system. Town proprietors subdivided divisions of land into numbered lots which were then distributed at random. They did this in the name of fairness and impartiality. Not all soil was of equal quality and this lottery system gave every proprietor an equal chance of obtaining especially good, or bad, land.[18]

By the eighteenth century, the region's land distribution policies had undergone significant changes. New Englanders abandoned the process of communal settlement and replaced it with a system that enccuraged individual settlement and land speculation. When Connecticut opened the northwest corner of the colony to settlement in the late 1730s, it divided the area into seven towns parceled into fifty-three shares and sold them at public auction. Here, obtaining and settling land was not a collective enterprise predicated on Puritan values but an individual process ruled by the logic of the marketplace. In addition, New Englanders discarded the practice of organizing town lands into divisions. The proprietors of Connecticut's northwest towns did not parcel up the land slowly over the course of decades but immediately divided it among themselves. Moreover, instead of cutting up their holdings into scattered house, field, and wood lots, they kept them together in large, thousand-acre lots. Such

---

17. Philip J. Greven, Jr., *Four Generations: Population, Land, and Family in Colonial Andover, Massachusetts* (Ithaca, NY, 1970), 41–71; Richard I. Melvoin, *New England Outpost: War and Society in Colonial Deerfield* (New York, 1989), 72; David Grayson Allen, *In English Ways: The Movement of Societies and the Transferal of English Local Law and Custom to Massachusetts Bay in the 17th Century* (Chapel Hill, NC, 1981), 30–36, 63–66, 125–29.

18. Greven, *Four Generations*, 45–60; John Frederick Martin, *Profits in the Wilderness: Entrepreneurship and the Founding of New England Towns in the Seventeenth Century* (Chapel Hill, NC, 1991), 149–61; Melvoin, *New England Outpost*, 59–63.

procedures encouraged the development of self-contained freehold farms. They also promoted land speculation as proprietors quickly sold off parts of their large claims to others for a profit.[19]

These New England precedents shaped how the Susquehannah Company distributed land. Before the Trenton Decree, many of the company's land policies were throwbacks to the seventeenth century. In response to the challenges of frontier settlement and the threat posed by Indians and Pennamites, the company promoted a communal system of settlement. It issued new town grants only after a requisite number of settlers had come forward to fill them. The company's proprietors also continued to organize their towns into divisions. Wilkes-Barre's inhabitants set off two hundred acres of land into a nucleated village containing fifty house lots. Soon after, they set off additional "meadow," "back," and "five-acre" lots. They then numbered the lots in these divisions and distributed them by lottery. In following such procedures, early Susquehannah Company towns replicated the seventeenth-century custom of noncontiguous landholding.[20] Timothy Pickering took note of this when he visited the Wyoming Valley in 1786. Speaking of Wilkes-Barre, Pickering explained that "each settler drew for his lot in each division," resulting in a situation where "his dwelling house is on the pitch pine plain, his meadow a mile or more from it, on one side, & his back-lot perhaps still farther removed." The Susquehannah Company also enacted policies that reflected more current practices. Drawing on the precedent recently set by the settlement of northwestern Connecticut, the company divided its towns (which were eventually set at a standard five square miles, or sixteen thousand acres) into fifty-three equal "settling rights" of three hundred acres (including three for the support of a school and minister). These were distinct from a "proprietors' right" in the entire Connecticut claim, which constituted six hundred acres of land.[21]

After the Trenton Decree, the Susquehannah Company transformed its land policies in ways that made the Connecticut claim more attractive to both land speculators and independence-seeking settlers. There were even signs of

19. Charles S. Grant, *Democracy in the Connecticut Frontier Town of Kent* (New York, 1961), 10–20.

20. For the various sorts of land divisions made in early Susquehannah Company towns, see Book of the Fifteen Towns, PHMC. William E. Price describes the division on Wilkes-Barre in "A Study of a Frontier Community in Transition: The History of Wilkes-Barre, Pennsylvania, 1750–1800" (Ph.D. diss., Kent State University, 1979), 61–69. Unlike many seventeenth-century New England towns, it does not appear that Wyoming's Yankees systematically held land back for later distribution.

21. Extracts from Timothy Pickering's Journal, Aug. 18, 1786, SCP 8:384; Julian P. Boyd, "Connecticut's Experiment in Expansion: The Susquehannah Company, 1753–1803," *Journal of Economic and Business History* 27 (1931): 53–54.

change before this event. In Putnam, Braintrim, Springfield, and other towns established in the mid to late 1770s, Yankee settlers abandoned the practice of organizing town lands into divisions. Instead, they started to issue settling rights in the form of consolidated three-hundred-acre grants.[22] This new method of distributing land was firmly entrenched by the time Yankee settlements spread to Wyalusing Creek, Wysox Creek, Sugar Creek, and other tributaries of the upper Susquehanna in the 1790s. In 1803, Robert Rose noted that "the Connecticut Townships on the Crs. [Creeks] are laid off in long & narrow lots, as for example Juddsburg where they are 80 ps. [perches] wide & extend 600 back." Distributing settling-rights in the form of consolidated, three-hundred-acre farmsteads rather than scattered home, meadow, and wood lots was far more convenient to settlers. This new system of dividing town lands does not mean that settlers lost sight of their need for various types of land to sustain themselves. In describing the layout of Juddsburgh's settling rights, Rose pointed out that the lots all extended from Sugar Creek, "so as to give each person a part of the bottom land" for tillage, back into hills that furnished land fit for pastures and woodlots.[23] In addition, by the mid 1790s the minimum number of proprietors needed to settle a town had been reduced to eight and the size of a proprietor's right had increased to two thousand acres.[24] Finally, instead of waiting for a complete cohort of settlers before creating a town, the Susquehannah Company promoted settlement on a first come, first serve basis. This benefited Yankee migrants by allowing them to pick land that suited them rather than randomly obtaining it by lottery.[25]

These new methods of parceling out land reflect a configuration of community that had a profound impact on agrarian resistance. The consolidation of settling rights and the turn from a communal to an individual method of settlement point to the development of communities predicated on household independence. The creation of unified farmsteads promoted the emergence of more autonomous rural households. The Yankee families who took up land in northern Pennsylvania after the Revolutionary War did not live in communities

---

22. The Susquehannah Company established the towns of Putnam, Braintrim, Springfield, and Claverack between 1774 and 1778 and laid out their settling rights in consolidated 300-acre lots: see, Classification of the Seventeen Townships, PHMC, 60–62.

23. Robert Rose to Samuel Hodgdon, July 28, 1803, *SCP* 11:401. It is worth noting that a tract of land 80 perches wide and 600 deep contains 300 acres of land—the size of a standard settling right in the Susquehannah Company.

24. Minutes of a Meeting of the Susquehannah Company, Feb. 18–20, 1795, *SCP* 10:215–16.

25. There is no mention of settlers obtaining lands by lottery after the Revolutionary War. There is, however, abundant circumstantial evidence that settlers were allowed to pick their lands as they filled a town. For instance, see John Franklin to Caleb Benton, June 26, 1787, *SCP* 9:14.

where the division of land into house, meadow, and wood lots promoted, even necessitated, the close cooperation of households. Moreover, they were worlds away from the common field system of the seventeenth century that took even basic decisions concerning farming out of the hands of individual household heads and put them into the hands of the wider community.

Though such households were more self-contained, it does not mean that they were self-sufficient. Rural life, and especially along the frontier, still depended on cooperation between neighbors. Nevertheless, the ties of mutuality that pervaded backcountry settlements were rooted in a voluntary communalism that emerged out of a common struggle for survival and independence rather than the formal communitarianism that marked so many early New England towns.[26] In communities where the common pursuit of independence tied together relatively autonomous families, agrarian resistance could both flourish and wither. When it forwarded their independence, Yankee settlers joined ranks in opposing Pennsylvania and its landholders. But when it was not clear that resistance promoted independence, or at least did not promote the independence of everyone, then settler unity could quickly unravel. To fully understand the relationship between resistance, accommodation, and independence, the focus needs to turn from the fabric of frontier communities to the experience of individual settler households.

Farms

Yankees fought and negotiated with Pennsylvania and its landholders as they labored to carve farms out of forests. By the turn of the century, the procedures for establishing a farm in the sort of heavily forested land that predominated in Northeast Pennsylvania were well established and widely practiced. Pioneers initiated the process of farm building by creating a rough clearing in the forest. There were two techniques, sometimes used in combination, to accomplish this. Sometimes settlers simply "girdled" trees. That is, they cut away a band of bark that kept the trees from leafing and eventually caused them to die where they stood. Even before they were finally brought down and removed, the dead trees let in enough light for crops to be planted in their midst. The alternative to girdling trees was simply cutting them down. This approach was faster but more labor intensive. It appears that this second

---

26. Good examples of the formalized communalism that governed life in many early New England towns can be found in, Greven, *Four Generations*; Kenneth A. Lockridge, *A New England Town: The First Hundred Years* (New York, 1970); and Melvoin, *New England Outpost*, esp. 72, 152–81.

method became the preferred one among New Englanders by the mid eighteenth century.[27]

Instead of creating open fields, the early stages of frontier development produced a jumbled, unkempt landscape. While journeying through western New York in the 1820s, the English traveler Basil Hall came across pioneer farms "covered with an inextricable and confused mass of prostrate trunks, branches and trees, piles of split logs, and of squared timbers, planks, shingles, great stacks of fuel." He noted that even more established farms were scattered with "numerous ugly stumps of old trees" and the "scorched and withered remnants of the ancient woods." In the midst of this clutter, settlers constructed rude log cabins and lean-tos to shelter themselves and their livestock. When he made his first visit to the Wyoming Valley in 1786, Timothy Pickering encountered such "wretched" settlers' "hovels." He described them as being "generally built with logs, but in the very worst manner" and noted that "in a great part of them there is no chimney, but a hole is left in the roof, thro' which the smoke escapes."[28]

Techniques of agriculture and animal husbandry also distinguished the pioneering phase of farm building. Even as they cleared the forest, settlers turned to planting gardens and sewing crops. The stumps and tree trunks that littered pioneers' rude clearings made the creation of orderly, plowed fields an impossibility. Instead, settlers broke the ground with hoes and planted their grains broadcast in the midst of stumps and tree trunks. Though settlers grew wheat, oats, rye, and barley, Indian corn was a preferred pioneer crop. It possessed a very high bushel-to-acre yield (a very important consideration in the early years of settlement when pioneers struggled to clear enough land and plant enough crops to feed their families). Livestock were an important component of frontier farming. Cattle and pigs were popular with backcountry settlers because they provided food and, in the case of oxen, animal power needed to haul trees and pull plows. In addition, raising livestock was a labor-saving strategy. Instead of fencing in and feeding their animals, pioneer farmers turned them loose to browse on forest underbrush. William Davy, an English traveler who visited the Susquehanna Valley in the mid 1790s, pointed to the prevalence and success of this practice, observing that "the Woods here are so full of

27. William Cronon, *Changes in the Land: Indians, Colonists, and the Ecology of New England* (New York, 1983), 116–18. For detailed descriptions of pioneer farming procedures, see Michael Williams, *Americans and Their Forests: A Historical Geography* (New York, 1989), 58–62, 67–75, 94–100, 121–22, 139; and Charles Brooks, *Frontier Settlement and Market Revolution: The Holland Land Purchase* (Ithaca, NY, 1996), 60–74.

28. Basil Hall quoted in Williams, *Americans and Their Forests*, 121; Extracts from Timothy Pickering's Journal, Aug. 18, 1786, SCP 8:484.

Walnuts, Chestnut, Hickory & Hazle Nuts & Acorns that great quantities of Hogs are made fat by feeding on them alone."[29]

The investment of time and labor steadily transformed raw frontier freeholds into productive backcountry farms. A season or two after they seated themselves on the land, settlers began preparing the ground for more intensive use. Whatever logs and brush remained from their initial cutting would be burned to clear the ground and enrich the soil. Over the following years, settlers laboriously pulled the charred remains of stumps from their fields. Eventually, the plow replaced the hoe as the settlers' main agricultural implement. Frontier farmers also planted orchards and, with time, the fruit they bore joined the yield of their fields and gardens. Backcountry inhabitants continued the practice of letting their livestock browse in the woods, but they also created meadows that allowed them to harvest and store fodder for the winter months. Finally, though most ordinary settlers continued to build with rough-hewn logs, they replaced rude pioneer cabins and lean-tos with more substantial houses and out buildings. As their fields and herds grew, backcountry families achieved a competency and could even contemplate selling surplus produce.

Even with industry, skill, and a good deal of luck, building a farm and securing a subsistence was always a struggle. Climate and soil fertility constrained farm families' productive capabilities as did more unpredictable events such as drought, the death of livestock, or crop disease. Yankee migrants who settled on lands away from the Susquehanna River and its major tributaries encountered something that they found disappointingly similar to the life they left behind in New England: the thin soils, hard labor, and slim returns of hill farming. While passing between Tioga Point and Wilkes-Barre in the late 1790s, Isaac Weld described the rough terrain that characterized much of the upper Susquehanna Valley and commented that most of the families he lodged with had "barely enough" provisions to feed themselves. On one occasion, Weld left one hungry household and crossed the Susquehanna River in search of better lodging only to find that the inhabitants on the opposite bank "were still more destitute." When the Duc de le Rochefoucault-Liancourt traveled through the same territory a few years later he was also struck by the poverty he encountered. He attributed it to the settlers themselves, characterizing them as "poor, lazy, drunken, quarrelsome, and extremely negligent in the culture of their lands."[30] Robert Rose more accurately linked the settlers' penury to the quality of the soil. In many areas he found the

---

29. Quote from William Davy found in Peter C. Mancall, *Valley of Opportunity: Economic Culture along the Upper Susquehanna, 1700–1800* (Ithaca, NY, 1991), 175.

30. Isaac Weld, *Travels through the States of North America, and the Provinces of Upper and Lower Canada*, 2 vols. (1807; reprint, New York, 1968), 1:343–45, 348; Duc de la Rochefoucault-Laincourt, *Travels through the United States of North America, The Country of the Iroquois, and Upper Canada in the Years 1795, 1796, and 1797*, 2 vols. (London, 1799), 1:93.

land "not worth five cents an acre." He noted that along the tributaries of the Susquehanna River near the New York State line (the same areas populated by many die-hard Wild Yankees) tillable land was usually restricted to "a very narrow slip" and that land on the surrounding hills was "of little value."[31]

In comparison to poor hill-country settlers, Yankees whose farms lay on fertile, riverside lands achieved a comfortable subsistence. Turn-of-the-century descriptions of Wilkes-Barre and the Wyoming Valley paint a picture of improvement and growing prosperity. After traveling the difficult road from Tioga Point, Isaac Weld was pleased to find that Wilkes-Barre contained more than 150 houses, a church, a courthouse, and a jail. Around the same time that Weld made his visit, Timothy Pickering described the growing size and productivity of Wyoming Valley farms. He claimed that the average freehold in the valley contained three hundred acres of land, of which thirty were cleared. By Pickering's reckoning, these improved acres produced just over ninety bushels of mixed grains and one-and-a-half tons of hay. Since the average farm family and its livestock needed between thirty and fifty bushels of grain for their support, this would have left a substantial surplus for settlers to exchange for goods, cash, or credit.[32]

Besides the intrinsic quality of their land, the prosperity of backcountry settlers was tied to the amount of labor they invested in their farms. Even a tract of land with great agricultural potential was worthless until somebody cleared and improved it. Labor was, in turn, a factor of time: a settler who had occupied a tract for five years had more opportunity to improve it than one who had been on his land for only five months. If a pioneer devoted all his time to the task, he could clear (but not destump) between ten and twelve acres of forest in a year. However, because farmers had to spend working hours on planting, cutting firewood, splitting fence rails, and other tasks, clearing land was a much slower process. Pioneer families in eighteenth-century Vermont cleared between one and three acres a year. In turn-of-the-century western New York, farmers cleared, on average, three or four acres a year.[33] Though exact figures varied from region to region and family to family, the average rural household needed between sixteen and twenty-five acres of improved land to support

---

31. Robert Rose to Samuel Hodgdon, Sept. 10, 1803, and Rose to Hodgdon, July 28, 1803, *SCP* 11: 410, 401.

32. Weld, *Travels through the States of North America*, 351; Timothy Pickering to Alexander Hamilton, Oct. 13, 1791, *SCP* 10:151. My figures for the amount of grain needed to support a farm family are drawn from Bettye Hobbs Pruitt, "Self-sufficiency and the Agricultural Economy of Eighteenth-Century Massachusetts," *WMQ* 41 (July 1984): 342–45.

33. Michael Bellesiles, *Revolutionary Outlaws: Ethan Allen and the Struggle for Independence on the Early American Frontier* (Charlottesville, VA, 1993), 53; Williams, *Americans and their Forests*, 63–64, 114–17.

itself. The low end of this range represents what would have been required to provide a bare subsistence, keeping in mind that frontier families who let their livestock forage in the woods were able to make do with even fewer improved acres. The upper end signifies the point at which a family could expect to move from a comfortable competency to producing a marketable surplus. No matter which, it is clear that pioneers had to devote several years of labor to their farms before they could expect to secure their basic needs, let alone produce a surplus that would allow them to turn a profit. Robert Rose touched on this when he informed his employers that some time would pass before they could expect to receive payment from Yankee settlers because "the difficulty of clearing the land is so great that some years expire before a man can raise a subsistence for his family from it."[34]

The time-labor factor of farm building favored Connecticut claimants in long-settled communities in and around the Wyoming Valley over those who lived in newly established settlements to the north. The productivity gap that separated the two is revealed in the land assessments calculated for the federal direct tax of 1798. The average value of an acre of land in the Wyoming Valley was $2.44. In the bastions of Wild Yankee resistance to the north, the average value of an acre of land was $1.67.[35] Another way to rate the prosperity of settlers is to look at the number of improved acres they possessed, for cleared land translated into tillage that would grow crops and meadow that would support livestock. This standard of measure again illustrates the economic disparity between older and newer settlements. In 1804, the settlers who lived along the upper reaches of Sugar Creek possessed, on average, nine acres of improved land. In contrast, Connecticut claimants who lived in Claverack, a settlement located at the confluence of Sugar Creek and the Susquehanna River and one of the Compromise Act's fifteen towns, possessed an average of forty-five improved acres. Since a farm family needed between sixteen and twenty five acres of improved land to provide for its needs, the possession of twenty cleared acres can be used as a rough dividing line between households that struggled to maintain a mere subsistence and those who had reached a humble prosperity. A much higher proportion of settlers in older towns close to the Susquehanna River met this twenty-acre mark than those seated in newly formed backwoods communities. Only two of Claverack's inhabitants found in Wysox Township's 1804 tax rolls possessed farms with under twenty acres of cleared

34. Robert Rose to Samuel Hodgdon, July 28, 1803, CCP 2:40. For calculations of the amount of improved acres needed to support a family see Bettye Hobbs Pruitt, "Self-sufficiency and the Agricultural Economy," 342–45; and Christopher M. Jedry, *The World of John Cleaveland: Family and Community in Eighteenth-Century New England* (New York, 1979), 63.

35. USDT, List H: Summary Abstract, Fifth Assessment District, Luzerne County.

land. Across the township as a whole, one out of three settlers held twenty or more improved acres. In comparison, in Burlington Township, which adjoined Wysox to the west and contained many of the settlers who lived along the upper reaches of Sugar Creek, only one out of ten taxables had reached a similar level of farm development.[36]

Patterns of prosperity and poverty in Northeast Pennsylvania closely matched those of resistance and accommodation. Connecticut claimants in older, riverside towns were far more likely to open negotiations with Pennsylvania and its landholders than those in raw, isolated settlements. They did so because they could better afford to purchase state deeds and because this cost, when compared to the value and long-term productivity of their lands, was a reasonable investment. Meanwhile, hardscrabble farmers who barely eked out a subsistence from their holdings bridled at the thought of paying for the land twice. Because backwoods settlers were too poor to repurchase their farms, low prices and generous terms of credit were needed.

The process of frontier development also helps to explain why Yankee resistance ultimately unraveled when it did. The poverty that dogged backcountry inhabitants was, for most, a temporary condition rooted in the realities of frontier agriculture. With the passage of time, settlers slowly improved the productive capabilities of their farms and increased their ability to purchase Pennsylvania deeds. This created an atmosphere that was both corrosive to resistance and conducive to accommodation. By analyzing tax assessments from Luzerne County's Wysox Township—which, up until 1804, included that bastion of Wild Yankee resistance, Sugar Creek—it is possible to chart this process. Specifically, the changing ratio between unimproved and improved acreage documented in tax rolls provides a rough index of how far down the path toward rural prosperity the township's inhabitants had come. In 1799 there were more than eighteen acres of unimproved land in the district for every acre that had been improved. By 1801 there were slightly more than eleven unimproved acres for every improved acre, and three years later, there were just over nine acres of unimproved land for every cleared acre. If the town of Claverack (which constituted the oldest settlement is Wysox Township) is considered alone, the ratio of unimproved to improved land plummets to three to one. It is also possible to get a rough sense of individual settlers' progress through these tax assessments. In 1799 Wysox Township's taxables possessed, on average, eleven and a half acres of improved land. By 1804 the mean had jumped close

---

36. Wysox Assessment of 1804 and Burlington (Canton) Assessment of 1804, TPM. For the names of the inhabitants of the town of Claverack, see Classification of the Seventeen Townships, PHMC.

to fourteen acres and, if the Sugar Creek's newer settlements are left out of the equation, it rises to seventeen acres.[37]

Taken together, these figures illustrate that settlers were transforming the district from a place where forests dominated, to one where farmsteads increasingly replaced woods. Though these aggregate figures show that settlers were collectively clearing more acres and moving toward rural competency, they hide that improved land was not evenly distributed. Recently arrived migrants and the sons of long-settled inhabitants just starting out in the world possessed far fewer cleared acres than their more established neighbors. Amos Bennett, who first came to Northeast Pennsylvania in 1778, took up land in Wysox Township in 1791. He had cleared thirty acres by 1799 and fifteen more by 1804. In comparison, Henry Cornelius, who moved to Pennsylvania from Kinderhook, New York, after 1800, had only managed to clear six of the hundred acres he held by 1804.[38]

Even if a large proportion of a settlement's inhabitants remained determined to oppose Pennsylvania, it only took a minority of compromise-minded settlers to undermine resistance. Robert Rose's visit to Sugar Creek in the summer of 1803 illustrates this. The three men whom Rose convinced to turn against the Connecticut claim—Ezra Goddard, Luther Goddard, and Stephen Ballard—were all well-established settlers (Stephen Ballard had arrived along the creek in 1792 and the Goddards came four years later) who had reached a more advanced stage of farm development than many of their neighbors. While Sugar Creek inhabitants possessed an average of nine acres of improved land in 1804, these three men possessed sixteen, thirteen, and twenty-eight acres respectively. Moreover, the Goddard brothers jointly ran grist and saw mills that added to their wealth and economic standing. These defectors became the vanguard of the thirty Sugar Creek settlers who opened up negotiations with the Landholders' Association shortly after Rose's visit.[39] Eventually, every Yankee settlement reached a tipping point where a critical mass of its inhabitants turned away from violence and toward negotiation as a means of keeping their farms. Once this point was reached, it was difficult for Yankee hardliners to maintain their opposition. Their only recourse was to join their more compromise-minded neighbors and to make the best terms they could with the state and its landholders or, failing this, to move on to a different location and begin the process of farm building anew.

37. Wysox Assessments of 1799, 1801, 1804; Burlington (Canton) Assessment of 1804, TPM.
38. Heverly, *Pioneer and Patriot Families*, 1:182 and 2:19.
39. Burlington (Canton) Assessment of 1804, TPM; Heverly, *Pioneer and Patriot Families*, 1:222–23, 266–67; Robert Rose to Samuel Hodgdon, July 28, 1803, CCP 2:40–41.

Markets

The formation of commercial markets is another aspect of frontier development essential to understanding the move from resistance to reconciliation. Even if they had developed farms able to turn out a surplus, Yankees who contemplated purchasing Pennsylvania deeds still had to have a means for transforming produce into payments. Rural folk could barter for most of their day-to-day needs, but the prospect of paying off the state or distant land speculators required more sophisticated, formalized networks of exchange through which settlers could acquire cash or credit.

By the turn of the century, Northeast Pennsylvania possessed (or was in the process of obtaining) the three components essential for the creation of a regional market: valuable commodities, inhabitants willing to engage in commercial exchange, and the transportation networks necessary to link them to the wider world. The upper reaches of the Susquehanna and Delaware valleys possessed great commercial potential. The area embraced thousands of acres of forests to be harvested and transformed into farms. In addition, it connected the growing settlements and rich agricultural lands of central and western New York to markets in Philadelphia and, later, Baltimore. The region also hosted a rapidly growing population. After having been nearly depopulated by the Revolutionary War, the population of the upper Susquehanna Valley grew to thirty-five thousand in 1790 and exceeded seventy-five thousand by 1800.[40]

Settlers in Northeast Pennsylvania and across the early America backcountry produced a number of "pioneer" commodities—goods that required very little labor and capital to turn out or that were byproducts of the process of farm building. One such item was lumber. Settlers cut down acres of trees as they fashioned farms out of forests. They simply burned much of this timber in the process of clearing fields and used more of it to build fences, construct cabins, and fuel fireplaces. However, an industrious settler could turn the trees he cleared from the land into a source of profit by selling them. Though requiring little capital or extra labor, marketing lumber was not feasible for many settlers. The problem was that backwoodsmen had to get the trees they cut off their land. Timber could be dragged short distances with a team of oxen, but a settler had to have access to a stream or river to move it farther. Moreover, the profit a settler could achieve by selling lumber was not high enough to make it worth the trouble (and danger) of moving cumbersome logs over long distances. It was only later in the nineteenth century that demand (and prices) for

---

40. Mancall, *Valley of Opportunity*, 180.

wood increased enough to produce a lumbering boom across northern Pennsylvania.[41]

Producing maple sugar was another option for pioneers in the North. Building on techniques they learned from Indians, settlers tapped sugar maples and boiled down the sap into syrup. The syrup could then be strained and dried to produce a crude brown sugar. Besides the cost of buying an iron kettle to boil down sap into syrup, producing maple sugar required little in the way of capital. Making sugar also fit well into the cycle of farm labor. Settlers tapped trees and produced sugar in late winter and early spring during the seasonal lull in farm labor before spring planting. Producing maple sugar was also reasonably lucrative considering the amount of time, tools, and labor it required but it certainly did not provide settlers with a cash windfall. In the early 1790s William Cooper purchased maple sugar from Otsego County farmers for six pence a pound. At such rates, a settler would have to turn out a lot of sugar to make a significant profit.[42]

Its low capitalization costs, ease of production, and profitability made potash the most attractive pioneer commodity to frontier settlers. With a few alternations, the process of burning the timber that littered freshly cut clearings could be transformed into a profitable venture. Instead of burning tree trunks and branches where they lay, settlers who intended to produce potash would gather them together in great piles in order to burn them more effectively. Settlers could sell their ashes to local merchants who would process them further. An acre of hardwoods usually produced sixty to one hundred bushels of ashes. In 1790 William Cooper purchased ashes for six pence a bushel, giving settlers $3.25 to $6.25 for every acre of hardwood they burned. Farmers interested in a better rate of return entered into the next phase of the production process. They washed their ashes down with water to extract the lye and then boiled it down into potash. Besides the considerable price of a boiling kettle—they sold for fifty dollars in western New York in the early nineteenth century—the costs of producing potash were low and the extra labor minimal. The process also transformed bulky timber into a compact, easily transportable commodity. Finally, it was profitable. Potash and its more refined counterpart, pearl ash, were used to produce soap, glass, saltpeter, dyes, and other manufactured goods. William Peacock, an agent for western New York's Holland Land Company, calculated that an acre of hardwoods would produce up to five hundred pounds of potash which, in turn, sold for

---

41. Ibid., 199–200, 227; Williams, *Americans and Their Forests*, 94–100, 160–67.
42. Mancall, *Valley of Opportunity*, 195–96; Alan Taylor, *William Cooper's Town: Power and Persuasion on the Frontier of the Early American Republic* (New York, 1995), 119–20, 432.

between $2.50 and $3.00 per hundred-weight (or between $12.50 and $15 per acre) in 1810.[43]

Once settlers had cleared enough land to support themselves and produce a surplus, they could market farm commodities in addition to those they drew from the forest. The process of farm building enabled Northeast Pennsylvania's settlers to enter into a profitable grain market. Europe's Napoleonic Wars produced surging prices for grain that benefited turn-of-the-century American farmers. With prices rising, backcountry inhabitants whose crops could once not bear the costs of transportation now found themselves able to sell their grain for a profit. The growth of market agriculture in the upper Susquehanna Valley is reflected in the increasing amounts of grain its farmers sent to Philadelphia and Baltimore. In 1790, the regions' farmers exported 150,000 bushels of grain. By 1795 this figure had expanded to 180,000 bushels and continued to go up through the early nineteenth century. Livestock represented another valuable farm commodity. That cattle could walk themselves to market over rough terrain was especially important in frontier regions with rudimentary road networks. Like pioneer commodities, livestock required relatively little labor to produce. Moreover, though they were certainly an element in the creation of a "settled" landscape, free-ranging animals that survived and multiplied in the woods were as much a gift of the forest as lumber, ash, or maple sugar.[44]

Besides producing a range of valuable commodities, the inhabitants of Northeast Pennsylvania were willing to engage in market exchange. The vast majority of early America's rural inhabitants did not possess enough land, livestock, or tools to be truly self-sufficient. To secure even their basic needs, farm families had to barter with neighbors and purchase goods from local stores. The latter sort of transaction ultimately tied them to regional, national, and international markets. Those households that did possess the wherewithal to meet their essential needs did not see self-sufficiency as an end to itself. Rural consumers could only obtain rum, tea, coffee, and the numerous other goods that made the difference between living and living well through contact with wider commercial networks.[45] This does not mean that farm folk always existed in harmony with market forces. In the summer of 1789 settlers from around

---

43. Taylor, *William Cooper's Town*, 108–9; Brooks, *Frontier Settlement and Market Revolution*, 64–65.
44. Mancall, *Valley of Opportunity*, 176; Taylor, *William Cooper's Town*, 105–6; Brooks, *Frontier Settlement and Market Revolution*, 66–69.
45. In recent decades the romantic image of the self-sufficient farmer has been laid to rest. See Pruitt, "Self-sufficiency and the Agricultural Economy"; and T. H. Breen, "An Empire of Goods: The Anglicanization of Colonial America," *Journal of British Studies* 25 (1986): 467–99.

Tioga Point, short on food and outraged by the high prices demanded by local traders, turned violent. In a letter to Henry Drinker, Samuel Wallis described how gangs of settlers in search of grain had "gone in arm'd body's & taken it from those who had carry'd [it] there for sale."[46] This episode represents a departure from the thousands of peaceful transactions that took place in the region between settlers and storekeepers. Frontier migrants did not seek to escape the marketplace. Rather, they hoped to acquire land so they could engage in it as producers rather than as dependent, landless workers.

Market exchange, like agrarian resistance, was one of many tools settlers used to secure freeholds and achieve independence. In the first few years of settlement, securing a subsistence was extremely difficult. Pioneer families often failed to clear enough tillage to feed themselves and forest predators and pests took a heavy toll on livestock. Newly arrived frontier migrants often had to buy food and other necessities to make ends meet. This is why pioneer commodities such as lumber and potash were so important. Harvesting and selling these goods gave settlers a way to earn cash and credit with which they could make purchases. Frontier farmers certainly cut lumber and made maple sugar to satisfy their own needs. But the only reason they took the trouble to produce potash in large quantities was to engage in market exchange. And produce it in large quantities they did. John Nicholson established potash and pearl ash works at Wilkes-Barre and near the mouth of Towanda Creek. These ventures proved unprofitable, not because of a lack of ash or a market for it, but because so many people were producing these commodities that the market became glutted, forcing prices down.[47]

Northeast Pennsylvania's commercial prospects had to be enhanced by improvements in transportation before this potential could be fully realized. The 1790s marked the beginning of a spate of road-building projects across the region. As early as 1788, Tench Coxe, Henry Drinker, James Wilson, John Nicholson, and other prominent speculators pledged hundreds of pounds toward the construction of roads that would connect the upper Delaware and Susquehanna River valleys to southeastern Pennsylvania. A year later, prominent Philadelphia residents established "A Society for Promoting the Improvements of Roads and Inland Navigation in the State of Pennsylvania." Led by financier Robert Morris, the group focused its efforts on the Susquehanna Valley. Besides these private efforts, the state embarked on its own program of road construction in the Wyoming region. Pennsylvania completed a road connecting Philadelphia to Sunbury and built others between Northampton and

---

46. Wallis quoted from Mancall, *Valley of Opportunity*, 172.
47. Mancall, *Valley of Opportunity*, 201.

the mouth of the Tioga River and between Wilkes-Barre and Wyalusing. By 1803, the all-weather Lancaster Turnpike had been extended to the Susquehanna River, increasing travel between the upper valley and Philadelphia.[48]

Besides building roads, economic boosters and the state worked on improving river transportation. The Susquehanna and Delaware rivers had always been at the heart of the region's transportation network. However, nature had imposed limits on both of these trade conduits. The Delaware River watered a relatively small hinterland. The Susquehanna River, though it embraced a huge swath of territory, was too shallow to navigate at its lower reaches. From the time of first settlement, craft of any size descending the river had to stop at Middletown (where the Conewago Falls presented the first obstruction to boats) and offload their cargos onto wagons that would take them over a hundred miles of road to Philadelphia. Innovations in boat design finally opened the length of the river to commercial traffic. In 1794 boatmen piloting new river "arks" (flat-bottomed, shallow draft boats ranging from sixty to ninety feet in length and fifteen to twenty feet in width) began running the Susquehanna's falls and rapids and taking their cargos directly to Havre de Grace from whence they could be loaded on shallops bound for Baltimore. These large craft could only navigate the river in the spring and fall when heavy rains raised water levels, but even this was a vast improvement over the old procedure. By 1800 Baltimore was replacing Philadelphia as the destination for commodities flowing down the Susquehanna. The opening of the river to navigation revolutionized the economy of Northeast Pennsylvania by effectively and efficiently tying it to national and international markets.[49]

The timing of these improvements in transportation was critical to the progress of reconciliation between the state and Connecticut claimants in the fifteen towns. The new roads and innovations in river navigation that appeared in the 1790s and early 1800s most directly benefited these river-side communities. By the turn of the century, the inhabitants of the fifteen towns lay astride the corridor that linked western and central New York and the upper Susquehanna Valley to merchants in Philadelphia and Baltimore. They knew that any surplus they produced would enjoy ready access to markets, which would enable them to acquire the money they needed to pay for Pennsylvania deeds.[50]

The market ties that created an atmosphere conducive to reconciliation spread only as far as roads and rivers would carry them. Economic isolation remained

---

48. Subscription List for Road for the Pennsylvania Landholders, Feb. 28, 1788, *SCP* 9:329–30; Mancall, *Valley of Opportunity*, 208; James Weston Livingood, *The Philadelphia-Baltimore Trade Rivalry, 1780–1860* (New York, 1970), 27–52.
49. Livingood, *Philadelphia-Baltimore Trade Rivalry*, 27–52.
50. Mancall, *Valley of Opportunity*, 171, 176, 206–13.

pronounced in the hill country of northern Pennsylvania. Pennsylvania could not hope to enforce its laws among settlers it could not reach nor entice them with economic opportunities that lay beyond their grasp. Backwoods settlers continued to complain of "the badness of the roads to their farms, & the difficulty of clearing the land, & getting its produce to market." While traveling along the Susquehanna in 1795, the Duc de la Rochefoucault-Liancourt described the conditions that continued to isolate die-hard Wild Yankees from state power and commercial opportunity. On one occasion, his party followed a road that led north out of the Wyoming Valley only to discover that it was little more than an eighteen-inch wide footpath that wound around "fallen trees, and led along the edges of a precipice."[51] With roads in poor condition or nonexistent, hill-country settlers found themselves largely cut off from regional commercial networks. Without markets, even farmers who could produce a surplus lacked the means for turning crops, livestock, or other commodities into cash or credit. Backwoods settlers who did manage to get goods to market saw their profits eaten up by higher transportation costs and offset by the time and difficulty of such trips. Travel by water was also limited for backwoods Yankees. While Wysox Creek, Wyalusing Creek, Sugar Creek, and other tributaries of the Susquehanna were navigable by canoe and certainly facilitated communication among neighboring settlers, they were not deep or wide enough to carry significant freight.

It was only in the first decade of the nineteenth century that hill-country Yankees came firmly into contact with the marketplace and the forces of accommodation. Pennsylvania's landholders were well aware of the isolation that cut off backwoods settlers from regional commercial networks and shielded them from state authority and did what they could to put through roads between the settled parts of Pennsylvania and the tracts they claimed to the north. In trying to obtain government funding for this project, they pointed out that, besides opening up great expanses of land to settlement, such a program of road building would help to subdue "any remaining disposition to disorder in the county of Luzerne" by creating an "easy road . . . by which a force, if necessary, may be rapidly moved to that place."[52] Nonetheless, roads of any account did not appear in areas dominated by Wild Yankees until the turn of the century. The construction of roads between Tioga Point and Towanda Creek and between Wysox Creek and Wyalusing Creek only began in the early 1790s and took several years to complete. The upper reaches of Sugar Creek, another hotbed of Yankee dissent, were not effectively linked to the wider world by

---

51. Robert Rose to Samuel Hodgdon, July 10, 1803, *SCP* 11:395–96; Rochefoucault-Liancourt, *Travels through the United States*, 1:33.

52. Subscription List for Road for the Pennsylvania Landholders, Feb. 28, 1788, and Observations by the Committee of the Pennsylvania landholders, Mar. 5, 1788, *SCP* 9:329–33.

roads until the nineteenth century—around the same time that the area's inhabitants abandoned resistance and came to terms with Pennsylvania and its landholders.[53]

Roads may have enabled isolated settlers to reach markets, but stores brought the market to them. Starting in the late 1790s stores began to crop up among backwoods Yankee settlements and joined those in more established river-side communities. For example, Ezra Goddard entered into store keeping when he brought a small stock of goods up Sugar Creek to Juddsburgh in 1796. Elisha Keeler followed suit when he opened a store along Wyalusing Creek in 1804. These backwoods entrepreneurs and others brought consumer goods to their neighbors and, more important, furnished them with a means for transforming their produce into cash or credit.[54]

The development of commercial networks transformed how Connecticut claimants perceived their relationship to Pennsylvania. Those who lacked market ties remained more fully wed to a subsistence culture that stressed the primacy of local authority and encouraged farmers to commit economic resources to assure their family's subsistence rather than to take advantage of commercial opportunities. Settlers who perceived the world through this cultural lens saw state authority as a threat to their status as independent yeomen. Commercially connected Yankees developed a different perspective. Instead of viewing the roads and rivers that tied them to the rest of the state as avenues through which their communities would be invaded by surveyors and land agents, they understood them as profitable paths of egress through which they could channel their surplus to outside markets. Settlers who sold surplus produce to merchants in Wilkes-Barre and Tioga Point for shipment down the Susquehanna were more likely to see the purchase of a Pennsylvania deed as a way to secure commercial ties, and their independence, than as an obstacle to household autonomy.[55] The role that commerce played in bringing peace to Northeast Pennsylvania is also intimately tied to geography. The rivers and streams that served as conduits for commerce flowed south toward market centers in Philadelphia and Baltimore. Settlers who had any ambition to rise above a bare subsistence and gain the comfortable competency and prosperity offered by commerce had to deal with Pennsylvania.

53. Craft, *History of Bradford County*, 249–50.
54. Heverly, *Patriot and Pioneer Families*, 1:233–34, 266.
55. Works that discuss the relationship between subsistence agriculture, market connections, and the outlook of yeomen farmers include James A. Henretta, "Families and Farms: Mentalité in Pre-Industrial America," *WMQ* 35 (Jan. 1978): 1–32; Michael Merrill, "Cash is Good to Eat: Self-Sufficiency and Exchange in the Rural Economy of the United States," *Radical History Review* 4 (1977): 42–71; and Daniel Vickers, "Competency and Competition: Economic Culture in Early America," *WMQ* 47 (Jan. 1990): 3–29.

By the nineteenth century, the settler unity on which Yankee resistance depended was crumbling. The pursuit of personal independence, which had once motivated opposition, now moved many Connecticut claimants toward accommodation with Pennsylvania and its landholders. The consequences of this were demonstrated in November 1804 when Constable Howard Spalding arrived along Sugar Creek carrying warrants against forty-six settlers under the Intrusion Act. Instead of resisting, most of the wanted men fled into the hills. Only Phineas Pierce, Michael Bird, and John Barber opposed the constable's arrival. The three leveled their guns at Spalding and warned that they would shoot him before they would be taken. However, the men backed down when Spalding declared his determination to do his duty. Pierce and Bird later repented for their actions and offered to pay for state titles. Many of the settlers who had run off followed suit and surrendered themselves to state authorities. Only John Barber, who was suspected of having taken a hand in Edward Gobin's shooting, remained defiant.[56]

This confrontation marked the collapse of agrarian resistance in Northeast Pennsylvania. In the 1780s or 1790s, a lone constable who entered a Yankee settlement to serve warrants would have been mobbed, tarred and feathered, or worse. But by the 1800s the insurgency had ebbed. Through a combination of compromise and force, Pennsylvania officials and the Landholders' Association convinced many Yankees that the only way to secure their property was to relinquish their Connecticut deeds. In the end, Sugar Creek's settlers agreed to pay the value of their lands in a state of nature or to quit their farms if they were compensated for their improvements. With this breakthrough, Robert Rose asserted that "the Connecticut claim may now be said to be perfectly abandoned."[57] This did not, however, spell an end to conflict in the region. At the center of the Wyoming controversy's final battles stood a handful of prominent settlers who had to balance their roles as community leaders against their interests as backcountry entrepreneurs.

---

56. James Ralston to Thomas McKean, Nov. 17, 1804, and Affidavit of Howard Spalding, Constable, Nov. 7, 1804, CCP 2:104.

57. Robert Rose to Samuel Hodgdon, Nov. 28, 1804, CCP 2:106.

CHAPTER 7

"ARTFUL DECEIVERS"

Yankee Notables and the Resolution of the Wyoming Controversy

In rural communities across early America, a few leading inhabitants stood above their neighbors in terms of wealth and social status. In Northeast Pennsylvania, one such man was Bartlett Hinds. A Revolutionary War veteran who often went by the title "Captain," Hinds was no ordinary frontier settler. A native of Boston, Massachusetts, he came to the Susquehanna Valley in 1800. Once there, he developed a four-hundred-acre tract along Wyalusing Creek that he had purchased from the one-time governor of Connecticut Samuel Huntingdon and, in the capacity of a resident land agent, promoted Huntingdon's efforts to sell and settle thousands of additional acres he held in Pennsylvania under the Connecticut claim. Hinds did not migrate to the frontier alone but brought his wife, daughter, three sons, a brother, and half-a-dozen other families with him. He soon emerged as the chief inhabitant of a growing backcountry community known as "The Hinds Settlement." In keeping with his position as a leading man and revolutionary veteran, Captain Hinds organized his settlement's Fourth of July celebrations. One year he even orchestrated an ingenious thirteen-gun salute (one for each of the rebellious colonies) to America's independence. Using a technique practiced by frontiersmen to clear land, Hinds cut a line of thirteen trees until they were just ready to fall. Then, with the stroke of an ax, he caused the first, "driver," tree to topple which, in turn, caused the other trees to fall with a thundering crash that resembled "the roar of cannon."[1]

---

1. Emily C. Blackman, *History of Susquehanna County, Pennsylvania* (Philadelphia, 1873), 287–89. For an example of how Hind's tree-felling stunt was used by settlers to clear land, see

In the early nineteenth century, Northeast Pennsylvania began to shed its raw frontier character and start down the road to becoming a market-connected agricultural hinterland. This process of improvement enhanced the position of a group of local notables whose reputation, wealth, and authority placed them above other settlers and made them key players in the region's struggle for property and power.[2] Samuel Preston, land agent to Pennsylvania landholder Henry Drinker, penned a letter to his employer in 1803 outlining the central role Yankee notables played in the Wyoming controversy. Preston divided the Connecticut claimants who occupied Drinker's lands into two categories: a few leading men who were resident proprietors of the Susquehannah and Delaware companies and a much larger number of ordinary settlers. He described the former as "swindlers" and "artful deceivers" who sought to profit from their investments in the Connecticut claim and the latter as the "ignorant deceived" who, though they were primarily concerned with protecting their individual holdings, were cajoled into supporting their leaders' more extensive claims. In sum, Preston believed that Yankee notables were essential to the maintenance of settler resistance and the pivot point on which the course of events in Northeast Pennsylvania would turn.[3]

Yankee notables may have occupied a pivotal position but it was not an easy one. Leading men found that they had to reconcile self-interest with what was best for their communities. On the one hand, the power and influence of leading men was rooted in their locales. It rested in their neighbors' willingness to recognize their authority and was contingent on their ability to protect and promote their neighbors' interests. On the other, Yankee notables formed a rising class of backcountry entrepreneurs who at times went beyond their communities to secure wealth, power, and legitimacy. These overlapping identities did not always coexist in harmony. This was especially true in the first decade of the nineteenth century when Pennsylvania and hard-pressed Yankee settlers forced them to decide between the two. Intentionally or not, the choices they made helped to pave the way to the final settlement of the Wyoming dispute.

Alan Taylor, *Liberty Men and the Great Proprietors: The Revolutionary Settlement of the Maine Frontier, 1760–1820* (Chapel Hill, NC, 1990), 64.

2. For a discussion of the role of leading men in the revolutionary frontier's agrarian disturbances, see Taylor, *Liberty Men*, 155–77; and Richard M. Brown, "Back Country Rebellions and the Homestead Ethic in America, 1740–1799," in *Tradition, Conflict, and Modernization: Perspectives on the American Revolution*, ed. Richard M. Brown and Don E. Fehrenbacher (New York, 1977), 87–91.

3. Samuel Preston to Henry Drinker, Mar. 8, 1803, HDP, Journal and Land Records, 1789–1809.

Closing the Wyoming Controversy

No single event marked the end of the Wyoming controversy. Instead, numerous episodes of negotiation brought the dispute to a close. One of these began to unfold in Athens on July 4, 1808. That day, Deputy Marshall Jacob Hart prepared to serve a writ of ejectment against Elizabeth Mathewson. The widow of deceased Yankee stalwart Elisha Mathewson, Elizabeth held land in the town under the Connecticut claim. Henry Welles, a Pennsylvania landholder, challenged her right to the property. Henry's father, George, had obtained Pennsylvania deeds covering the majority of Athens in 1798 and succeeded in buying out most of the town's Yankee proprietors in the following years. Only two Connecticut claimants, including Elisha Mathewson, refused to sell. George's son and Elisha's widow carried on the dispute, which culminated in Deputy Hart's arrival in Athens. But the confrontation between Wells and Mathewson ended in compromise rather than conflict. On the night of July 3, Hart came in secret to Elizabeth's home and told her that if she made a show of resisting the writ, he would not serve it. The next day, the widow loaded an old musket and waited. As Hart had promised, he approached Mathewson's house and, seeing that she was armed, retreated from the scene. In October 1808, Elizabeth finally came to terms and turned over the disputed property (except for her home and tavern and the land on which they stood) to Welles for two hundred dollars.[4]

Reconciliation between Yankee settlers and Pennsylvania moved forward with growing momentum after 1804 and was largely complete by 1810. By decade's end, most Connecticut claimants had come to terms with the state and the Landholder's Association, and those who remained unreconciled lacked the numbers and unity needed to maintain an effective resistance. Stubborn holdouts eventually left the state or grudgingly purchased Pennsylvania deeds. Even leading Wild Yankees like John Franklin turned their backs on insurgency and violence. When Elizabeth Mathewson asked Franklin for aid in her dispute with Henry Welles, he only offered her ten dollars to help engage a lawyer.[5]

Pennsylvania subdued the last murmurs of Yankee dissent with new legislation. In 1807 the state expanded the terms of the Compromise Act to include categories of Connecticut claimants not formerly covered by the law. Specifically, the legislature authorized state commissioners to examine and confirm

---

4. Louise Welles Murray, *A History of Old Tioga Point and Early Athens* (Wilkes-Barre, PA, 1907), 353–56, 359–60, 382–86, 388–91; David Craft, *History of Bradford County, Pennsylvania* (Philadelphia, 1878), 277–78; H. C. Bradsby, *History of Bradford County, Pennsylvania* (Chicago, 1891), 415.

5. Murray, *History of Old Tioga*, 384–85.

the titles of Connecticut claimants who held lands in the fifteen towns but did not necessarily occupy them and of those who had obtained property in the towns *after* the Trenton Decree. Less than a year after this amendment went into effect, the Pennsylvania Assembly officially recognized the successful resolution of land disputes in the fifteen towns by dissolving the commission that administered the compromise law.[6] Pennsylvania also made moves, though limited, to extend the terms of the Compromise Act to settlers living outside of the fifteen towns. In 1810 the state briefly resurrected the law and used it to quiet the inhabitants of Bedford and Ulster.

Yankee notables stood at the forefront of this reconciliation. When Pennsylvania extended the Compromise Act to Bedford and Ulster, John Franklin, Elisha Satterlee, Joseph Kinney, and many other one-time Wild Yankee leaders discarded their Connecticut deeds in favor of state titles. In addition to purchasing land from the state, Joseph Kingsbury, who once considered settlers who accepted Pennsylvania deeds to be "traitors unworthy to live among full blooded Yankees," accepted a position as clerk to the commissioners of the Ulster-Bedford Act and later worked for them as a surveyor.[7] This spirit of cooperation was also apparent among Athens's leading men. In 1809 they joined together to help Henry Welles, who had so recently challenged the Connecticut deed of widow Mathewson, secure a seat in Pennsylvania's House of Representatives. Once in office, Welles led an attempt to get Athens included, along with Ulster and Bedford, under the provisions of the Compromise Act. Later, in 1817, Athens's leading inhabitants promoted a piece of legislation popularly known as the "Settlers' Bill." The law would have guaranteed state-awarded compensation for Connecticut claimants not covered by the Compromise Act who lost their lands as a result of the Wyoming controversy. Henry Welles's son, Charles, authored both of the petitions sent to the state assembly in support of the bill. Though both of these initiatives failed, they demonstrate that Northeast Pennsylvania's leading men were settling their differences—at least as far as contested land titles were concerned.[8]

Ironically, the final battle in Northeast Pennsylvania's struggle for property and power was fought between two prominent and intermarried Yankee families. In 1813 Elizabeth Mathewson commenced a lawsuit to recover three town lots in Athens that her husband had leased to her brother, Elisha

---

6. Amendments to the Compromise Act, Apr. 9, 1807, and Act Ending the Work of the Commission Under the Compromise Act, Mar. 28, 1808, *SCP* 11:519–21, 528–29.

7. Journal of the Commissioners of the Ulster-Bedford Act, PHMC; Joseph Kingsbury to John Jenkins, June 28, 1801, *SCP* 11:96.

8. Murray, *History of Old Tioga*, 393, 427–28, 431–34, 449–51, 459–60.

Satterlee. Six years earlier, in a move that poisoned relations between the two families for years to come, Elisha gained control of the leased land when he purchased a Pennsylvania deed to the property that superseded the Mathewson's Connecticut title. Elizabeth reopened the battle of the town lots when she discovered that the Pennsylvania deed held by her brother was faulty. The brother and sister waged an on-again off-again legal battle over the next fourteen years. The case eventually ended up before the Pennsylvania Supreme Court. In 1827 the court upheld the Satterlee family's possession of the disputed land but awarded Elizabeth Mathewson ten thousand dollars to compensate her for her losses.[9]

The Mathewson-Satterlee controversy demonstrates just how much conditions had changed in Northeast Pennsylvania. In the eighteenth century, the Mathewsons and Satterlees were united and at the forefront of Yankee resistance. But by the first decades of the nineteenth century, the struggle over property had divided these two families and many other Connecticut claimants. Moreover, instead of leading the fight for the Connecticut claim, Yankee notables like Elisha Satterlee promoted the process of accommodation. The conflict between Elizabeth Mathewson and Elisha Satterlee was not settled among Yankees and through violence but in Pennsylvania's highest court.

Yankee Notables

How and why the Wyoming controversy came to an end cannot be fully understood without considering Northeast Pennsylvania's Yankee notables. John Franklin, Elisha Satterlee, Joseph Kingsbury, and other leading settlers had once been at the forefront of resistance. After 1800, however, these same individuals turned toward reconciliation. The first step in deciphering their change of heart lies in understanding where they stood socially and economically with respect to their neighbors and the world beyond the backcountry.

Yankee notables may have constituted a local backcountry elite, but they were a far cry from powerful eastern gentlemen like those who headed up the Pennsylvania Landholders' Association. The association's leading members laid claim to hundreds of thousands of acres, were involved in commerce and manufacturing, and surrounded themselves with the trappings of wealth and power. Samuel Meredith, John Nicholson, and Henry Drinker lived in a world of bright carriages, spacious homes, and liveried servants. They claimed membership in a

9. Craft, *History of Bradford County*, 277–78; Murray, *History of Old Tioga*, 422–24, 459, 474.

national elite who dominated economic and political life in the early republic.[10] In contrast, the political connections enjoyed by backcountry leading men were restricted to those they made as militia officers and local magistrates, and the scope of their commercial activities was limited to marketing surplus farm produce, selling off small tracts of land, and operating mills. Instead of carriages, servants, and mansions, frontier notables were content with a good horse, a couple of dependable farm hands, and a frame house.

Yankee leading men could often not even match the wealth of more modest Pennsylvania landholders who resided in the Wyoming region. Samuel Stanton, a prominent Yankee settler whom Samuel Preston described as "the best man from Connecticut" in his neighborhood and the only one "not addicted to drunkenness" laid claim to almost nine hundred largely undeveloped acres valued at $1,530 and a small frame house worth $210. In terms of the size and value of his land holdings, he was head and shoulders above ordinary Yankees. Neighboring settlers possessed farms between one and five hundred acres. The average holding was a three-hundred-acre farm worth about $420 dollars.[11] Stanton may have stood out among his fellow New Englanders, but his wealth hardly compared to that of Henry Drinker's resident land agent, Samuel Preston. In 1798 he possessed a two-story frame home valued at $1,220. A tax assessment recorded eight years later listed Preston as owning two hundred acres of land (of which two-thirds were improved) and a number of outbuildings worth $1,090 and three mills worth $300. While Preston managed numerous commercial ventures and oversaw the development of Stockport, a thriving backcountry trade center, Stanton, according to local tradition, had to struggle to keep his family from starving when they first came to the frontier. Although knee-deep in land rights, prominent Connecticut claimants like Stanton could easily fall short of the money and labor needed to clear the land, make improvements, or even assure their families a bare subsistence.[12]

In terms of wealth, many leading Connecticut claimants were not far removed from the average Yankee settler. Jonas Ingham, Minor York, and Elisha Keeler were widely recognized as Wyalusing Creek's leading men. In 1798 the average value of a home along the creek was just over $24, the average farm contained 260 acres, and the average per-acre value of land was about a $1.30.

---

10. Thomas M. Doerflinger, *A Vigorous Spirit of Enterprise: Merchants and Economic Development in Revolutionary Philadelphia* (New York, 1987), 21–30. For a discussion of the wealth, influence, and outlook of gentlemen-speculators in Massachusetts see Alan Taylor, *Liberty Men*, 31–60.

11. Samuel Preston to Henry Drinker, May 22, 1799, HDP; USDT, Wayne County, Pennsylvania, no. 371.

12. Phineas G. Goodrich, *History of Wayne County* (Honesdale, PA, 1880), 188–89, 217; USDT, Wayne County, Pennsylvania, no. 368:593, 599.

Minor York was Wyalusing Creek's most prosperous settler. He possessed a $200 home, a frame barn, and three hundred acres of land worth $1,200, or $4 an acre. Ingham, who arrived in Northeast Pennsylvania in 1789, was by no means rich but held the land and resources needed to move down the path toward prosperity. He owned a home valued at $150, a small log barn, and six hundred acres of land worth $850, or about $1.45 an acre. At the lowest end of the scale was Elisha Keeler. He lived in a cabin worth only $20, possessed a crude log barn, and held title to a 350-acre farm valued at about $1.28 an acre. Keeler, whose property values fell slightly below the mean, probably maintained a standard of living familiar to most settlers.[13]

Those unfamiliar with life in the backcountry easily missed many of the signs that denoted a person as a leading man. Robert Rose described Yankee notable Ezra Goddard as "one of the ruder animals in existence," but he was perceptive enough to see that, in spite of appearances, Goddard was an "influential & comparatively wealthy" man.[14] The possession of a barn or other outbuildings, common among farmers in settled areas, was a mark of prestige in backwoods regions and testified to an individual's status as a leading man. Sugar Creek's most prominent settlers all had barns listed in their tax assessments. These buildings were, more often than not, rude log structures, but they signaled that their owners had the means and the ambition to develop their frontier freeholds into valuable farms capable of producing marketable surpluses of crops, fodder, and livestock. More than barns and outbuildings, mills signified their owners' preeminence. Yankee notables Ezra and Luther Goddard owed their status to the mills they jointly owned and operated. As millers, they turned their neighbors' grain into flour and their trees into lumber, providing crucial services that made them important figures in their settlement.[15]

The status and power of local notables, besides taking the demonstrable form of material possessions and money, were rooted in the less tangible ties of community life. A position of authority within an extensive kin network or the prestige of being a settlement's founding father could convey to an individual the title of leading man. Samuel Stanton owed much of his local influence to his status as his settlement's earliest homesteader. Such pioneers were valued not only because of the experience and advice they could offer to later migrants, but because their more developed farms often produced enough food to help support newcomers through their first difficult years along the frontier.

13. USDT, Luzerne County, Pennsylvania nos. 374: 40, 41, and 375 142, 148.
14. Robert Rose to Samuel Hodgdon, July 21, 1803, CCP 2:40.
15. USDT, Luzerne County, Pennsylvania, no. 375:155–57; Clement F. Heverly, *Pioneer and Patriot Families of Bradford County, Pennsylvania*, 2 vols. (Towanda, PA, 1915), 1:266–67.

Pennsylvania land agent Samuel Baird touched on how kinship contributed to local stature when he described Gordon Fowler, one of the chief inhabitants along Towanda Creek, as being "as formidable as an Eastern Patriarch" because of the "number of his Sons and Sons in law" who had settled around him.[16] The esteem and respect of friends and neighbors was another essential foundation of status in the backcountry. A settler's reputation for honesty, fair dealing, and concern for others could go a long way toward establishing his prominence in the community. Among Connecticut claimants, a man's community-mindedness was often judged with reference to his willingness to stand up for his neighbors against Pennsylvania and its landholders.

Notables and Neighbors

The local influence of leading men made them key figures in the choice between accommodation and resistance. According to Samuel Preston, Samuel Stanton took "great pains" to dissuade Yankee settlers from purchasing Pennsylvania deeds. He played on his neighbors' fear of dispossession by telling them that once they relinquished their Connecticut titles—and thus stripped themselves of any legal claim to their lands—Pennsylvania's landholders would eject them from their farms instead of selling them state deeds. Stanton also encouraged continued resistance by reminding settlers of "the success of Governor Chittenden & the Allen's in forming the State of Vermont" and asserting that they could accomplish a similar feat "with greater ease."[17]

Stanton was not the only Yankee notable who strove to shape the attitudes of his neighbors. In 1802 Major Theodore Woodbridge, whom Preston described as "a man of great merit & influence," seated himself on a twelve-hundred-acre tract that he claimed under a Delaware Company deed. Besides his sizable land holdings, Woodbridge's status as a leading settler rested on the kinship network he created by settling family members on his lands.[18] Soon after his arrival, he braced local resistance by declaring his intention of standing "between his Settlers and harm under an Ejectment." But in the following

16. David W. Maxey, "Of Castles in Stockport and Other Strictures: Samuel Preston's Contentious Agency for Henry Drinker," *PMHB* 100 (July 1986): 437; Samuel Baird to Thomas Cooper, Oct. 7, 1803, Letters from Pennsylvania Claimants to the Commissioners, PHMC; Heverly, *Pioneer and Patriot Families*, 1:335–39.

17. Samuel Preston to Henry Drinker, Sept. 19, 1797, and Preston to Drinker, Oct. 13, 1797, HDP, Journal; Extract of a Letter from Wayne County, July 21, 1801, CCP 1:76; Henry Drinker to Tench Coxe, Aug. 20, 1801, *SCP* 11:182.

18. Goodrich, *History of Wayne County*, 268–70; Samuel Preston to Henry Drinker, Mar. 8, 1803, HDP, Journal.

year James Ralston reported that Woodbridge had been instrumental in convincing his neighbors to renounce the Connecticut claim. For reasons that remain obscure, he again changed direction in 1804. According to Pennsylvania surveyor Jason Torrey, Woodbridge persuaded settlers to reject the proposals of the Pennsylvania Landholders and, using his authority as a justice of the peace, had Pennsylvania surveyors who entered his neighborhood arrested for trespassing.[19]

Pennsylvania and its landholders recognized the important role leading men played in shaping local opinion and went to great lengths to obtain their cooperation. In the summer of 1803, Thomas Cooper wrote to Robert Rose and urged him to contact several prominent Connecticut claimants who could supply him with information on intruders and, at the very least, help him find safe passage through areas controlled by Wild Yankees. On Wyalusing Creek, Cooper advised Rose to visit Minor York who, according to reports, had created "a great Schism" among his neighbors by abandoning the Connecticut claim. On Wysox Creek, Cooper recommended that Rose meet with another influential settler, William Means. Means represented a more entrepreneurial brand of leading man. A Susquehanna River boatman in his youth, he had become a prosperous merchant and the owner of a distillery, a tavern, a ferry, and other commercial ventures by the turn of the century. In addition, Means possessed houses and outbuildings worth $300 and a 311-acre farm of which an impressive 123 acres were improved. Cooper believed that since Means had "much property at stake" he would "be a friend of the Pennsya title" even though he held his lands under rights from the Susquehannah Company.[20]

For successful Yankee entrepreneurs like William Means, the risks of resistance eventually outweighed its benefits. In the spring and summer of 1801, three of Towanda Creek's most prominent settlers, Orr Scoville, Stephen Allen, and David Allen, signed petitions offering to relinquish their Connecticut deeds. Having promoted resistance along the creek in the 1790s, Scoville became more conservative after the turn of the century. His change of heart may have been rooted in his desire to retain possession of a costly frame house (the first one built in his neighborhood), a spacious barn, a mill, and a valuable farm. Similarly, the Allens possessed lucrative grist and saw mills in addition to their farms. The increasingly uncertain future of the Connecticut claim

---

19. Jason Torrey to Edward Tilghman, May 31, 1802, JTP; James Ralston to the Landholders' Committee, May 17, 1803, and Edward Tilghman to Thomas McKean, Nov. 25, 1804, RPLA; Jason Torrey to Edward Tilghman, Oct. 10, 1804, JTP.

20. Thomas Cooper to Robert Rose, July 2, 1803, CCP 2:31; Wysox Assessment of 1804, TPM.

threatened these improvements and doubtlessly encouraged their move toward accommodation.[21] Many of Athens's leading men also gave up resistance when it became clear that continued support for the Connecticut claim threatened their economic standing. The town's chief inhabitants lived in well-appointed homes worth hundreds of dollars, possessed tracts of land whose values reached into the thousands (James Irwin alone held fourteen town lots in Athens), and ran prospering mills and taverns. In every respect they had attained a level of wealth far beyond that of the average Yankee settler.[22] In 1801 several of Athens's leading men delivered a petition to the Landholders' Association that signaled their willingness to abandon resistance and purchase state titles. It was this defection that convinced John Franklin and other company officials that continued resistance was pointless and persuaded them to pursue a negotiated settlement.[23]

In contrast, cash-strapped leading men in isolated backwoods neighborhoods were far more likely to remain committed to resistance. Such men were less able to afford the cost of purchasing their lands from Pennsylvania (especially if they wanted to retain possession of the large tracts they often claimed under the Susquehannah and Delaware companies) and less willing to risk the censure of their even more penurious neighbors. Notables who lacked easy access to markets and maintained limited economic horizons saw no real commercial advantage in coming to terms with the state.[24] Nathaniel Allen, whom Robert Rose called the "most influential man" along Sugar Creek, epitomizes this brand of leading men. In 1798 he possessed a home valued at fifty dollars, a log barn, and rights to thousands of acres of land under the Connecticut claim. Though Allen was by no means rich, he possessed wealth that set him apart from his neighbors. That he served as one of the Susquehannah Company's leading surveyors and land agents enhanced his local status. Through his connections with the company, he established and promoted settlement in the town of Burlington. In

---

21. List of Connecticut Relinquishments, June–Aug. 1801, *SCP* 11:193. Orr Scovill's land holdings are described in Heverly, *Patriot and Pioneer Families*, 1:159; in *The Luzerne County Federalist*, Feb. 2, 1805, WHGS; and in the Wysox Assessment of 1799 and 1801 and the Burlington (Canton) Assessment of 1804, TPM. For the property holdings of David and Stephen Allen see the USDT, Luzerne County, Pennsylvania, no. 375:149; and Wysox Assessments of 1801 and 1804, TPM.

22. USDT, Luzerne County, Pennsylvania, nos. 374:43–49 and 375:162–66; Murray, *History of Old Tioga*, 359.

23. Letter to the Landholders' Association from the Rev. John Smith, July 20, 1801, MPLA.

24. Alan Taylor notes this same pattern in "Agrarian Independence: Northern Land Rioters After the Revolution," in *Beyond the American Revolution: Explorations in the History of American Radicalism*, ed. Alfred F. Young (DeKalb, IL, 1993), 229–31.

1800 he became a justice of the peace, further adding to his prestige.[25] Yet he embraced this parochial base of support and encouraged his neighbors—many of whom were too poor to pay for state titles—to oppose Pennsylvania and its landholders. On more than one occasion he took the lead in rallying Sugar Creek's Wild Yankees. Allen was likely involved in the mobbing of Thomas Smiley in 1801 as well as the shooting of Edward Gobin in 1804. He also headed up local efforts to guard against intruding surveyors and land agents. At numerous settler meetings, Allen spoke out against accommodation with the Landholders' Association and, on one occasion, assured his neighbors that their claim to the land was "as holy as the God of nature could make it."[26]

Leading Yankees, no matter what their level of wealth or outlook, found it increasingly difficult to navigate their way between prosecution by the state and persecution by Yankee militants. Pennsylvania punished notables who promoted resistance by bringing suits against them under the Intrusion Act. By November 1801, the state had issued warrants against a number of prominent Connecticut claimants. Besides prosecuting long-time Yankee radicals like John Franklin, John Jenkins, and Elisha Satterlee, Pennsylvania also brought charges against Nathaniel Allen, Theodore Woodbridge, Josiah Grant, and other key leading men.[27] Josiah Grant, described as "a prominent character" and a "large Speculator," had been very active in buying and selling Susquehannah Company rights during the 1790s.[28] In 1798 he moved from Vermont to the upper reaches of Wysox Creek to oversee his lands in the town of Graham. Determined to protect his fledgling settlement, and perhaps influenced by his experiences as a Green Mountain Boy in Vermont, Grant became a stubborn defender of Yankee property rights. His stance made him a target of legal action by Pennsylvania and the Landholders' Association. In November 1803, a Luzerne County court found Grant guilty of intrusion and conspiracy.[29] Ezekiel Hyde, a proprietor of the Delaware Company and the leading

---

25. Robert Rose to Samuel Hodgdon, July 21, 1803, CCP 2:38. For descriptions of Nathaniel Allen's property holdings, see USDT, Luzerne County, Pennsylvania no. 375:155; Bradsby, *History of Bradford County*, 391; Heverly, *Patriot and Pioneer Families*, 1:246; and Burlington (Canton) Assessment of 1804, TPM.

26. For Allen's role as a resistance leading, see *The Luzerne County Federalist*, Aug. 20, 1803, WHGS; Nathaniel Allen to John Jenkins, June 25, 1804, in Murray, *History of Old Tioga*, 420–21; and Robert Rose to Samuel Hodgdon, Aug. 11, 1803, CCP:2 43.

27. Summary of Court Proceedings of Luzerne and Wayne counties, Nov. and Dec. 1801, SCP 11:250–51; Robert Rose to Henry Drinker, Sept. 1, 1803, CCP 2:59.

28. For entries concerning Grant's activities as a speculator, see SCA Liber C:559–69; Liber D:31–33, 44–45; Liber E:217–28, 258, 264, 332, 334, 340–41, 418, 427; Liber F:70–74; and Liber H:209–10, 212–13, 225–26, 258–59.

29. Heverly, *Patriot and Pioneer Families*, 1:300; Robert Rose to Samuel Hodgdon, Aug. 11, 1803; Rose to Hodgdon, Sept. 17, 1803; and Rose to Hodgdon, Nov. 26, 1803, CCP 2:43, 58, 68.

inhabitant of the town of Usher, was another prominent Yankee who attracted the attention of state prosecutors. The Landholder's Association took steps to ruin him when they sent backcountry trouble-shooter Robert Rose to collect evidence against Hyde and to convince settlers to testify against him in court.[30]

Of course, state authorities and Pennsylvania speculators preferred to co-opt Yankee notables rather than attempt to ruin them in lengthy and unpredictable court proceedings. The Landholders' Association readily dropped charges against prominent settlers if they renounced the Connecticut claim and encouraged their neighbors to follow suit. The association scrapped their plans to prosecute Isaac Hancock, a prominent Wyalusing settler, after he agreed to give evidence against Ezekiel Hyde.[31] Hancock was not the only leading man to turn against the Wild Yankees. In the summer of 1801, David Paine and several other resident proprietors of the Susquehannah Company gave evidence against their one-time business associates and fellow resistance leaders. Their testimony eventually led to the indictment of John Jenkins, Elisha Satterlee, John Franklin, and other Connecticut claimants for intrusion and conspiracy.[32]

Local notables who encouraged resistance ran the risk of legal prosecution, but those who turned their backs on Yankee soil rights risked raising the ire of their neighbors. Minor York was one leading man who discovered that cooperation with the Landholders' Association carried significant risks. In the summer of 1803, York labored to convince his neighbors to relinquish their Connecticut deeds. He eventually persuaded forty settlers to sign a petition signaling their willingness to open negotiations with the Landholders' Association but lamented that, in doing so, he "had only gained himself enemies." Even Robert Rose had to admit that the influence York "had formerly possessed had been greatly destroyed by his siding with the Pennsylvanians." York's position was so tenuous that Rose avoided face-to-face meetings with him: he valued York as an informant but feared that his being seen with an association agent would only further undermine his position.[33] Isaac Hancock was another prominent settler who paid a price for switching his allegiance to Pennsylvania. After helping to bring a warrant against Ezekiel Hyde for intrusion, he lost the support and respect of his neighbors and became known as a "Pennamite." Likewise, John Tyler, a leading man of the Nine Partners Settlement who of-

30. Robert Rose to Samuel Hodgdon, June 30, 1804, SCP 11:491; Rose to Hodgdon, Nov. 2, 1803, and Rose to Hodgdon, Nov. 10, 1803, CCP 2:60, 64.
31. Robert Rose to Samuel Hodgdon, Nov. 2, 1803, CCP 2:60.
32. A List of the Names of Offenders Under Intrusion Law, Aug. 1801, and Daniel Smith and Charles Hall to Abraham Horn, 1801, CCP 1:87, 94.
33. Robert Rose to Samuel Hodgdon, Aug. 21, 1803; Rose to Hodgdon, July 3, 1803; and Rose to Hodgdon, July 10, 1803, CCP 2:49, 33, 36.

fered to work for the Pennsylvania landholders, was "much abused by ill will and ill language from some of his disaffected neighbors." Fearing for his safety, he soon severed his ties with the association.[34] Robert Rose recognized that many notables walked a dangerously thin line between local allegiance and self-interest and used this knowledge to his advantage. He sought out leading Wild Yankees knowing that if he could not persuade them to abandon resistance, that at least he could raise "suspicions of their intensions" in the minds of their followers.[35]

Some notables consistently promoted, or resisted, accommodation with Pennsylvania and its landholders. Others, like Bartlett Hinds, presented themselves as proponents of resistance or advocates of accommodation depending on who their audience was and which position best served their immediate interests. In June 1801, Hinds delivered a letter to Governor Thomas McKean signed by thirty settlers that proclaimed their loyalty to the laws of Pennsylvania and their willingness to relinquish their Connecticut deeds. But on returning to his backcountry home Hinds "reported divers falsehoods" about his meeting with the governor in order to derail negotiations with the state and its landholders. He claimed that McKean doubted the legitimacy of many Pennsylvania claimants' titles and advised settlers not to purchase land from the Landholders' Association.[36] When state officials caught wind of Hinds's duplicity they targeted him for prosecution under the Intrusion Act. Fearing his imprisonment and financial ruin, Captain Hinds reversed himself again. He repurchased his land from Pennsylvania and gave testimony that led to the prosecution of a dozen other settlers. As if this treachery was not enough to blacken Hinds's name, a rumor circulated that he had received five acres of land from Pennsylvania for every settler he helped to indict.[37] Captain Hinds's betrayal ultimately led to the severe drubbing he received at the hands of Wild Yankees in December 1802.

The struggle between resistance and accommodation did not bring every leading man into conflict with his community. Several Yankee notables maintained solidarity with their neighbors and continued to serve the needs of their settlements, even in the face of economic ruin and imprisonment. Nathaniel Allen was one prominent backcountry inhabitant who remained loyal to his community—Jonas Ingham was another. A native of Bucks County, Pennsylvania, Ingham

34. Jason Torrey to Henry Drinker, July 17, 1802, JTP.
35. Robert Rose to Samuel Hodgdon, Nov. 2, 1801, and Rose to Hodgdon, Aug. 11, 1803, CCP 2:60, 43.
36. Henry Drinker to Tench Coxe, Aug. 20, 1801, and Henry Drinker to John Tyler, June 9, 1801, HDP, Letterbook, 1800–1806; Extract of a Letter from Wayne County, CCP 1:76.
37. Blackman, *History of Susquehanna County*, 21–22; Document no. 1 attached to letter of Samuel Hodgdon and James Strawbridge to Landholders' Committee, Nov. 26, 1801, MPLA; List of Persons Presented Under the Intrusion Act, CCP 1:87.

settled along Wyalusing Creek in 1789 under a Connecticut title. His local influence rested on his relative wealth and on his outspoken support of the Connecticut claim. In 1804 the inhabitants of Luzerne County rewarded Ingham for his steadfastness by sending him to the state legislature as their representative. Once there, he worked to forward the interests of Connecticut claimants.[38] Under Jonas Ingham's leadership, Yankee settlers along the upper reaches of Wyalusing Creek maintained resistance long after most others had lost the ability to mount effective opposition to Pennsylvania and its landholders. As late as 1806, Wyalusing's settlers, guided by Ingham, successfully drove off a surveyor employed by Pennsylvania landholders. When he got word of the surveyor's approach, Ingham advised his neighbors "to make any kind of opposition they pleased only not to kill or hurt nobody, nor let anybody appear in arms." He knew any action that could be interpreted as armed insurrection would bring down the state militia on their heads. Settlers hiding in the woods fired guns into the air while the surveying party appeared while others, who did not carry firearms, surrounded and threatened the Pennsylvanians. Tensions rose when the surveyors ignored these challenges and continued their work. Ingham, fearing "some worse mischief would happen," told the settlers to break the surveyor's compass. Someone complied with his order and the surveyors retreated. After this encounter, Ingham continued to mediate between settlers and state officials. He defended Wild Yankees in court and later worked to arrange a settlement with Pennsylvania landholders agreeable to his neighbors.[39]

Eventually, every Yankee notable faced the choice between resistance and reconciliation. Some leading settlers—men like Bartlett Hinds—embraced the latter and fell afoul of Wild Yankees. Others, like Nathaniel Allen and Jonas Ingham, continued to support their neighbors and resistance and came into conflict with state authorities. The real distinction between Hinds and Allen and Ingham was not *if* they moved toward accommodation with the state but *how* they did so. Hinds pursued reconciliation with Pennsylvania at the expense of ordinary settlers. In contrast, the latter two leading men stuck to the path of resistance while that served the needs of their communities and only turned toward reconciliation when their neighbors were ready to move in that direction. No matter how they approached the prospect of accommodation, Yankee notables found the turn of the century a troubling time when their influence and authority was challenged by Pennsylvania, by their fellow settlers, and by the tension between self-interest and community.

38. For information on Allen's speculating activities see SCA Liber C:570–71; Liber F:80–85; Liber H:7; and Liber I:72–73, 229.
39. Craft, *History of Bradford County*, 443; Murray, *History of Old Tioga*, 406 n. 15.

Fraternal Order and Party Spirit

In the end, most Yankee notables chose the path of accommodation over that of resistance and helped to bring the Wyoming dispute to an end. Joseph Kingsbury was one of them. Kingsbury, once a prominent Wild Yankee, turned his back on violence after 1800. He even went so far as to aid Pennsylvania in extending the provisions of the Compromise Act over the towns of Ulster and Bedford in 1810. What accounts for this shift in attitude and behavior? On one level, Kingsbury simply numbered among those who decided that they could better secure their property and independence through reconciliation rather than resistance. But on another, he was also one of the many leading men whose growing attachment to Freemasonry and deepening involvement in party politics eventually undermined their commitment to agrarian resistance. By becoming a freemason, Kingsbury gained access to a new source of status and identity that existed beyond the bounds of their communities. Second, as a Federalist and, later, as a Democratic-Republican, Kingsbury participated in a process whereby state and national party organizations, rather than the Wyoming controversy, came to dominate notables' calculations of allegiance.

Freemasonry was central to Yankee notables' turn-of-the-century efforts to refashion themselves. The Masonic order was a select secret society which, besides advancing fraternity among Masons, promoted the economic well-being and social prestige of its members. Between 1790 and 1840, as many as 100,000 Americans became Masons. Many of these initiates were enterprising individuals who populated small commercial towns in the nation's rapidly expanding hinterlands.[40] Northeast Pennsylvania followed this national pattern. The chief inhabitants of Wilkes-Barre formed a Masonic lodge in 1794. Athens's leading men followed suit with the formation of the Rural Amity Lodge in 1796, and prominent settlers from around Towanda Creek established the Union Lodge in 1807. The Rural Amity Lodge had fourteen charter members, including such notables as Elisha Satterlee, Joseph Kingsbury, and Josiah Grant. Also among the lodge's original Masons was Zephon Flower, whose horse became the victim of a skimmington because of his work for the Pennsylvania Landholders' Association.[41]

---

40. Steven C. Bullock, "A Pure and Sublime System: The Appeal of Post-Revolutionary Freemasonry," *Journal of the Early Republic* 9 (fall 1989): 366–69; Alan Taylor, *William Cooper's Town: Power and Persuasion on the Frontier of the Early American Republic* (New York, 1995), 210–13; Jon Butler, *Awash in a Sea of Faith: Christianizing the American People* (Cambridge, MA, 1990), 235.

41. Craft, *History of Bradford County*, 177; Bradsby, *History of Bradford County*, 369, 307, 371; Heverly, *Pioneer and Patriot Families*, 1:189.

Like many who joined the Masonic order after the Revolution, Pennsylvania's Yankee notables were an ambitious, but marginal, local elite in search of legitimacy, prestige, and power. Josiah Grant looked to Freemasonry to bolster his status. The way people are commemorated in death speaks volumes about who they were while they lived. That Grant was buried with full Masonic honors suggests that Freemasonry was an important element of his identity.[42] A collective portrait of Athens's chief inhabitants presents a similar image of men striving to complement their economic accomplishments with the social capital provided by Masonic membership. Elisha Satterlee, John Spalding, John Shepard, Noah Murray, and Clement Paine were leading landholders in Athens and all were at the forefront of efforts to transform the town from a rough-and-tumble frontier settlement into a commercial center replete with inns, stores, and mills. This same spirit of improvement led these men to establish the Athens Academy—one of the region's first formal public schools—in 1797. But to fully satisfy their craving for distinction, these Yankee boosters felt the need to gain acceptance into the ranks of Freemasons and founded a Masonic lodge in order to make this aspiration a reality.[43]

Freemasonry offered Yankee notables a source of prestige and identity that transcended the traditional bonds of agrarian life. Through Masonry, leading men were able to nurture relationships based not on kinship or locale but on *association*: the voluntary formation of ties among like-minded peers. Although the standards for Masonic membership significantly widened after the Revolution, acceptance into the order still carried considerable prestige. This elitism appealed to Yankee notables who wished to gain recognition and acceptance from gentlemen beyond the backcountry who could provide them with patronage, credit, or commercial connections.[44] Bartlett Hinds was one prominent settler who looked outside his community for social distinction. Thus, in addition to the other markers that denoted him as a leading man, Hinds added Masonic membership. He discovered, however, that while it might have added to his standing in the wider world, Masonic membership offered him little advantage in his dealings with ordinary settlers. Local tradition has it that during his ordeal at the hands of Wyalusing's Wild Yankees, Hinds gave a Masonic hand signal, hoping that fellow members of the fraternity would come to his aid. One apparent Mason did attempt to help Hinds but was forced back by the mob.[45]

---

42. Craft, *History of Bradford County*, 46–47; Heverly, *Pioneer and Patriot Families*, 1:300.
43. Dorothy Ann Lipson, *Freemasonry in Federalist Connecticut* (Princeton, 1977), 8, 77; Stephen C. Bullock, *Revolutionary Brotherhood: Freemasonry and the Transformation of the American Social Order, 1730–1840* (Chapel Hill, NC, 1996), 207–8, 220–23; Craft, *History of Bradford County*, 123.
44. Bullock, *Revolutionary Brotherhood*, 184–86, and "A Pure and Sublime System," 360.
45. Craft, *History of Bradford County*, 46–47; Bullock, *Revolutionary Brotherhood*, 184–85, 207–8; Taylor, *William Cooper's Town*, 210–13.

Yankee notables' turn to Freemasonry also altered their relationship to agrarian resistance. It is no coincidence that many Yankee Masons, several of whom were once prominent Wild Yankees, took the lead in promoting accommodation with Pennsylvania. The sorts of settlers who became Masons were also the sorts of settlers who possessed substantial landholdings and commercial ventures. Masons filled the ranks of Yankee accommodationists because they, like many leading men, held valuable estates that made continued resistance seem risky and the costs of accommodation acceptable. On a deeper level, for men such as Noah Murray, Clement Paine, and Joseph Kingsbury, settling their differences with Pennsylvania and its landholders offered the same sorts of advantages that came with Masonic membership: access to a wider world of patronage, opportunity, and commerce. To these leading Yankees, advancing their interests no longer entailed shielding themselves and their communities from outsiders but forging ties beyond the backcountry.

The confrontation between Elizabeth Mathewson and Deputy Jacob Hart provides a final illustration of how Freemasonry altered Yankee notables' relationships with their fellow settlers, Pennsylvania, and agrarian resistance. The episode can only be fully understood in the context of the deepening inroads the fraternal order made among Northeast Pennsylvania's leading men. Both Hart and Elizabeth's recently deceased husband, Elisha, were Freemasons and it was in the spirit of Masonic brotherhood that Hart proposed the arrangement whereby he did not serve the writ of eviction against widow Mathewson. Thus Freemasonry brought a Pennsylvania deputy to the aid of a Yankee landholder against a Pennsylvania land claimant. What did not happen that July day is just as important as what did. Wild Yankees did not gather to protect Mathewson's property and punish Deputy Hart. Even the one-time Yankee firebrand John Franklin offered legal advice rather than armed force.[46] Athens's inhabitants, or at least its leading residents, had turned away from violence as a method of promoting their interests and toward instruments more befitting an aspiring local elite—the law and politics.

Political parties offered leading Yankees another opportunity to build identities and allegiances that extended beyond their backcountry settlements. At the turn of the century, Northeast Pennsylvania was politically out of step with much of the backcountry. Frontier farmers across America almost universally aligned themselves with the Anti-Federalists and, later, the Democratic-Republicans because of their populist rhetoric, localist outlook, and support for agrarian economic interests. Likewise, backcountry inhabitants generally opposed the Federalists whom they identified with the commercial, metropolitan agendas of elite merchants and land speculators. Yet Pennsylvania's Yankee

46. Murray, *History of Old Tioga*, 384–85, 390–91.

heartland was a Federalist stronghold and remained so into the nineteenth century, well after most other backcountry regions had gone over to the Republicans.[47]

Yankee settlers' regional heritage and preoccupation with the Wyoming controversy predisposed them to vote Federalist. Though the Federalist Party was the party of commercial and elite interests it was also the party of New England, and Connecticut claimants supported the Federalists out of loyalty to their Yankee homeland. More important, Yankees clung to the belief that an appeal to a federal court offered them the best chance of securing their claims and so supported the political party—the Federalists—that championed the power and authority of the national government. Simon Kinney, Joseph Kingsbury, Henry Spalding, and other leading Wild Yankees actively supported the Federalist Party. These "Sheshequinites," as Yankee Federalists came to be known, yoked party politics to efforts to win concessions for Connecticut claimants. In opposition to these Sheshequinites emerged a Republican faction made up mostly of Pennsylvania landholders, like Henry and Charles Welles, and leading Yankee settlers, like Minor York, Elisha Keeler, and Job Irish, who had switched their allegiance to Pennsylvania. That those who opposed the Connecticut claim gravitated toward the Republican Party only served to further cement the ties between Yankee hard-liners and the Federalists. Political affiliations at the turn of the century had much in common with patterns of allegiance during the Revolutionary War: "Federalist" and "Republican," like "Patriot" and "Tory," were labels pasted over much older and deeper divisions related to the region's struggle over property and power.[48]

The Wyoming dispute framed turn-of-the-century politics in Northeast Pennsylvania. During the 1799 gubernatorial race between Federalist James Ross and Republican Thomas McKean, a notice appeared in the *Wilkes-Barre Gazette* entitled "The PEACE and INTERESTS of the Government and People of Pennsylvania endangered: OR, The CONNECTICUT CLAIM To our Lands most injuriously aided." The polemic accused Ross of assisting Yankee intruders while he served as a senator in the state legislature. Here and elsewhere, local Republicans attempted to build up support among Pennsylvania claimants by associating their Federalist opponents with Yankee insurgents. During this same election, John Franklin traveled through Northeast Pennsylvania obtaining promises of support for Ross "on the ground that he was for

---

47. Saul Cornell, "Aristocracy Assailed: The Ideology of Backcountry Anti-Federalism," *Journal of American History* 76 (Mar. 1990): 1148–72; Murray, *History of Old Tioga*, 454; James E. Brady, "Wyoming: A Study of John Franklin and the Connecticut Settlement into Pennsylvania" (Ph.D. diss., Syracuse University, 1973), 306; Bradsby, *History of Bradford County*, 283–84; Taylor, *Liberty Men*, 209–15.

48. Bradsby, *History of Bradford County*, 283–84; Murray, *History of Old Tioga*, 454–58.

the Connecticut title." Franklin's tactic worked: Ross received 979 votes in Luzerne County, McKean only 259. When the two men again contended for the post of governor in 1802, the result was much the same. Ross received 680 votes in Luzerne County, McKean only 278. Tioga, Wysox, and Wyalusing, three Wild Yankee-dominated election districts in the upper portion of Luzerne County, proved to be the most pro-Federalist. While Ross took about 70 percent of the votes cast across the entire county, he obtained nearly 80 percent (158 out of 205) in these northern districts.[49]

Before 1810 Yankees' determination to defend their soil rights was so powerful that it transcended party affiliation. No matter if they were Federalists or Republicans, candidates well known for their support of the Connecticut claim did very well with Yankee voters. During state elections in 1801, John Franklin and Jonas Ingham both ran for the Pennsylvania Assembly even though Franklin was a Federalist and Ingham a "Stanch Republican." What made this cross-party ticket workable was that both Franklin and Ingham were well-known proponents of Yankee soil rights.[50] In 1801, 1802, and 1803 the Federalist John Franklin won landslide victories in Luzerne County that placed him in Pennsylvania's House of Representatives. Likewise, in 1801, Yankee stalwart John Jenkins, though a Republican, handily won the post of Luzerne County sheriff. In both cases, and despite their different party affiliations, Franklin and Jenkins received the lion's share of their support from areas dominated by Wild Yankees.[51] In 1802 Franklin obtained every vote but three in the election districts of northern Luzerne County; in 1803 he received every vote but ten. Similarly, Jenkins received 147 out of 151 votes in the election districts of Tioga and Wyalusing during his successful bid for county sheriff.[52]

Local political leaders joined ordinary voters in placing their attachment to the Connecticut claim before party allegiance. In 1801, Federalist Joseph Kingsbury wrote to Republican John Jenkins expressing his desire to "lay aside" partisan politics and "unite for the common good of Yankees." In that same year, Connecticut claimants created a "Yankee" or "half share Ticket" that brought together Federalists and Republicans in opposition to Pennsylvania and its landholders. Ebenezer Bowman observed in 1803 that while "at least eight tenths" of Luzerne County residents were Federalist, Republicans such as

---

49. *Wilkes-Barre Gazette*, Oct. 29, 1799, WHGS; Letter from Tench Coxe, Aug. 12, 1800, *SCP* 10:529; Craft, *History of Bradford County*, 192; Thomas Cooper to Thomas Mckean, Nov. 15, 1802, *SCP* 11:339.

50. Samuel Gordon to John Jenkins, Sept. 1801, *SCP* 11:202.

51. Bradsby, *History of Bradford County*, 282, 283–84, 288; Craft, *History of Bradford County*, 192; John Franklin to John Jenkins, September 16, 1801, *SCP* 11:198.

52. Bradsby, *History of Bradford County*, 282, 283–84, 288; Craft, *History of Bradford County*, 192.

John Jenkins and Ezekiel Hyde repeatedly won elections. He rightly concluded that this could only be accounted for by Yankees' "fixed determination to pursue their claim."[53]

Even as they provided Connecticut claimants with an instrument to wage their struggle against Pennsylvania, party politics also furnished Yankee notables with an alternative to violence. It is noteworthy that John Franklin, John Jenkins, Joseph Kingsbury, and other prominent settlers turned away from armed resistance around the same time they deepened their involvement in state-level politics. But even as politically savvy leading men forged a "Yankee Ticket" to push forward their interests, ordinary settlers were assaulting Pennsylvania surveyors and land agents. In other words, while notables and ordinary settlers may have still had a common goal (the preservation of their land claims) they increasingly divided on the tactics used to achieve it.

Leading men helped to transform Northeast Pennsylvania's political landscape in the second decade of the nineteenth century by bringing the region into the Republican fold. By 1805 John Franklin had retired from public life and no longer offered his personal magnetism to the Federalist cause. With the decline of settler resistance, Yankee notables began to look beyond their mistrust of Pennsylvania's Republican government and recognize how their political aspirations could be advanced by joining the Republican Party. For some time, the Republicans' proagrarian, populist outlook had attracted Yankee settlers. This development was especially pronounced outside of Luzerne County where the Federalist Sheshequinites were not so influential. Samuel Preston observed that Wayne County settlers from Federalist-dominated Connecticut "unanimously" turned to the Republicans when they arrived in the backcountry. Eventually, William Means, Joseph Kinney, Joseph Kingsbury, and many other leading men from Luzerne and Lycoming counties transferred their loyalty to the Republican Party. Nathaniel Allen, who started his political career at the end of the first decade of the nineteenth century, went straight into the Republican ranks.[54]

Yankee notables transformed local politics in one other crucial way: after 1810 they started to place party allegiance before loyalty to the Connecticut claim. Some even went so far as to form political ties with long-standing foes. Such an alliance took shape when Pennsylvania formed Bradford County out of the northern portions of Luzerne and Lycoming County in 1812. Yankee notables William Means, Nathaniel Allen, Joseph Kinney, and Joseph Kingsbury

53. Joseph Kingsbury to John Jenkins, June 28, 1801, and Ebenezer Bowman to Henry Drinker, Oct. 14, 1803, *SCP* 11:95–96, 420–22.
54. Samuel Preston to Henry Drinker, Nov. 14, 1799, HDP, Letterbook, 1786–1790; Bradsby, *History of Bradford County*, 298, 272–79.

dominated the new county's political apparatus. Means served as the county's first treasurer, Allen and Kinney both took posts as county commissioners, and Kingsbury accepted an appointment as county clerk. They joined forces with another Bradford County Republican, Henry Welles. Welles, who had so recently quarreled with Elizabeth Mathewson over her Athens town lots, became Bradford County's first representative to the state legislature.[55] That one-time insurgent leaders like Allen, Kinney, and Kingsbury could make common cause with a man like Henry Welles speaks volumes about how far Yankee notables had come down the road of reconciliation.

By 1812 partisan politics no longer responded to the ebb and flow of land disputes. Instead, politically active leading men began to use the Wyoming controversy (or memories of it) to merely mobilize voters. In 1817, Bradford County Republicans pushed for the passage of the "Settlers' Bill." Though the legislation had little chance of passage, it served an important political function during the year's gubernatorial election. Joseph Heister, the Federalist candidate and a man with longstanding ties to the Landholders' Association, opposed the law. Republicans showcased his opposition to the Settlers' Bill to undercut his standing among Northeast Pennsylvania's Yankees and backcountry inhabitants throughout the state. Likewise, in 1827, Bradford County Federalists helped to reignite a decade-old land dispute that had festered between Elizabeth Mathewson and Elisha Satterlee. They did so not to revive the Connecticut claim but to discredit their Republican foes, Charles and Henry Welles, among the county's inhabitants during an election year. The Federalists took the opportunity to remind voters that Henry Welles was the Pennsylvania landholder who had pushed Elizabeth Mathewson, a survivor of the Battle of Wyoming and a widow of one of the region's most venerated Yankee settlers, off her lands.[56]

Party politics and Masonry provided two avenues through which backcountry leading men reworked their relationship to their communities and to agrarian resistance. Whether these individuals took on the personae of Republicans, Federalists, or Freemasons, they all moved away from an identity based exclusively on family and community and toward one that transcended parochial boundaries and their commitment to the Connecticut claim. Both party politics and Freemasonry offered leading Yankees new ways of securing property and power that had little to do with community-sanctioned agrarian violence. They also led notables to discard a vision of independence rooted solely in the land and their locales and to adopt one that made room for a wider, more complex world of politics and commerce.

55. Bradsby, *History of Bradford County*, 298, 272–79.
56. Murray, *History of Old Tioga*, 449–51, 459–60.

Epilogue

Closing the Revolutionary Frontier

On March 1, 1831, the most notable of Northeast Pennsylvania's Yankee notables, John Franklin, died in his Athens home at the age of eighty-one. At the time of his death, he possessed a 580-acre farm, a sawmill, a horse, some livestock, and a house. Assessors valued Franklin's personal property at $316.20. His single most valuable possession was a clock worth $15. Franklin was well off but he was no commercially oriented backcountry entrepreneur. He never became a Freemason, never strayed from the Federalist Party, and until he joined Athens's Universalist church near the end of his life, stayed true to his Congregationalist roots. John Franklin died as he had lived—a New England yeoman farmer.[1]

John Franklin's life spanned the creation and closing of the revolutionary frontier. Indeed, his life was bound up in the forces that shaped this time and place in America's past. Franklin, like thousands of other land-hungry colonists, migrated to the backcountry in the wake of the Seven Years' War. Born in the western Connecticut town of Canaan on September 23, 1749, John married Lydia Doolittle in the winter of 1772 when he was twenty-three years old. He journeyed with his new wife to Pennsylvania's Wyoming Valley the following spring to occupy land under the Connecticut claim. Once there, John joined in the process of frontier development, building not one, but three, farms. He started out in the town of Plymouth, then moved a short distance in 1776 to lands his father

---

1. James E. Brady, "Wyoming: A Study of John Franklin and the Connecticut Settlement into Pennsylvania" (Ph.D. diss., Syracuse University, 1973), 309–12; Clement F. Heverly, *Pioneer and Patriot Families of Bradford County, Pennsylvania*, 2 vols. (Towanda, PA, 1915), 1:181.

held in Huntington. Later, in 1789, he moved his family up the Susquehanna River to Athens where he lived for the rest of his life. Besides being a husband and pioneer, Franklin was also a household head and community leader. John fathered three children with Lydia while living in Plymouth and Huntington and rose through the ranks of local officeholders to become a justice of the peace and militia captain. After the Revolutionary War, he rose to even higher levels of office, serving as sheriff of Luzerne County and multiple terms as a representative to the Pennsylvania Assembly. Franklin also suffered his share of setbacks. One of the worst came in 1778 when his wife died from smallpox. Unable to care for his three small children, he took them back to Canaan and placed them with relatives. Franklin soon returned to Wyoming and married Abigail Bidlack, the widow of Captain James Bidlack who fell at the Battle of Wyoming. Franklin never had any more children, but brought up the two sons and two daughters Abigail brought to their marriage.[2]

Franklin's life also reflects the conflict and contention that attended backcountry settlement. The revolutionary frontier was forged in heated conflicts, first between Indians and the colonists who dispossessed them from their land and, later, among settlers and landlords who clashed over property and the terms under which it would be held. These conflicts, in turn, overlapped and intermingled with the military, political, and social struggles sparked by the American Revolution. Franklin participated in all of these battles. He fought against Indians as a frontiersman and against the British and their Loyalist allies as an American soldier. Franklin served as a captain in the Westmoreland County militia during the Revolutionary War. He missed the Battle of Wyoming but experienced its destructive aftermath. His farm was one of the hundreds destroyed by the victorious invaders and he and his family joined the exodus of refugees fleeing the valley. It was during this exhausting flight that Lydia Franklin contracted smallpox and died. Franklin led Wyoming's Yankees on a number of scouting missions and reprisal raids later in the war, including General John Sullivan's violent rampage through Iroquois territory. Franklin carried two reminders of his Revolutionary War service till the end of his days. The first was a scar from a bullet wound he received in the shoulder in a skirmish with Indians during Sullivan's expedition. The second was a pocket watch he plundered from a British or Loyalist officer during one of his many forays up the Susquehanna Valley. Franklin did not lay down his arms after the war, but turned them against the Pennamites and Pennsylvania landlords who challenged the soil rights of his fellow Yankees after the Trenton Decree. Throughout the 1780s and 1790s, Franklin served as chief of the Wild Yankees and

2. Heverly, *Pioneer and Patriot Families*, 1:173–82.

stood as the most tenacious advocate of the Connecticut claim. Though his activities earned him arrest, imprisonment, and a second gunshot wound, Franklin never strayed from the defense of his and his neighbors' property rights.

Franklin's life demonstrates that the story of the revolutionary frontier is one of conflict and cooperation between settlers and land speculators. Indeed, he bridged these two supposedly antagonistic frontier types. While Franklin struggled to build a farm and raise a family, he also operated as a leading figure in the Susquehannah Company. Though his personal land holdings were modest, Franklin oversaw the distribution and development of hundreds of thousands of acres of frontier land and was deeply involved in one of the greatest speculating schemes in American history. One of the most important lessons that Franklin and the Wyoming controversy offer is that backcountry farmers, while certainly possessing an outlook that frequently put them at odds with wealthy gentlemen who coveted large tracts of frontier land, did not necessarily perceive society as an assemblage of innately antagonistic classes.

Ultimately, John Franklin's life is a testament to the pervasiveness and power of the concept of independence and of the profound impact its pursuit by thousands of ordinary settlers had on early America. The desire to obtain land and achieve independence fueled the waves of white settlement that washed over the backcountry and helped to spark the intense conflicts over property and power that marked the process of frontier expansion. No matter if frontier farmers fought against Indians, land speculators, government officials, the British Empire, or each other, the land and what its possession symbolized framed their efforts. The pursuit of independence likewise provides an underlying unity to different episodes of agrarian unrest and to the various tactics employed by diverse groups of rural insurgents. Whether the issue was debt laws and taxes that undermined the financial security of ordinary farmers, Indian policies and frontier banditry that threatened the physical security of settlers, or land disputes that imperiled the soil rights of backcountry yeomen, rural people's concerns about their ability to obtain, maintain possession of, and enjoy the fruits of freehold farms lay close to the surface of contention. Moreover, while some agrarian insurgents donned disguises and others did not, and one group of rural rebels spoke of Locke and the American Revolution while another remained silent, their movements were not essentially isolated, localized eruptions of dissent. While keeping in mind that time, place, events, and tactics distinguished one resistance movement from another, an aggressive drive to secure land and independence linked agrarian unrest across the revolutionary frontier.

Fully recovering the dimensions of this farmer's revolution demands that we reconsider our understandings of the American Revolution. The relationship between these two revolutions was not causative but catalyzing. The farmer's revolution started in the mid eighteenth century when large numbers of colonists started to make their way into the backcountry and before the America's independence movement gained momentum. For its part, the American Revolution first bloomed in the colonies' seaport cities and did not require frontier inhabitants to germinate it. Either of these revolutions could have taken place without the other, but only in an attenuated form. Backcountry settlers used the struggle for American independence to legitimate their own battles for personal independence. In addition, the social and political instability created by the Revolution created opportunities for frontier insurgents that otherwise would not have existed. Likewise, though the battle for American independence and the revolution that it sparked could have proceeded without the participation of backcountry settlers, it is doubtful that it would have been as radical or perhaps even successful. America's independence movement may have started in the cities, but its triumph was only assured when rural folk joined the cause. The pervasive disputes over property and power that plagued America's hinterlands were in no small measure responsible for the friendly reception the Revolution received in the countryside. The notion that national independence offered a solution to America's most pressing problems found fertile soil in the minds of backcountry inhabitants who were already anxious about their prospects for achieving personal independence.

The story of the farmer's revolution also recasts the sources of the American Revolution. On the one hand, it challenges the perspective that the Revolution's origins lay purely in the realm of ideas—that political ideologies born in Europe and nurtured in America by the local elites sparked America's independence movement. Again, events along the revolutionary frontier demonstrate that ordinary farmers did not need the English Whig writers or Enlightenment philosophers to mount determined and, at times, radical struggles for property and power. On the other hand, the Wyoming controversy also demonstrates that the origins of the Revolution do not necessarily lay in pervasive economic distress and class conflict. Indeed, the unrest that plagued America's revolutionary frontier emerged as much out of opportunity and optimism as out of hardship and despair. More often than not, it was the threat of dependency and a lack of material security rather than the reality of it that drove backcountry inhabitants to take up arms. All told, the farmer's revolution and, by extension, the American Revolution were products of ordinary folks' struggles for personal independence—struggles in which class conflict was more "circumstantial" than inherent and in which confrontations between farmers and gentlemen were joined and, at times, overshadowed by battles between Indians and whites, and by contention among and within settler households.

Coming to terms with the farmer's revolution broadens and transforms our understanding of the American Revolution in other ways. It broadens it by including ordinary backcountry inhabitants, be they Indians or white settlers, in the revolutionary narrative. It transforms it because, with these new characters, the story of the American Revolution goes from being a simple tale of triumph to a more complex one that includes plenty of defeat and tragedy. The farmer's revolution was a contest with winners and losers. Among the defeated were clearly the Indians who hoped to keep their hold on the land. Also among the losers was the British Empire who found that its vision of imperial expansion in North America was overpowered by a far more aggressive and effective one spearheaded by tens of thousands of white pioneers.

The fate of the ordinary settlers who battled for independence along the revolutionary frontier is far more complex and ambiguous. In some cases they suffered serious setbacks. Government forces crushed agrarian insurrections in North Carolina in the 1770s, in Massachusetts in the 1780s, and in Pennsylvania in the 1790s. However, government authorities and the wealthy gentlemen who stood behind them were far less effective in dealing with smoldering backcountry insurgencies like the ones that plagued mid Maine, Northeast Pennsylvania, and Vermont in the late eighteenth and early nineteenth centuries. There were no clear victories here but a series of compromises in which neither side obtained all that it sought. Yet in some important respects agrarian insurgents came out on top. In the hands of Thomas Jefferson and many others, the image of America as a land of independent yeoman farmers became a powerful discourse of American nationhood in the early republic. Moreover, the idea of America as a nation established to promote the aspirations and independence of ordinary white men took concrete form in the nineteenth century with the emergence of universal white male suffrage and, later, federal laws that attached free land grants to westward settlement.

No matter who won and who lost the struggle for America's revolutionary frontier, what is clear is that with John Franklin's passing and the passing of his generation, many of the forces that had given birth to it dissipated or lost their resonance. As white settlers pushed Indians westward, states resolved their jurisdictional disputes, and settlers and speculators came to terms with one another, conflict in the backcountry declined. Ultimately, the revolutionary frontier that Franklin and thousands of other backcountry inhabitants made came to a close because, quite simply, it ceased to be a frontier. The process of settlement and farm building eventually transformed the backcountry from a contentious world of crude log cabins and stump-studded fields into a more stable, ordered, and productive agricultural hinterland that was fully integrated into the nation's political, social, and economic mainstream. The pursuit of independence that had helped to create America's unruly revolutionary frontier ultimately helped to tame it.

Selected Bibliography

Manuscript Collections

Connecticut Historical Society, Hartford, Connecticut
Susquehannah Company Account Books
Historical Society of Pennsylvania, Philadelphia, Pennsylvania
    Asylum Company Papers
    Connecticut Claims Papers
    Henry Drinker Papers
    Journal of Samuel Fothergill
    Minutes of the Pennsylvania Landholders' Association
    Records of the Pennsylvania Landholders' Association
    James Strawbridge Papers
Massachusetts Historical Society, Boston, Massachusetts
    Timothy Pickering Papers
New York Historical Society, New York, New York
    William Walker Papers
Pennsylvania Historical and Museum Commission, Harrisburg, Pennsylvania
    Book of the Fifteen Townships
    Classification of the Seventeen Townships, Luzerne County
    Journal of the Commissioners of the Ulster-Bedford Act
    Letters from the Pennsylvania Claimants to the Commissioners
Swem Library, The College of William and Mary, Williamsburg, Virginia
    The United States Direct Tax of 1798 (microfilm)
Tioga Point Museum, Athens, Pennsylvania
    Bradford County Tax Assessments, 1796–1806

Wyoming Historical and Geological Society, Wilkes-Barre, Pennsylvania
  Samuel Meredith Papers
  Jason Torrey Papers

Primary Sources

Boyd, Julian P., and Robert J. Taylor, eds. *The Susquehannah Company Papers*. 11 vols. Ithaca, NY, 1962–71.
Duc de la Rochefoucault-Liancourt. *Travels through the United States of North America, The Country of the Iroquois, and Upper Canada in the Years 1795, 1796, and 1797*. 2 vols. London, 1799.
Egle, William H., ed. *Pennsylvania Archives*. 2nd ser. Vol. 18. Harrisburg, 1890.
Hazard, Samuel, ed. *Colonial Records of Pennsylvania*. Vol. 9. Harrisburg, 1852.
———. *Pennsylvania Archives*. 1st ser. 12 vols. Philadelphia, 1854.
Lincklaen, John. *Travels in the Years 1791 and 1792 in Pennsylvania, New York, and Vermont: Journals of John Lincklaen, Agent of the Holland Land Company*. New York, 1897.
Luzerne County Federalist.
MacKinney, Gertrude ed. *Pennsylvania Archives*. 9th ser. Vol. 1. Harrisburg, 1931.
Minutes of the Annual Conferences of the Methodist Episcopal Church for the Years 1773–1828. New York, 1840.
Raup, Hallock F., ed. "Journal of Griffith Evans, 1784–1788." *Pennsylvania Magazine of History and Biography* 65 (April 1941): 202–33.
Reed, George Edward, ed. *Pennsylvania Archives*. 4th ser. Vol. 4. Harrisburg, 1900.
Weld, Isaac. *Travels through the States of North America and the Provinces of Upper and Lower Canada*. 2 vols. 1807. Reprint, New York, 1968.
Wilkes-Barre Gazette.

Secondary Sources

Alford, Violet. "Rough Music or Charivari." *Folklore* 70 (December 1959): 505–18.
Aron, Stephen. *How the West Was Lost: The Transformation of Kentucky from Daniel Boone to Henry Clay*. Baltimore, 1996.
———. "Pioneer and Profiteers: Land Speculation and the Homestead Ethic in Frontier Kentucky." *Western Historical Quarterly* 23 (May 1992): 179–98.
Bellesiles, Michael A. *Revolutionary Outlaws: Ethan Allen and the Struggle for Independence on the Early American Frontier*. Charlottesville, 1993.
Blackman, Emily C. *History of Susquehanna County, Pennsylvania*. Philadelphia, 1873.
Bogin, Ruth. "Petitioning and the New Moral Economy of Post-Revolutionary America." *William and Mary Quarterly* 45 (July 1988): 397–402.
Botscharow-Kamau, Lucy Jayne. "Neighbors: Harmony and Conflict on the Indiana Frontier." *Journal of the Early Republic* 11 (winter 1991): 507–29.
Boyd, Julian P. "Attempts to Form New States in New York and Pennsylvania, 1786–96." *New York State Historical Association Quarterly Journal* 12 (July 1931): 264–66.

———. "Connecticut's Experiment in Expansion: The Susquehannah Company, 1753–1803." *Journal of Economic and Business History* 27 (1931): 38–69.
Bradsby, H. C. *History of Bradford County, Pennsylvania.* Chicago, 1891.
Brady, James E. "Wyoming: A Study of John Franklin and the Connecticut Settlement into Pennsylvania." Ph.D. diss., Syracuse University, 1973.
Brooke, John L. "A Deacon's Orthodoxy: Religion, Class, and the Moral Economy of Shay's Rebellion." In *In Debt to Shays: The Bicentennial of an Agrarian Rebellion*, edited by Robert A. Gross, 205–38. Charlottesville, 1993.
Brooks, Charles E. *Frontier Settlement and Market Revolution: The Holland Land Purchase.* Ithaca, 1996.
Brown, Margaret L. "William Bingham, Eighteenth-Century Magnate." *Pennsylvania Magazine of History and Biography* 61 (October 1937): 378–434.
Brown, Richard M. "Back Country Rebellions and the Homestead Ethic in America, 1740–1799." In *Tradition, Conflict, and Modernization: Perspectives on the American Revolution*, edited by Richard M. Brown and Don E. Fehrenbacher, 73–94. New York, 1977.
Bullock, Steven C. "A Pure and Sublime System: The Appeal of Post-Revolutionary Freemasonry." *Journal of the Early Republic* 9 (fall 1989): 359–73.
———. *Revolutionary Brotherhood: Freemasonry and the Transformation of the American Social Order, 1730–1840.* Chapel Hill, 1966.
Butler, Jon. *Awash in a Sea of Faith: Christianizing the American People.* Cambridge, MA, 1990.
Bushman, Richard L. *From Puritan to Yankee: Character and the Social Order in Connecticut, 1690–1765.* Cambridge, MA, 1967.
———. " 'This New Man': Dependence and Independence, 1776." In *Uprooted Americans—Essays in Honor of Oscar Handlin*, edited by Richard Bushman et al., 77–96. Boston, 1979.
Calloway, Colin G. *The American Revolution in Indian Country: Crisis and Diversity in Native American Communities.* New York, 1995.
Camenzind, Krista. "Violence, Race, and the Paxton Boys." In *Friends and Enemies in Penn's Woods: Indians, Colonists, and the Racial Construction of Pennsylvania*, edited by William A. Pencak and Daniel K. Richter, 201–20. University Park, 2004.
Cayton, R. L., and Fredrika J. Teute, eds. *Contact Points: American Frontiers from the Mohawk Valley to the Mississippi, 1750–1830.* Chapel Hill, 1998.
Chaffee, Amasa F. *History of the Wyoming Conference of the Methodist Episcopal Church.* New York, 1904.
Cornell, Saul. "Aristocracy Assailed: The Ideology of Backcountry Anti-Federalism." *Journal of American History* 76 (March 1990): 1148–72.
Countryman, Edward. " 'Out of the Bounds of the Law': Northern Land Rioters in the Eighteenth Century." In *The American Revolution: Explorations in the History of American Radicalism*, edited by Alfred F. Young, 37–70. DeKalb, IL, 1976.
Craft, David. *History of Bradford County, Pennsylvania.* Philadelphia, 1878.
Cronon, William. *Changes in the Land: Indians, Colonists, and the Ecology of New England.* New York, 1983.
Darlington, James W. "Peopling the Post-Revolutionary New York Frontier." *New York History* 74 (October 1993): 341–81.

Davis, Natalie Zemon. "The Reasons for Misrule: Youth Groups and Charivaris in Sixteenth-Century France." *Past and Present* 50 (February 1971): 41–75.

Doerflinger, Thomas M. *A Vigorous Spirit of Enterprise: Merchants and Economic Development in Revolutionary Philadelphia.* New York, 1987.

Dutrizac, Charles D. "Empire, Provinces, Frontier: Perspectives on the Pennsylvania-Maryland Boundary Dispute, 1681–1738." Ph.D. diss., University of Western Ontario, 1986.

———. "Local Identity and Authority in a Disputed Hinterland: The Pennsylvania-Maryland Border in the 1730s." *Pennsylvania Magazine of History and Biography* 115 (January 1991): 35–61.

Egle, William H. *History of the Counties of Dauphin and Lebanon in the Commonwealth of Pennsylvania: Biographical and Genealogical.* Philadelphia, 1883.

———. "The House of Lancaster to the Rescue." *Proceedings and Collections of the Wyoming Historical and Geological Society* 6 (1901): 97–105.

Ellis, David Maldwyn. "Rise of the Empire State, 1790–1820." *New York History* 56 (January 1975): 5–28.

———. "The Yankee Invasion of New York, 1783–1850." *New York History* 32 (January 1951): 3–17.

———. "Yankee-Dutch Confrontation in the Albany Area." *New England Quarterly* 45 (June 1972): 262–70.

Eslinger, Ellen. "Migration and Kinship on the Trans-Appalachian Frontier: Strode's Station, Kentucky." *Filson Club Historical Quarterly* 62 (January 1988): 52–66.

Fennell, Dorothy E. "From Rebelliousness to Insurrection: A Social History of the Whiskey Rebellion, 1765–1802." Ph.D. diss., University of Pittsburgh, 1981.

Fischer, Joseph R. *A Well-Executed Failure: The Sullivan Campaign Against the Iroquois, July–September, 1779.* Columbia, 1997.

Fossler, Linda. "Samuel Wallis: Colonial Merchant, Secret Agent." *Proceedings of the Northumberland County Historical Society* 30 (December 1990):107–15.

Franz, George W. *Paxton: A Study of Community Structure and Mobility in the Colonial Pennsylvania Backcountry.* New York, 1989.

Gates, Paul W. "The Role of the Land Speculator in Western Development." *Pennsylvania Magazine of History and Biography* 66 (July 1942): 314–33.

Glover, Edwin A. *James Strawbridge, Esquire.* Elkland, PA, 1954.

Goodall, David J. "New Light on the Border: New England Squatter Settlements in New York during the American Revolution." Ph.D. diss., State University of New York at Albany, 1984.

Goodrich, Phineas G. *History of Wayne County.* Honesdale, PA, 1880.

Graffagnino, J. Kevin. " 'The Country My Soul Delights In': The Onion River Land Company and the Vermont Frontier." *New England Quarterly* 65 (March 1992): 24–60.

Grant, Charles S. *Democracy in the Connecticut Frontier Town of Kent.* New York, 1961.

Greven, Philip J., Jr. "Family Structure in Seventeenth-Century Andover, Massachusetts." *William and Mary Quarterly* 23 (April 1966): 234–56.

———. *Four Generations: Population, Land, and Family in Colonial Andover, Massachusetts.* Ithaca, 1970.

Gross, Robert. *The Minutemen and Their World.* New York, 1976.

Handlin, Oscar. "The Eastern Frontier of New York." *New York History* 18 (January 1937): 50–75.
Harvey, Oscar Jewell, and Ernst G. Smith. *History of Wilkes-Barre, Luzerne County, Pennsylvania.* 6 vols. Wilkes-Barre, 1927–30.
Hatch, Nathan O. *The Democratization of American Christianity.* New Haven, 1989.
———. "In Pursuit of Religious Freedom: Church, State, and People in the New Republic." In *The American Revolution: Its Character and Limits*, edited by Jack P. Green, 389–94. New York, 1987.
Henderson, Elizabeth. "The Northwestern Lands of Pennsylvania, 1790–1812." *The Pennsylvania Magazine of History and Biography* 60 (1936): 131–60.
Henretta, James A. "Families and Farms: *Mentalité* in Pre-Industrial America." *William and Mary Quarterly* 35 (January 1978): 1–32.
Heverly, Clement F. *History of the Towandas, 1776–1886.* Towanda, PA, 1886.
———. *Patriot and Pioneer Families of Bradford County, Pennsylvania.* 2 vols. Towanda, PA, 1915.
Hinderaker, Eric, and Peter C. Mancall, *At the Edge of Empire: The Backcountry in British North America.* Baltimore, 2003.
Hindle, Brooke. "The March of the Paxton Boys." *William and Mary Quarterly* 3 (October 1946): 461–86.
Hoerder, Dirk. "Boston Leaders and Boston Crowds, 1765–1776." In *The American Revolution: Explorations in the History of American Radicalism*, edited by Alfred F. Young, 233–71. Dekalb, IL, 1976.
Hoffman, Ronald, Thad W. Tate, and Peter J. Albert, eds. *An Uncivil War: The Southern Backcountry during the American Revolution.* Charlottesville, VA, 1985.
Humphrey, Thomas J. "Crowd and Court: Rough Music and Popular Justice in Colonial New York." In *Riot and Revelry in Early America*, edited by William Pencak, Matthew Denis, and Simon P. Newman, 107–24. University Park, 2002.
———. *Land and Liberty: Hudson Valley Riots in the Age of Revolution.* DeKalb, IL, 2004.
Huston, Reeve. *Land and Freedom: Rural Society, Popular Protest, and Party Politics in Antebellum New York.* New York, 2000.
Ingram, Martin. "Ridings, Rough Music, and Mocking Rhymes in Early Modern England." In *Popular Culture in Seventeenth-Century England*, edited by Barry Reay. London, 1985.
Jedry, Christopher M. *The World of John Cleaveland: Family and Community in Eighteenth-Century New England.* New York, 1979.
Jennings, Francis. *Empire of Fortune: Crowns, Colonies, and Tribes in the Seven Years War in America.* New York, 1988.
———. " 'Pennsylvania Indians' and the Iroquois." In *Beyond the Covenant Chain: The Iroquois and Their Neighbors in Indian North America, 1600–1800*, edited by Daniel K. Richter and James H. Merrell, 75–91. Syracuse, 1987.
Kars, Marjoline. *Breaking Loose Together: The Regulator Rebellion in Pre-Revolutionary North Carolina.* Chapel Hill, 2002.
Karsky, Barbara. "Agrarian Radicalism in the Late Revolutionary Period, 1780–1795." In *New Wine in Old Skins: A Comparative View of Socio-Political Structures and Values Affecting the American Revolution*, edited by Erich Angermann et. al, 87–114. Stuttgart, Germany, 1976.

Kay, Marvin L. Michael. "The North Carolina Regulation, 1766–1776: A Class Conflict." In *The American Revolution: Explorations in the History of American Radicalism*, edited by Alfred F. Young, 71–123. DeKalb, IL, 1976.

Kim, Sung Bok. "The Impact of Class Relations and Warfare in the American Revolution: The New York Experience." *Journal of American History* 69 (September 1982): 326–46.

———. *Landlord and Tenant in Colonial New York: Manorial Society, 1604–1775*. Chapel Hill, 1978.

Klein, Rachel N. "Ordering the Backcountry: The South Carolina Regulation." *William and Mary Quarterly* 38 (October 1981): 661–80.

———. *Unification of a Slave State: The Rise of the Planter Class in the South Carolina Backcountry, 1760–1808*. Chapel Hill, NC, 1990.

Knouff, Gregory T. " 'An Arduous Service': The Pennsylvania Backcountry Soldiers' Revolution." *Pennsylvania History* 61 (January 1994): 45–74.

———. *Soldiers' Revolution: Pennsylvanians in Arms and the Forging of Early American Identity*. University Park, 2004.

———. "Whiteness and Warfare on a Revolutionary Frontier." In *Friends and Enemies in Penn's Woods: Indians, Colonists, and the Racial Construction of Pennsylvania*, edited by William A. Pencak and Daniel K. Richter, 238–57. University Park, 2004.

Kulikoff, Allan. *The Agrarian Origins of Capitalism*. Charlottesville, 1992.

———. *From British Peasants to Colonial American Farmers*. Chapel Hill, 2000.

Lipson, Dorothy Ann. *Freemasonry in Federalist Connecticut*. Princeton, 1977.

Livingood, James Weston. *The Philadelphia-Baltimore Trade Rivalry, 1780–1860*. New York, 1970.

Lockridge, Kenneth. "Land, Population, and the Evolution of New England Society, 1630–1790." *Past and Present* 39 (April 1968): 62–80.

Lynd, Staughton. *Class Conflict, Slavery, and the United States Constitution*. Indianapolis, 1967.

Mancall, Peter C. *Valley of Opportunity: Economic Culture along the Upper Susquehanna, 1700–1800*. Ithaca, 1991.

Mark, Irving. *Agrarian Conflicts in Colonial New York, 1711–1775*. New York, 1940.

Martin, James Kirby. "The Return of the Paxton Boys and the Historical State of the Pennsylvania Frontier, 1764–1774." *Pennsylvania History* 38 (April 1971): 117–33.

Martin, John Frederick. *Profits in the Wilderness: Entrepreneurship and the Founding of New England Towns in the Seventeenth Century*. Chapel Hill, 1991.

Maxey, David W. "Of Castles in Stockport and Other Strictures: Samuel Preston's Contentious Agency for Henry Drinker." *Pennsylvania Magazine of History and Biography* 100 (July 1986): 413–46.

McConville, Brenden J. *These Daring Disturbers of the Public Peace: The Struggle for Property and Power in Early New Jersey*. Ithaca, 1999.

———. "The Rise of Rough Music: Reflections on an Ancient New Custom in Eighteenth-Century New York." In *Riot and Revelry in Early America*, edited by William Pencak, Matthew Denis, and Simon P. Newman, 87–106. University Park, 2002.

Meginness, John Franklin. *History of Tioga County Pennsylvania*. Chicago, 1897.

Melvoin, Richard I. *New England Outpost: War and Society in Colonial Deerfield*. New York, 1989.

Merrill, Michael. "Cash Is Good to Eat: Self-Sufficiency and Exchange in the Rural Economy of the United States." *Radical History Review* 4 (1977): 42–71.
Miner, Charles. *History of Wyoming.* Philadelphia, 1845.
Murray, Louise Welles. *A History of Old Tioga Point and Early Athens.* Wilkes-Barre, 1907.
Newman, Paul Douglas. *Fries's Rebellion: The Enduring Struggle for the American Revolution.* Philadelphia, 2004.
Newman, Simon P. *Parades and the Politics of the Street: Festive Culture in the Early American Republic.* Philadelphia, 1997.
Nobles, Gregory H. *American Frontiers: Cultural Encounters and Continental Conquest.* New York, 1997.
———. "Breaking into the Backcountry: New Approaches to the Early American Frontier, 1750–1800." *William and Mary Quarterly* 46 (October 1989): 641–70.
Onuf, Peter S. "Liberty, Development, and Union: Visions of the West in the 1780s." *William and Mary Quarterly* 43 (April 1986): 179–213.
———. *The Origins of the Federal Republic: Jurisdictional Controversies in the United States, 1775–1787.* Philadelphia, 1983.
Ousterhout, Ann M. "Frontier Vengeance: Connecticut Yankees vs. Pennamites in the Wyoming Valley." *Pennsylvania History* 62 (summer 1995): 330–63.
———. *A State Divided: Opposition in Pennsylvania to the American Revolution.* New York, 1987.
Pearce, Stewart. *Annals of Luzerne County.* Philadelphia, 1866.
Peck, George. *Early Methodism within the Bounds of the Old Genesee Conference from 1788 to 1828.* New York, 1860.
Preston, David L. "Squatters, Indians, Proprietary Government, and Land in the Susquehanna Valley." In *Friends and Enemies in Penn's Woods: Indians, Colonists, and the Racial Construction of Pennsylvania,* edited by William A. Pencak and Daniel K. Richter, 180–200. University Park, 2004.
Price, William E. "A Study of a Frontier Community in Transition: The History of Wilkes-Barre, Pennsylvania, 1750–1800." Ph.D. diss., Kent State University, 1979.
Pruitt, Bettye Hobbs. "Self-sufficiency and the Agricultural Economy of Eighteenth-Century Massachusetts." *William and Mary Quarterly* 41 (July 1984): 333–64.
Purvis, Thomas L. "Origins and Patterns of Agrarian Unrest in New Jersey, 1735–1754." *William and Mary Quarterly* 39 (October 1982): 600–627.
Reed, Newton. *Early History of Amenia.* Amenia, NY, 1875.
Richards, Leonard L. *Shays's Rebellion: The American Revolution's Final Battle.* Philadelphia, 2002.
Sarsfield, Luke A. "Matthias Hollenback: Early Wyoming Valley Entrepreneur." Ph.D. diss., New York University, 1973.
Schwartz, Philip J. *The Jarring Interests: New York's Boundary Makers, 1664–1776.* Albany, 1979.
Shannon, Timothy J. *Indians and Colonists at the Crossroads of Empire.* Ithaca, 2000.
Shaw, Peter. *American Patriots and the Rituals of Revolution.* Cambridge, MA, 1981.
Siles, William Herbert. "A Vision of Wealth: Speculators and Settlers in the Genesee Country of New York." Ph.D. diss., University of Massachusetts, 1978.
"Sketch of the Life of Lt. Col. John Jenkins." *Proceedings and Collections of the Wyoming Historical and Geological Society* 18 (1922): 249–51.

Slaughter, Thomas P. "Crowds in Eighteenth-Century America: Reflections and New Directions." *Pennsylvania Magazine of History and Biography* 105 (January 1991): 3–34.
———. *The Whiskey Rebellion: Frontier Epilogue to the American Revolution*. New York, 1986.
Smith, Barbara Clark. "Food Rioters and the American Revolution." *William and Mary Quarterly* 51 (January 1994): 3–38.
Stefon, Frederick J. "The Wyoming Valley." In *Beyond Philadelphia: The American Revolution in the Pennsylvania Hinterlands*, edited by John B. Frantz and William Pencak, 133–52. University Park, 1998.
Stewart, Steven J. "Skimmington in the Middle and New England Colonies." In *Riot and Revelry in Early America*, edited by William Pencak, Matthew Denis, and Simon P. Newman, 41–86. University Park, 2002.
Szatmary, David P. *Shays' Rebellion: The Making of an Agrarian Insurrection*. Amherst, 1986.
Taylor, Alan. "Agrarian Independence: Northern Land Rioters after the Revolution." In *Beyond the American Revolution: Explorations in the History of American Radicalism*, edited by Alfred F. Young, 221–45. DeKalb, IL, 1993.
———. " 'The Art of Hook and Snivey': Political Culture in Upstate New York during the 1790s." *Journal of American History* 79 (March 1993): 1372–96.
———. "The Early Republic's Supernatural Economy: Treasure Seeking in the American Northeast, 1780–1830." *American Quarterly* 38 (spring 1986): 6–34.
———. " 'A Kind of Warr': The Contest for Land on the Northeastern Frontier, 1750–1820." *William and Mary Quarterly* 46 (January 1989): 3–26.
———. *Liberty Men and Great Proprietors: The Revolutionary Settlement on the Maine Frontier, 1760–1820*. Chapel Hill, 1990.
———. "Nathan Barlow's Journey: Mysticism and Popular Protest on the Northeastern Frontier." In *Maine in the Early Republic*, edited by Charles E. Clark et al., 100–117. Hanover, NH, 1988.
———. " 'Stopping the Progress of Rogues and Deceivers': A White Indian Recruiting Notice of 1808." *William and Mary Quarterly* 42 (January 1985): 90–103.
———. " 'To Man Their Rights': The Frontier Revolution." In *The Transforming Hand of Revolution: Reconsidering the American Revolution as a Social Movement*, edited by Ronald Hoffman and Peter J. Albert, 231–57. Charlottesville, 1995.
———. *William Cooper's Town: Power and Persuasion on the Frontier of the Early American Republic*. New York, 1995.
Taylor, Robert J. *Colonial Connecticut: A History*. Millwood, NY, 1979.
———. "Trial at Trenton." *William and Mary Quarterly* 26 (October 1969): 521–47.
Thompson, E. P. "The Moral Economy of the English Crowd in the Eighteenth Century." *Past and Present* 50 (1971): 76–131.
Tillson, Albert H., Jr. "The Localist Roots of Backcountry Loyalism: An Examination of Popular Political Culture in Virginia's New River Valley." *Journal of Southern History* 54 (August 1988): 387–404.
Turner, Orsamus. *History of the Pioneer Settlement of Phelps and Gorham's Purchase, and Morris' Reserve*. Rochester, 1852.
Ulrich, Laruel Thatcher. "Martha Ballard and Her Girls: Women's Work in Eighteenth-Century Maine." In *Work and Labor in Early America*, edited by Stephen Innes, 70–105. Chapel Hill, 1988.

———. *A Midwife's Tale: The Life of Martha Ballard Based on Her Diary, 1785–1812.* New York, 1991.
Underdown, David. "The Taming of the Scold." In *Order and Disorder in Early Modern England*, edited by Anthony Fletcher and John Stevenson, 116–36. New York, 1985.
Upham, Charles W. *The Life of Timothy Pickering.* 2 vols. Boston, 1873.
Vaughn, Alden T. "Frontier Banditti and the Indians: The Paxton Boys' Legacy." *Pennsylvania History* 51 (January 1984): 1–29.
Vickers, Daniel. "Competency and Competition: Economic Culture in Early America." *William and Mary Quarterly* 47 (January 1990): 3–29.
———. *Farmers and Fishermen: Two Centuries of Work in Essex County, Massachusetts, 1630–1850.* Chapel Hill, 1994.
———. "Working the Fields in a Developing Economy: Essex County, Massachusetts, 1630–1675." In *Work and Labor in Early America*, edited by Stephen Innes, 49–69. Chapel Hill, 1988.
Wallace, Anthony F. C. *King of the Delawares: Teedyuscung, 1700–1763.* Freeport, NY, 1970.
Warfle, Richard T. *Connecticut's Western Colony: The Susquehannah Affair.* Hartford, 1979.
Webster, Eleanor M. "Insurrection at Fort Loudon in 1765, Rebellion or Preservation of the Peace?" *Western Pennsylvania History Magazine* 47:2 (April 1964): 125–40.
Whittenburg, James P. "Planters, Merchants, and Lawyers: Social Change and the Origins of the North Carolina Regulation." *William and Mary Quarterly* 34 (April 1977): 215–38.
Wigger, John H. "Taking Heaven by Storm: Enthusiasm and Early American Methodism, 1770–1820." *Journal of the Early Republic* 14 (summer 1994): 167–94.
Wilkinson, Norman B. *Land Policy and Speculation in Pennsylvania, 1779–800: A Test of the New Democracy.* New York, 1979.
———. "The 'Philadelphia Fever' in Northern Pennsylvania." *Pennsylvania History* 20 (January 1953): 41–56.
Williams, Michael. *Americans and Their Forests: A Historical Geography.* New York, 1989.
Williamson, James R., and Linda A. Fossler. *Zebulon Butler: Hero of the Revolutionary Frontier.* Westport, CT, 1995.
Wyckoff, William. *The Developer's Frontier: The Making of the Western New York Landscape.* New Haven, 1988.
Young, Alfred F. "English Plebeian Culture and Eighteenth-Century American Radicalism." In *The Origins of Anglo-American Radicalism*, edited by Margaret and James Jacob, 183–213. London, 1984.
Zuckerman, Michael. *Peaceable Kingdoms: New England Towns in the Eighteenth Century.* New York, 1970.

Index

Abbot, Benjamin, 83
Abbot, Nathan (Jr.), 83
Abbot, Nathan (Sr.), 84, 89, 92
accommodation
   and farm building, 166
   and Freemasonry, 191
   geographic patterns, 153, 171–72
   and local notables, 179, 183–84
   and market formation, 167, 171–73
   obstacles to, 152
   and party politics, 194–95
   See also Wyoming controversy: resolution of
AcModer, John Jay, 78, 101
agrarian independence, 8, 200
   and agrarian unrest, 8, 11, 67–68, 88, 145–46, 198
   and the American Revolution, 9–10, 198–200
   and decline of Yankee resistance, 149
   and frontier migration, 110
   and frontier settlement, 10–11, 198
   and kinship/locale, 54–56
   and market exchange, 170
agrarian insurgents, 65–66
   disguise, use of, 137–39
   motivations of, 66–68
   See also Green Mountain Boys; White Indians; Wild Yankees
agrarian resistance. *See* agrarian unrest

agrarian unrest, 65–66
   and agrarian independence, 8, 11, 67–68, 88, 145–46, 198
   and American Revolution, 137, 139, 140, 198–200
   and class conflict, 66–67, 75, 81–82, 199
   and jurisdictional disputes, 6–7
   and land disputes, 6
   in Maine, 6, 65, 200
   and "moral economy," 144, 145–46
   and rebellion, 7
   and religion, 141–43
   and traditions of popular protest, 136–37, 138–39, 145
   in Vermont, 6, 65, 69, 200
   See also Yankee resistance
Albany Congress of 1754, 19–20
allegiance
   and ethnicity, 51–53
   and kinship/locale, 54–55, 155–56
   patterns of, 49–56
   and pursuit of property, 53–55
   and regional culture, 51–53
   See also Revolutionary War: patterns of allegiance
Allen, David, 183
Allen, Ethan, 78, 79, 100
Allen, Nathaniel, 184–85, 194–95
Allen, Stephen, 183
Allensburgh, 83, 100

212 INDEX

American Revolution, 9–10, 137, 139, 140, 198–200
Armstrong, John Jr., 45
Athens, 99, 142, 177–78
   local notables of, 184, 189–90
authority
   contests over, 39–49
   local constructions of, 43–44

Baily, Joseph, 111
Baldwin, Waterman, 44, 59, 61, 62, 99
Ballard, John, 155
Ballard, Nathan, 155
Ballard, Stephen, 143, 148, 155, 166
Baptist Church, 141–42
Beach, Zerah, 79–81, 98, 99
Bedford, 178
Bennett, Amos, 111
Benton, Caleb, 79, 100
Bingham, William, 98, 126
Black Boy riots, 7, 26
Board of Trade, 41
Bortle, Capt. John, 78, 80
Bortle, Peter, 109
Boyd, Maj. John, 44, 48
Bradford County, 194–95
Budd, Frederick, 83, 93
Burlington, 165, 184
Butler, Zebulon, 1, 3, 29, 47, 53, 79–80

Cady, Zebulon, 81n, 83, 92
Carney, William, 83
charivari. *See* rough music
class conflict, 66–67, 75, 81–82, 199
Claverack, 100, 122, 159n, 164–65
community building
   and kinship networks, 154–55
   and landholding patterns, 156, 159–60
Compromise Act, 122, 124, 153, 177–78
Confirming Act, 68, 95–96
Connecticut
   annexation of Wyoming region, 40–41
   land shortage in, 16–17
   1662 royal charter, 16
Connecticut claimants
   conflict with Paxton settlers, 52–53
   factionalism among, 68–69, 74–75, 122, 151
   moves toward reconciliation, 150
   and party affiliation, 192
   poverty among, 162
   See also Wild Yankees

Cooley, Preserved, 53–54
Cooper, Thomas, 122–23, 124
Coxe, Tench, 5, 98, 127–28, 170

Delaware (Indians), 2, 19, 21, 22, 32
Democratic–Republicans, 124, 191–92, 194–95
Donnell, Henry, 120, 132
Drinker, Henry, 98, 126, 170
Dudley, Anna, 87
Dudley, Gideon, 83, 109
Dudley, Joseph, 83, 87, 90, 93
Dudley, Martin, 74, 84–86, 92, 108–9

Earl, Benjamin, 81n, 83, 90
Earl, Daniel, 81n, 83, 90
Earl, Joseph, 86, 87, 90, 91
Earl, Solomon, 83, 89
Ellicott, Andrew, 128
Erwin, Arthur, 3, 113

farm building
   and decline of resistance, 165–66
   and household subsistence, 163–64
   pioneer phase of, 160–62
   time–labor factor of, 163, 166
Federalists, 191–92
Fenn v. Dorrance, 96
fifteen towns, the, 122, 153, 178
Finn, James, 70, 96, 143
flood of 1784, 58
Flower, Zephon, 135, 189
food riot, 169–70
Fort Stanwix Treaty of 1768, 23
Franklin, Jehiel, 108, 118
Franklin, John, 33, 72, 99, 196–97
   arrest of, 72–73
   death of, 196
   and Federalist Party, 192–92
   and half-share men, 80–81
   negotiations with Pennsylvania, 127–28
   political career of, 117–18, 192–94
   prosecution under Intrusion Act, 130
   and reconciliation with Pennsylvania, 177–78
   release from prison, 92
   service in Revolutionary War, 32–33, 197
   and the Susquehannah Company, 77–80, 198
   and Wild Yankees, 197–98
Franklin, Roswell, 108
Freemasonry, 189–91

Gobin, Edward, 132
Goddard, Ezra, 148, 156, 166, 173, 181
Goddard, Luther, 148, 156, 166, 181
Goodrich, Elihu C., 104
Gore, Obadiah, 74, 96
Grant, Josiah, 185, 189–90
Green Mountain Boys, 7, 65–66, 138, 185

half shares, 80–81
half-share men, 80–81, 81n, 82–87
Hamilton, Joseph, 79, 98, 100, 127
Hancock, Isaac, 186
Hart, Jacob, 177, 191
Hinds, Bartlett, 143, 175, 187, 190
    attack on, 133–34
Hodgdon, Samuel, 98, 126
Hollenback, John, 91
Horn, Abraham, 126–27, 129
households, rural
    and generational ties/tensions, 85–86, 89–90
    subsistence needs of, 163–64
    and women, 60–61
Hyde, Ezekiel, 101, 185–86, 194
Hyde, John, 83, 93

independence. *See* agrarian independence
Indians, 14, 19
    and agrarian unrest, 7, 23–31, 34–35
    dispossession of, 19, 22, 23, 35–36
    insurgents disguised as, 31, 132, 137–38, 139
    violence against, 25–26
    and Wyoming Valley, 19
    Also see Delaware; Iroquois
Ingham, Jonas, 180–81, 187–88, 193
Intrusion Act, 102, 114, 124, 129–30, 153
Irish, Job, 118, 192
Ironcutter, John, 26
Iroquois, 19–21, 23, 32
Irwin, James, 102, 184

Jeffersonian Republicans. *See* Democratic-Republicans
Jenkins, John, 74, 99,
    political career of, 193
    prosecution under Intrusion Act, 117, 130
    service in Revolutionary War, 32–33
    and the Susquehannah Company, 76, 78, 80
Jennings, John, 23, 28, 110
Jersey settlers, 45–46
Judd, William, 70
Juddsburgh, 155, 173

Keeler, Elisha, 173, 180–81, 192
Kilborn, Aaron, 83, 85, 92
Kilborn, Joseph, 86, 88
Kilborn, Timothy, 83
Kingsbury, Joseph, 178, 189, 192, 194–95
kin networks
    and community building, 154–55
    and local notables, 181–82
    and migration, 108, 110–11
    and Paxton settlers, 55
    and pursuit of independence, 54–55, 56
    and settler allegiance, 155–56
Kinney, Joseph, 81n, 117, 118, 178, 194–95
Kinney, Thomas, 88, 93

land clearing
    methods, 160–61
    rates of, 163
land distribution policies
    and community, 156, 159–60
    in New England, 156–59
    and the Susquehanna Company, 158–59
land prices, 97, 101, 153
land speculation, 97, 119, 97–98, 102, 104
land speculators
    and agrarian unrest, 6, 75, 97
    and Connecticut land companies, 98–99
    and settlers, 100–101
    and Pennsylvania, 98
    Wild Yankees as, 108–10
    and Yankee resistance, 75–78, 80–81, 88–89, 95
land values, 164, 180
leading men. *See* local notables
Liberty Men. *See* White Indians
local notables, 179–82
    and accommodation, 179, 183–84
    in Athens, 184, 189–190
    and community/kin networks, 181–82
    cooperation with Pennsylvania, 186
    and Freemasonry, 189–91
    friction with neighbors, 186–87
    influence of, 182–83
    and party politics, 191–95
    and Pennsylvania landholders, 179–80
    prosecution of, 185–86
    and Yankee resistance, 184–85, 187–88
    wealth of, 180–81
    along Wyalusing Creek, 180–81
    and the Wyoming controversy, 176
Locke, John, 140–41
Loop, Capt. Peter, 78, 80

Loyalists. *See* Tories.
Luzerne County, 68, 74, 97–98, 116–17, 192–93

Manville, Ira, 83
maple sugar, 168
Marcy, Zebulon, 91, 96
market formation
  and accommodation, 169, 171–73
  and agricultural surplus, 169
  in Northeast Pennsylvania, 167–73
  and "pioneer commodities", 167–69
  and pursuit of independence, 170
  and transportation networks, 170–71
  and stores, 173
markets
  and frontier migration, 111–12
  and frontier settlers, 169–70
Mathewson, Elisha, 32–33, 74, 84, 99, 191
Mathewson, Elizabeth, 177, 178–79
Mathewson v Satterlee, 178–79, 195
McKinestry, John, 100
Mead, David, 37, 46, 54, 64
Means, William, 183, 194–95
Meredith, Samuel, 126
Methodist Episcopal Church, 141–42
migration
  and kin/community ties, 108, 110–11
  motives for, 107, 110–12
  from New England, 106–7
  to Northeast Pennsylvania, 105–6, 107–8
  and Yankee resistance, 113–18
Murray, Noah, 142, 190

New Purchase, 23, 27
Nicholson, John, 98, 119, 170
North Carolina Regulation, 7, 142, 200
Northeast Pennsylvania
  formation of markets in, 167–73
  Freemasonry in, 189
  grain exports, 169
  land, value of, 164
  party politics in, 191–95
  population of, 167
  poverty of inhabitants, 162
  religious denominations, 142
  road construction, 170, 172–73
  soil quality, 162–63
  transportation networks, 170–71

Ogden, Amos, 23, 28, 30, 45
Ogden, Nathan, 3, 28
Okely, John, 44

Paine, Clement, 104, 190
Paine, David, 109, 186
party politics, 191–95
  and accommodation, 194–95
  and Connecticut claimants, 192
  and Wild Yankees, 192–93
  and Wyoming controversy, 192–95
  and Yankee resistance, 193–94
Patterson, Alexander, 43, 46–47, 48, 49, 56–57
Paxton Boys. *See* Paxton settlers
Paxton Riots, 7, 25–26
Paxton settlers
  alliance with Susquehannah Company, 27
  conflict with Yankees, 52–53
  and ethnicity, 53
  kinship among, 55
  and violence, 28–30
Pennamites. *See* Pennsylvania claimants
Pennamite–Yankee Wars. *See* violence: Pennamite–Yankee
Pennsylvania
  1799 gubernatorial election, 192–93
  efforts to end Yankee resistance, 121–26, 128
  negotiations with Yankees, 42, 47–48
  prosecution of Pennamites, 48–49
  settler dissent toward, 50
Pennsylvania claimants
  attacks on Connecticut claimants, 28, 30, 33, 56–57, 62–63
  and ethnicity, 52–53
  prosecution by Pennsylvania, 48–49
  resistance to Pennsylvania's authority, 46–47
  surrender Wyoming Valley, 29
  as targets of Yankee violence, 94, 113, 115–16, 131–32, 151–52, 188
Pennsylvania Landholders' Association, 126–27
  efforts to end Yankee resistance, 128–30, 154
  and local notables, 186
  negotiations with Susquehannah Company, 127–28
Pennsylvania Regulation, 7, 200
Pepoon, Silas, 104–5, 127
personal independence. *See* agrarian independence
Pickering, Timothy, 70–71, 92
  describes settlers' homes/farms, 161, 163
  and *Fenn v. Dorrance*, 96
  kidnapping of, 65, 74–75

as land speculator, 98, 126
target of Wild Yankees, 73–74
views on Yankee insurgents, 82–83
pioneer farming, 161–62
Plunket, William, 29
Plunket's expedition, 29, 41
Pope's Day, 138–39
potash, 168–69
Preston, Samuel, 112, 176, 180
Privy Council, 22
property
contest over, 56–60
views of, 81
See also violence: against property

Ralston, James, 128, 129
Revolutionary frontier, 6
Revolutionary War
and agrarian violence, 31–35
patterns of allegiance, 50–52
and racial conflict, 32
in Wyoming region, 32, 58
Rose, Robert, 148–49, 151–52, 186–87
rough music, 136
Rutty, Ezra (Sr.), 100, 111

Satterlee, Elisha, 99, 179, 190
and Freemasonry, 189
prosecution under Intrusion Act, 117, 130
reconciliation with Pennsylvania, 178
service in Revolutionary War, 32–33
and the Susquehannah Company, 104, 109
Scoville, Orr, 115, 183
Seely, John, 46
Sessions, Resolved, 107, 115–16, 118
Settlers' Bill, 178, 195
Shays's Rebellion, 7, 65, 69–70, 200
Shoemaker, Henry, 46, 49, 57
Singer, Casper, 115–16, 118
Six Nations. *See* Iroquois
skimmington. *See* rough music
Slocum, William, 96, 99
Smiley, Thomas, 132–33, 143
Smith, Garret, 83, 91
Smithfield, 131, 150
South Carolina Regulation, 7
Stanton, Samuel, 180, 181, 182
Stewart, Charles, 23, 29, 45, 51
Stewart, Lazarus, 24–25, 27, 53
alliance with Susquehannah Company, 27
death of, 32
murder of Nathan Ogden, 28
and Paxton Riots, 25–26

Strawbridge, James, 104–5, 114–15, 126
Strong, Solomon, 99, 100
Stump, Frederick, 26
Sugar Creek, 155, 159, 164–66, 148–49, 174
resistance along, 120, 131–32
Sullivan's expedition, 32
Susquehannah Company, 16–17
changing organization of, 79–80
decline of, 127
land distribution policies, 158–59
and land speculation, 102, 104
negotiations with Pennsylvania, 127–28
and Pickering's kidnapping, 73–74
revival of, 77–80
town-founding efforts of, 99–102
and Yankee resistance, 77–81
Susquehanna Valley. *See* Northeast Pennsylvania
Swift, John, 45, 62, 74, 84, 99
as land speculator, 99, 110
service in Revolutionary War, 32–33

Taylor, Daniel, 83
Teedyuscung, 19, 21–22
Territorial Act, 125–26, 130, 153
Thomas, Joel, 110, 113
Tioga Point, 69, 170, 172–73
Tioga River (south branch), 100, 131
Tories, 34–35, 51–52
Trenton Decree, 35–36, 41–42
Tunkhannock Creek, 69, 94, 98, 150
Turner, Seth, 104
Tyler, John, 83

Ulster, 100, 131, 178
Universalist Church, 141–42
Usher, 133

Vanderlip, Frederick, 51
violence
against property, 30–31
against women, 61–63
Indian–white, 25–26
and legacy of Indian–European conflict, 23–31, 34–35
Pennamite–Yankee, 28–30, 33–34, 56–57, 59–60
and race, 24, 26, 30, 32, 34–35
See also Revolutionary War; Wild Yankees

Wallis, Samuel, 94, 98
Wayne County, 150, 151, 194
Welles, George, 134, 177

Welles, Henry, 177, 178, 192, 195
Westmoreland, town of, 41
Westmoreland County, 41
Whitehaven, 83
White Indians, 6, 65–66, 138, 142
Wild Yankees, 4, 66
  age and status of, 83–85, 84n
  and alleged separatist plot, 70
  attacks on Pennsylvanians, 94, 113, 115–16, 131–32, 151–52, 188
  attacks on Yankee moderates, 132–35
  in disguise, 65, 132, 133, 137–39
  as land speculators, 108–110
  legal harassment of Pennsylvanians, 116–17
  manipulation of state authority, 116–18
  and party politics, 192–93
  and Pickering's kidnapping, 83
  prosecution of, 130, 147
  rhetoric of, 140–44, 146
  targets of, 131–35
  See also half-share men; Yankee resistance
Wilkes-Barre, 58, 158, 163, 170, 171
Williamson, Dr. Hugh, 49–50
Woodbridge, Maj. Theodore, 182–83, 185
Woodward, David, 83
Wyalusing Creek, 108, 171–72, 173
  leading men along, 180–81
  resistance along, 131, 151, 188
Wyoming, Battle of, 1–2, 32
Wyoming controversy, 5–6
  and Continental Congress, 41
  Indian involvement in, 18–23
  and Indian soil rights, 19–20
  jurisdictional dimension of, 39–42
  and local notables, 176
  origins of, 14–18
  and party politics, 192–95
  resolution of, 177–82
  and Seven Years' War, 20–21
  summary of, 3–5
  violence of, 24
  women's involvement in, 60–63
Wyoming dispute. See Wyoming controversy
Wyoming region. See Northeast Pennsylvania

Wyoming Valley, 1
  Indian inhabitants of, 19
  Pennsylvania garrison of, 47
  population of, 40
  productivity of land, 163
  violence in, 2–3
  See also Northeast Pennsylvania
Wysox Creek, 150, 159, 172
Wysox Township, 164–65

Yankee insurgents. See Wild Yankees
Yankee notables. See local notables
Yankee resistance
  and American Revolution, 137, 144
  culture of, 121, 135–46
  decline of, 149, 153–54, 165–66
  and economic isolation, 171–72
  and electoral politics, 117–18
  and farm building, 165–66
  geographic patterns of, 69, 131, 153, 171–72
  and half-share men, 80
  and land speculation, 94–95, 96–97, 99–102, 104–5
  and localism, 90–91
  localization of, 120–21, 131–35
  and local notables, 184–85, 187–88
  and local social networks, 83–84, 86–87, 89–90
  and migration, 113–18
  and party politics, 193–94
  persistence of, 150–52
  and pursuit of independence, 143, 144, 145–47
  and religion, 143
  and rough music, 136–37
  and settler-speculator alliance, 75–78, 80–81, 88–89, 95
  along Sugar Creek, 120, 131–32
  along Wyalusing Creek, 131, 151, 188
  See also Wild Yankees; half-share men
Yankees. See Connecticut claimants
Yankee surveyors, 114
York, Minor, 88, 180–81, 183, 186, 192

www.ingramcontent.com/pod-product-compliance
Lightning Source LLC
Chambersburg PA
CBHW020410230426
43664CB00009B/1244